The
World
of
Wines

Andre,
Hope this book will
tell you something about
a thing you like so
much.

Merry Christmas
Annette.

BY THE SAME AUTHOR:

A Notebook for the Wines of France (Alfred A. Knopf, New York, 1961)

by Creighton Churchill

WITH MAPS BY AVA MORGAN

THE
WORLD
OF
WINES

Collier Books, New York, New York
Collier-Macmillan Limited, London

Wine, Woman, Baths—
By Art or Nature warme—
Us'd or Abus'd—do Man
Much good—or harme.

—Code of the *Civitas Hippocratica*
(Medical School of Salerno—10th cent.)

Foreword

The appearance of *The World of Wines* in an updated, as well as a popular-priced edition, at long last justifies the author's original purpose in writing it. There are thousands of potential wine lovers in many countries—the United States is not unique—whose lives could be enhanced appreciably provided they were just a bit more knowledgeable, and hence courageous, about wines. So many of us have been falsely led into thinking we don't like wine. Hesitant to dive off into a sea of confusing labels, inhibited by the "wine snobs" nesting so jealously on their sophistications, or perhaps just having tried the wrong wine once (the wrong wine for us)—we decide there is no wine for us.

The potential wine lover, the average man, is not always to blame for this attitude. How can he be expected to win against certain producers or importers who peddle undrinkable, poor quality wines under the cloak of "catchy" packaging or high-pressure marketing devices—which often cost more than the contents of the bottle itself? Or how widely is it known that a large majority of restaurants keeps a stock of wines in the cellar, in case the customer demands one—yet keeps the wine list itself out of sight because the sale of other, stronger alcoholic beverages means a higher check? Or that many another restaurant accomplishes the same end by charging a two or three hundred per cent profit on wines? True, more often than not one gets what one pays for in wines. The so-called great ones are expensive, and with good reason: they are scarce, and difficult to produce. Yet that does not mean that there are not many satisfying and rewarding wines—ready and waiting to enhance any food or any meal—within reach of the average pocketbook. But the potential wine lover—and sometimes even the mighty connoisseur himself—must know where to look, without relying solely on the oftentimes unreliable advice of the local liquor store. This, in effect, is the aim and hope behind these pages.

The men (and women) who make good wines, honest wines, and likewise the people who deal in them, are unfailingly good, honest people. Wine makers, after all, are farmers, a part and parcel of the soil they work. Closer to nature herself than many of us, they are happy people, proud of the rewards they reap from nature—and their sense of honest accomplishment in every day's work of life spreads itself contagiously to those others whose task it is to shepherd wines on their long journey from the vineyard to the wine lover. In the course of many years it has been the author's privilege to make hundreds of lasting friendships among those who make and deal in wines. Would that space did not prevent mention of them all. But among the many whose advice and material assistance have so indelibly contributed to these pages, heartfelt thanks and recognition must be given at least to a few: Michel L. Dreyfus, Henri Malval, Warren Strauss, Peter Sichel, Frederick L. Haverly, Kendrick Pearson of New York; Charles M. Fournier, Konstantin Frank of Hammondsport, New York; James R. Lowe, Louis A. Benoist, Otto E. Meyer of San Francisco; Robert Mondavi of St. Helena, John Daniel, Jr., of Rutherford, Myron S. Nightingale of Fresno, Douglas Warner of Livermore, California; Hubert Beauville, Mme. Emile La Planche of Paris; Guy Faiveley, Jacques Chevignard, Comte Georges de Vogüé, Robert Drouhin, Cyprian Maufoux of Burgundy; Comte Bertrand du Vivier, Geoffroy deLuze of Bordeaux; Raymond Lillet of Podensac (Gironde); Michel Delas of Tournon-sur-Rhône; Ronald E. H. White of Rome; Dr. Richard Müller and Walter Müller of Reil (Mosel); Fritz Rall of Worms, Germany; Ferando de Terenas Latino, Antonio Julio Pereira, Fernando Van Z. Guedes, Antonio C. Sarmento of Portugal; Fernando Calleja of Madrid; Diego Ochagavia, Jésus M. Satún, Pedro López de Heredia of the Rioja (Spain); and Lazlo Terelmes of Budapest.

Creighton Churchill

New York
February, 1971

Contents

ELEVEN

The Service of Wines, *213*

TWELVE

The Selection and Storage of Wines, *224*

List of Maps and Chart

Tables

Wine—What Is It?

What is wine? What is the best wine? How did wine come to be? We hear these questions every day—and little wonder! How many liquids there are that come in a bottle today called wine.

Let us answer the last question first, even though it can be little more than speculation—for although wine is an integral part of the history of man, it is also buried in man's history.

Wine is as ancient as the Bible—in fact, it is mentioned several hundred times in the Bible, where the framers of our religion generally appear to have approved of it, though they always took pains to urge its temperate use. One of Noah's first acts after the waters had subsided was to plant a vineyard, legendarily supposed to be in Illyria, now eastern Yugoslavia. And we are all familiar with the miracle at Cana, when Jesus transformed water into wine for the guests at a wedding.

Elsewhere in the Middle East, wine was made in Egypt and in Persia by very much the same methods as are employed today in Europe, California and elsewhere—except that our modern techniques of aging and preserving wine are more efficient and, resultantly, we drink far better wines than our forebears did. The wines of two thousand years ago were coarse and hard, and the ancients usually watered them when they drank them.

Wine, properly speaking, is made from what are known as wine grapes, which—although closely related—are not the same variety of grape as table or eating grapes. The wine grape, known botanically as the *Vitis vinifera*, is smaller, more acid in taste and much less palatable than a table grape *(Vitis labrusca)*—and though the latter also makes wines of a sort, most wine drinkers of the world spurn them.

History naturally does not record what special or single type of the several hundred forms of *Vitis vinifera* was used to make the first wine, but the variety appears to have had its home in the Middle East—and like so many of the good things that man eats or drinks today, wine was in all probability not invented, but came about by accident. One might say that God must have clearly ordained that man drink wine, because every single one of the ingredients of wine is packaged, so to speak, by nature herself, and may be found in the ripe wine grape or in the surrounding air. Man has almost never needed to do more than supervise nature's simple receipt.[1]

When the mature grape is crushed (the tradition of using bare feet in ancient times still exists in many parts of the world today), yeasts, which are ever-present in the atmosphere, commence feeding on the natural sugar in the juice, and in turn convert part of this juice to alcohol. This fermentation or chemical conversion can also occur with a peach or a cherry, or even a dandelion blossom— but usually the fruit wines that we know today have had sugar added, and have been fortified with more alcohol than they acquired by natural fermentation. Thus they technically fall into the category of cordials or liqueurs, or else what the French call *apéritifs*, drinks best consumed before or after meals, not during them. Nature's bacteria are capable of producing only a certain amount of alcohol, and natural wine from the wine grape, which rarely contains more than 14 per cent alcohol (and usually less), almost always seems to be best with food. The sole exceptions are wines such as Sherry, Port and Madeira, which are all fortified with extra alcohol, and happen to be as delightful and appropriate with certain foods as without them.

What wines seem to go best with what foods is a subject we will cover in Chapter XI—but in the meantime, the best advice to be given any wine drinker is this: If you don't like a particular wine

---

[1] Only modern vintners—seeking to outdo nature's formula—add to or supplement natural grape juice with certain elements, such as cultured yeasts, tannin, etc.

when you try it, don't give up—try another! There are literally hundreds of different varieties, enough to match varying tastes, so that some individual wine will surely suit nearly every one of us, provided we are persistent enough to find it. Just as some people become sick the first day at sea and swear on the Bible never to travel again if God will only deliver them safely back to dry land, the mistake many of us make is to decide, at the first try, that we just don't like wine. Yet there are sweet wines, dry wines, strong and less strong wines, sparkling, red, white and pink (*rosé*) wines. They come from France, Germany, Italy, Spain, California and many another place—and they are all quite different. Once you have found one you like you will discover, in turn, that your taste will rapidly grow to others—and in a most surprising fashion.

As we have mentioned, wines fit with food—and one is always making the enjoyable discovery that certain wines fit better with certain foods than others. The right wine never fails to enhance the right food, and vice versa. Yet wine is also a food in itself, and we should not forget it has been an integral part of nutrition for peoples of many lands for uncountable generations. Even today peasants of many European nations thrive on a simple diet of bread, cheese—and wine. Furthermore, it whets the appetite and aids digestion, and because the roots of the wine grape often penetrate the subsoil deeper than the roots of the trees of the forest, the grape contains many valuable vitamins and trace minerals that we do not ordinarily get in our day-to-day diet.

Wine nourishes a brief, rosy, but harmless viewpoint which is very different from the oftentimes unfortunate effect of hard liquor; and there is mounting, and entirely sound, medical evidence that it reduces the cholesterol content of the blood—thought to be an important factor in certain heart ailments. Contrary to popular opinion, it does not produce gout. And though you may have heard that is bad for the liver, the true facts are, because wines go so well with foods, many people, especially Europeans, are tempted to consume far more rich food than is good for them—washing it down with good wine to aid the lagging digestion, and thus creating a vicious circle of gluttony. The French, for example, are always talking about their "bad livers," sometimes blaming it on wine, and many a Frenchman spends his "vacation" at

THE VINEYARDS OF
Europe
and North Africa

Morgan

NETHER-
LANDS
Amsterdam
R.RHEIN
(RHINE)

G E R M A N Y

Bonn

R. DONAU (DANUBE)

Vienna

Bern
SWITZERLAND

A U S T R I A

Budapest

R O M A N I A

R. PO

Belgrade

Bucharest

CORSICA

R. TIBER

Y U G O S L A V I A

Rome

I T A L Y

Sofia
B U L G A R I A

SARDINIA

G R E E C E

M E D I T E R R A N E A N   S E A

SICILY

Tunis

Athens

TUNISIA

one of his country's famous spas or watering spots, such as Vichy or Evian, where the water one drinks is reputedly a curative for the liver. Yet it always seems to be overlooked that all these spas have skilled medical staffs in attendance whose function it is to put the patient on a strict diet, which does not necessarily always exclude wine! It is the diet, no doubt, that largely accomplishes the cure.

Since the avowed purpose of this volume is to discuss wines of all countries that may be both available and of good value to wine drinkers in the United States and England, the reader may be puzzled to observe that more than one-third of these pages is devoted to the wines of France and Germany—which two nations, taken together, actually produce only a fraction of the world's wines. The point to be emphasized is that the production of good wine—leaving out the comparatively minute human factor —fundamentally depends on a subtle combination of three vital elements: 1) soil; 2) a wine grape or grapes appropriate to this same soil; and 3) climate. Without all three of these elements present—in fact, in almost perfect harmony—good and great wines are simply not made by man, however hard he tries. Although the wine grape is cultivated in many parts of the world, there is a marked difference among the types and qualities of wines from different climatic zones, and from different soils. Over the years, the soils and climates of France and southern Germany have proved to be the best for wines.

In terms of climate, there exist on all the continents certain definite northern and southern limits, beyond which the wine grape either does not produce profitably, or else makes a wine so coarse and unpalatable that no one nowadays cares much about drinking it. In Europe this geographical range extends roughly from the 30th to the 50th parallels, north of which almost no wine is produced—with the exception of a little bulge of celebrated vineyards along the Rhine and Moselle rivers in Germany, and a handful of distinctly experimental ones in southern England. Algeria and Israel, close to the southernmost boundary of the European zone, produce quantities of wine that are hardly rated at all by connoisseurs, although Algerian wines were for a long time the source, or at least the basis for blends, of most of the common wines (*ordinaires*) drunk in France. Further south, as long ago as 5000 B.C., the wine grape was raised along the Nile in Egypt—until it was found that wines brought down from Greece were better. The Romans, in turn, drank Greek and what are now Italian, Portuguese and Spanish wines until Gaul was developed—after which their most prized vintages came from their Gallic outposts, now France and Germany.

Thus history has shown that, in addition to the consideration of soils, man has progressively found the wines of northern countries more delicate and desirable—greater, as the term goes—than those of the south, which tend to be coarser and less subtle. This is very amply illustrated on our own continent in California, the largest wine-producing area in North America, where the wines from the northernmost limit of the wine-growing zone—the region around San Francisco Bay—are acknowledgedly the best of the state. As one proceeds southward, California wines increasingly resemble the bland and comparatively less delicate products of other warm, sunny lands, such as Italy and Algeria. Mexican wines, the southernmost product of our North American continent, are nothing anyone wants to bring home. And below the equator nature's same rule holds: the wines of Chile and Uruguay definitely outshine those of Peru and Brazil; Australia and Africa make their best wines in the colder parts of their wine-producing zones, those closest to the South Pole.

Many people who have drunk wines, even for years, have been sorely perplexed (though not always admitting it!) by their names and their numbers, and particularly by the specialized language on the labels. In the United States alone we see hundreds of wines from more than a dozen different countries, and with all of them the nomenclature of their labels—not to mention the pronunciations!— affords grounds for confusion, and often seems to have little or no logic. Yet it is not quite so difficult or discouraging as it might appear, once one catches on to certain fundamental patterns. A wine almost invariably derives its name from one of three sources: either the name of the principal grape from which it is made (the case with most Californian, Alsatian or Chilean wines); the geographical area from which it comes (Bordeaux, Burgundy, Chianti); or, in the case of the finest wines, mostly European, a particular vineyard or parcel of soil (Château Haut-Brion, Clos de Vougeot, Schloss Johannisberg).

There are some irritating exceptions, of course, many of which we will discuss in detail in later chapters. One of the arch crimes of wine producers of nearly all wine-producing countries is the fallacious use of names stolen from other parts of the world—"type names," or what are known as "generics." For example, the sweet, luscious dessert wine called Sauternes derives from a region in southwestern France, but because of its world-wide fame, and because in general they use the same grapes, Californian and Australian producers copy the name, even though there is no similarity whatever in the three wines. Burgundy is also a term that is bootlegged the world over. Another case is Champagne, which may only legally be called Champagne in France itself if it comes from the so-called Champagne district and is manufactured from certain prescribed grapes.[2] But the name Champagne is purloined by the Californians and many others to enhance almost anything white or pink with a fizzle. Yet another type of hoax involves the wine known as Liebfraumilch, one of the most popular of all the German wines, especially outside of Germany. Liebfraumilch (Milk of the Holy Virgin) is regrettably a name that may be legally attached to almost any wine from the southern part of the Rhine. Thus it is a common (and highly profitable) practice to use it for any and all wine not meriting a more specific or noble title. And many a wine drinker is led to believe that Liebfraumilch, which is produced by the thousands of gallons, springs from a tiny vineyard (itself the source of excellent wine) near the city of Worms. In all fairness, it must be added here that the Germans are less given to these practices than most.

Obviously, were one to decide to go to all the trouble of becoming an expert on wines, which would involve knowing all the best wines, one would begin by learning the names (and the tastes!) of those wines from all the most famous plots of soil on which the wine grape has traditionally flourished over the last thousand years

---

[2] Other French sparkling wines must by law be called *mousseux;* and most other nations adhere to the request of the French and avoid the term Champagne.

or so. For the great majority of us, this would require far too much "homework," not to mention a rather staggering expense. As we shall see, there are many short cuts to a knowledge and appreciation of wines that do not require the scope of an expert. But it is still well to remember—for those who would ask the question "Can some wines really be so *much* better than others?"— that the finest of them do indeed come from the appropriate grapes cultivated on time-tested soil, ground that has the ideal chemical properties for the wine grape, the best exposure to the sun and just the right amount of rainfall, as well as protection from winds and frosts. There are not too many of these ideal spots on the face of the earth: this is why fine wines bring, in most cases, such high prices. Yet there is the redeeming truth that most people who pursue even a mild interest in wines somehow, sooner or later, acquire an ability to recognize the qualities of the best. Even though they may never have tasted the actual best, they become singularly equipped to distinguish the sheep from the goats. And a great majority of them will have begun as the average man must do: finding a wine he likes, sticking to his taste for it as long as the taste lasts—and, of course, continuously experimenting.

TWO

Wines of France

THE VERSATILE WINELAND

In the pre-Christian world the Greeks were the active colonizers of the *Vitis vinifera*, or wine grape. They were followed by the Romans, who were in turn succeeded—beginning in the Middle Ages and continuing virtually into our own day—by the Church. We shall have a good deal more to say about the Church's role over the centuries in fostering and developing the wine grape: there is almost no wine-producing portion of the world, including our own California, which is in this respect not heavily in the Church's debt.

The first known planting of the wine grape in France took place about 600 B.C. at a Greek colony on the Mediterranean, near what is now the city of Marseille. Its culture soon spread up the Rhône Valley and northward to Alsace, as well as to other parts of France and the German Rhineland. Even in the days of Julius Caesar, the wines of Gaul were being talked about in Rome—and under Roman domination the industry showed such promise that about a hundred years later the Roman emperor, Domitian was forced to take steps to suppress it, fearing that these Gallic wines might compete too seriously with and blanket the fame of Rome's own traditional vineyards.

Domitian ordered all the vines of Gaul destroyed—but the wines of this amazingly versatile northern territory were not so easily downed. The ban was soon forgotten or overlooked, and virtually from that day on, France has been the acknowledged, indisputable queen of all the wine-producing nations on earth. Nor is there even a shred of evidence that her preeminence in the world of wines ever will vanish or fade. As we have emphasized, great wines derive primarily from soils—and within her perimeter France has not only a wide variety of soils, but also nearly all the proven best.

France is smaller than Texas, with a population of almost six times that of the Lone Star State—and nearly everyone in France drinks wine! The annual consumption for each French man, woman and child is somewhat more than thirty-five gallons—which amounts roughly to a pint a day.[1] This is not to say that every French child drinks a pint of wine daily, although many French children do drink wine, usually watered, instead of milk. Many of their fathers think nothing of consuming a bottle of it as the standard accompaniment to each of the day's two major meals! The French, like so many European peoples, consider wine to be as much a food as a beverage or thirst-quencher. France devotes over three and a half million acres (about one-third of her acreage in wheat!) to the production of more than one billion gallons of wine—and as though this shouldn't be enough to take care of the national thirst, she imports another half million gallons. Formerly this latter supply came largely from Algeria; now it also comes from Spain, Greece, Tunisia, Morocco and Corsica. Only in Italy— half the size of France, but producing as much wine as France and Algeria put together—is the making of wine more important to the national economy.

FRENCH LABELS AND VINTAGES

In both the United States and England the great majority of fine imported wines are French, and this situation will no doubt continue—even with a rising spiral of prices and an ever-increasing demand. But it must be emphasized that these imported French wines are not the ones which the French people ordinarily drink themselves on a daily basis. France has always been a frugal nation, and her citizens would not dream of drinking their best wines— except on very special occasions—when they can reap a nice profit on them abroad. Thus the ordinary Frenchman drinks a

[1] By contrast, the average American drinks slightly more than one gallon a year.

comparatively unsavory, coarse blend of his country's inferior wines, often put together with North African, Greek or Iberian wines as a base—and sends most of his choicest products to England and Belgium, Switzerland, the United States and West Germany. France's wine exports are a mere trickle compared to her immense production and prodigious national consumption, but most of these common wines of France, the *ordinaires*, never see a bottle or a label—and are thus of no concern to us here.

One often hears that the way to become knowledgeable about wines is to learn to read a label. In general, this is sound advice— except that in the case of French wines the matter of becoming an infallible expert in the field of labels may require the devotion of a good part of a lifetime. No country in the world, even that of the method-minded Germans, has stricter or more sensible regulations about the production of its wines than France—and corresponding-ly looser and more illogical laws about its labels! French law prescribes the type of wine grapes to be used on a specific piece of soil, the maximum production per acre, the minimum alcoholic content of the wine and the exacting methods by which the vines of each locality are to be pruned each year. Even setting the exact day when the grapes may be picked in the autumn was, until recently, carefully regimented by local authorities. Out of a hun-dred or so wine grapes in popular use in France today, usually only one or two are authorized for a given piece of soil or for a region that is rarely larger than an average county in the United States. These officially sanctioned grapes are the ones tradition has proven to be the best suited for the soil and climate—and only the Lord can help a French winegrower who is caught deviating from the official formula, overproducing or otherwise seeking to adulterate his product. By contrast, one often wishes that Divine Providence could be called upon to intervene on behalf of the unknowing con-sumer, when it comes to labels.

The regulations governing the French wine industry are known as *Appellations Contrôlées* (controlled appellations)—two words of prime importance to anyone seeking a knowledge of French wines for, with few minor exceptions, they must by law appear on the label of any genuine French wine of real quality.[2] They

---

[2] The only two important exceptions are Champagne, a name officially controlled and a guaranty in itself; and (until recently) wines from Alsace, which were not

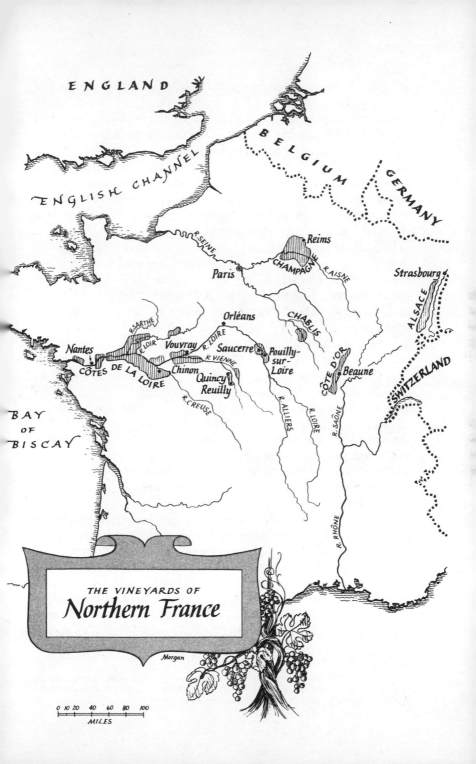

THE VINEYARDS OF
Northern France

Morgan

0 10 20 40 60 80 100
MILES

are thus not only the consumer's basic guidepost to that quality, but also his skeleton key, so to speak, to the mysteries of French labels. These two words guarantee that the wine actually comes from where the label specifies it does—whether this be a large district, such as Bordeaux; or a more confined region, such as Beaujolais; or in the case of the very finest wines, a specific vineyard. Hence, unless some merchant or vintner has managed to outsmart the authorities, an *Appellation Contrôlée* wine will not be a cheap blend of wines from different localities, nor will it contain a base of vinous red ink from Algeria or Greece.

In addition to the words *Appellation Contrôlée*, labels of the finer French wines will usually bear the vineyard name, and on occasion the terms *Grand Vin*[3] or *Grand Cru* (variously indicating great vineyard, growth or crop), or *Premier* (first) *Cru*. As we shall see later, *Grand Cru* and *Premier Cru* are both terms authorized in certain of France's vinicultural districts for wines from vineyards of superior quality. Unfortunately, while French law prescribes what shall be put on a label, it does not by any means specify a limit as to what may not, and many terms applicable to one district are often bootlegged by vintners of other districts with the hope of misleading or confusing the innocent consumer. In other words, the laws have spikes in them for malpractices in the vineyards, yet afford a veritable featherbed for anyone who might seek to embellish his labels! It is for this purpose—the reader's guidance through the frequent pitfalls of conflicting or confusing terms on French labels—that many of the tables which follow have been prepared.

Another example of the Frenchman's method of persuading the buyer that his wines are better than the next man's is to print the word *Monopole* on the label. This grandiosely implies that he owns a monopoly on a certain formula, vineyard or *cru*, and the reader should of course be forewarned that what counts more than any merchant's monopoly on anything is what the wine is like when the cork is pulled. Perhaps the best possible rule of thumb to be given about French

regulated by the *Appellations Contrôlées* laws until October, 1962. Labels of certain other lesser (though good quality) French wines use the initials *V.D.Q.S.* (*Vins Délimités de Qualité Supérieure*), which freely translated means wines of superior quality from a delimited area.

[3] The term *Grand Vin*, which is apt to appear on the label of *any* French bottle, has official status and meaning only in Alsace. The most accurate translation for the word *grand* as used in the unofficial sense is "super."

labels as a whole is this maxim: the simpler the label, the more genuine the wine is apt to be. Just as a truly beautiful woman requires a modicum of lipstick and make-up, so with a wine. Beware of exotically shaped bottles that look more appropriate to perfume than to wine. Cultivate a healthy suspicion of ornate or indecorous labels, of ribbons and medallions, of the word *Grand* attached to nearly anything but *Cru*, of *Monopoles*, names in quotes or catchy trade names. French law requires that all coined names or trade names[4] be accompanied by the words *marque déposée* (registered trademark). But many a French vintner somehow manages either to omit the term or else print it in pinpoint type in a place where the eye will be sure to miss it. One of the best examples of an honest French label known to the writer is that of one of the several owners of the tiny white-wine vineyard of Montrachet in Burgundy, traditionally one of France's greatest. Printed in simple, readable type, it provides all the components of information that the consumer should need, and nothing more, in the following order:

The name of the vineyard: *Montrachet*.

The term *Appellation Contrôlée*, certifying that the vineyard is officially recognized.

The year the wine was made.

The vinter's name and address (a guaranty that he stands behind the wine's quality and authenticity).

Why further dress up a born princess?

A French wine without a year on its label is generally a wine that is a blend of two or more years—or else it is a wine of a year of such lowly repute that the vintner has decided he can perhaps sell it better without disclosing its birth date. Wine years, good or bad, are known as "vintages"—or sometimes, "vintage years"—and, as we have mentioned, most of the world's finest wines come from the northernmost countries of the wine belt, parts of the world where the weather can be treacherously variable. In 1956 and 1960, for example, the vineyards of France and Germany were not favored by nature, and the wines were almost universally inferior. In most cases the vines had not flowered in time for the grapes to ripen under the hot suns of the long August and September days;

---

[4] An excellent example is Nectarose (rosy nectar), as used for an otherwise almost unidentified *rosé* wine.

thus the grapes did not contain enough natural sugar to create the necessary alcohol and the wine was proportionately too acid. In some places no wine was made at all; in others, what wine there was went to the blenders of "regional" or "district" wines—wines that may, or need not, be sold with the year on the label, depending upon the success of the blend.[5]

Good and bad years often vary according to locality, thus as part of each of the following sections on the various French wine districts, the reader will find specific recommendations for the vintage years, in addition to a summary (see page 232) giving the general characteristics of recent vintages for wines of France, Germany, Spain, Portugal and Italy. But it should be emphasized that these are only intended to serve the reader as a general guide. Vintage charts and other recommendations can only give an overall picture at best, and like all other statistics, they have their outstanding exceptions. Ordinarily no reputable vintner will put his name and label on a bottle of wine stemming from a very poor year—just as, by the same token, many a United States and British importer bought only a handful of wines of the outstandingly poor year of 1960. On the other hand, it can happen through some quirk of nature, or by extra skill or luck, that a French vintner will make an excellent wine (or contrive a superior blend) in an off year. Under these circumstances, he is prouder than ever to market the wine under his own name, instead of dumping it less profitably on the blenders.[6] Such off-year wines, when found either on the advice of a reliable local dealer or by chance, are always good bargains. And their discovery usually constitutes an invaluable bit of evidence in one's private search for the names of honest foreign vintners and domestic importers.

---

[5] In 1952, 1953, 1955, 1959, 1961, 1962, 1964 and 1966 the opposite happened, and wines of these years are the recent best; 1959, a highly productive year, promoted at the time as the "Year of the Century," was almost too good. Because of the virtual "hothouse conditions" nature imposed in this particular growing season, many elements and tastes were exaggerated, and many of its wines are not typical. The vintages of 1961 and 1962, though in general excellent, were in short supply.

[6] This high-minded practice of the best French vintners, sacrificing their poorer wines to protect their reputations, often results, paradoxically, in better blends (wines labeled simply Bordeaux, Médoc, Châteauneuf-du-Pape) for a poor year than a good year. In a "great" or a very good year, every vineyard owner wants to market his own wines under his own label—leaving the blenders with only the poorest to pick from.

THE VINEYARDS OF
Southern France

Morgan

CHALONNAISE
MÂCONNAIS
BEAUJOLAIS

R. SAÔNE

Mâcon

Lyon

HERMITAGE

R. CHARENTE
Cognac

R. GIRONDE

R. DORDOGNE

CÔTES DU RHÔNE

Die

R. RHÔNE

Bordeaux

BORDEAUX

R. GARONNE

CHÂTEAUNEUF-
DU-PAPE

ARMAGNAC

CÔTES DE
PROVENCE

Marseille

LANGUEDOC

BÉARN

Pau

Cassis
Bandol

ROUSILLON

Banyuls

S   P   A   I   N

BAY OF BISCAY

MEDITERRANEAN

SEA

0 10 20   40   60   80   100

SUMMARY

Although a familiarity with labels always goes hand in hand with an appreciation of the best in French wines, the French systems of labeling unfortunately do not provide for either clarity or consistency. Two convenient rules of thumb: 1) look for the words *Appellation Contrôlée* (or the initials *V.D.Q.S.*) on a label, both of which are a guarantee of an authentic wine, and 2) remember that, within reason, the simpler and less complicated or ornate the label (or bottle), the better the quality of the wine is apt to be. An honestly made French wine needs only to be described on its label in terms of four elements: the name of the vineyard or locality, the official appellation, the year and the vintner's name and address.

Never be a slave to the vintage charts. French vintages vary from very bad to very great as a result of quirks of weather, and the recent best years for France as a whole were 1952, 1953, 1955, 1959, 1961, 1962, 1964 and 1966. But fine wines are often made by good producers or blenders in certain localities in off years, constituting excellent bargains.

"Regional" blends from poor years are frequently of better quality than from the great ones.

BORDEAUX:
HUB OF THE WINE WORLD

The vineyard district of Bordeaux, which takes its name from France's second-largest city, is a vast and enormously productive agricultural area lying in the southwest corner of France, near the Spanish border. It is France's most prolific wine district: the home of the great red clarets and the white sweet Sauternes—considered by many connoisseurs to be the two finest wines in the world—and of many other wines less well known.

The Bordeaux area is drained by two rivers, the Garonne and the Dordogne, which join about eighty miles from the sea to form the tidal Gironde. The ancient city lies on the Garonne, within ample reach of high tide, just above the confluence of the two streams. It is one of France's busiest ports—and distinctly a wine port. Its citizenry lives and breathes (and tastes and drinks) wines from morning until night. Along the length of the city's famed Quai des Chartrons are some of the oldest and most celebrated winehouses in the world, establishments of bottlers and blenders and shippers, most of whose ancestors have been engaged in the international wine trade for many hundreds of years. To say that these people are proud of their tradition would be a naive understatement.

The great low-lying peninsula that shields the city from the temperamental waters of the Bay of Biscay and the Atlantic Ocean is loosely called the "Graves." *Graves* means gravel or a gravel bank—and in that very particular part of the peninsula where the wines are literally known as Graves, the roots of the vines sometimes penetrate thirty feet or more of gravel to obtain the necessary moisture and nourishment. This Graves region would be an American building contractor's dream— but let it not be thought that any Bordeaux vineyard owner would part, for any recompense in the world, with one shovelful of his precious gravelly soil for so menial a structure as a concrete footing or a cement block! In some parts of the Bordeaux wine district certain vintners, out of a dedicated sentiment for land and wine that we would find hard to understand in the New World, have themselves buried in their vineyards. Here are perhaps the most unique graveyards on earth; a lone tombstone stands untended amid the waving vines, and there are no little strips of lawn to be lovingly cared for by those left behind. Obviously the soil is far too precious for such foolishness.

The wines of the region technically known as the Graves, which lies to the west and south of the city, are about equally divided between reds and whites. (See map, page 21) Most vineyards make both. The reds, the best of which are to be numbered among France's finest, tend to be dark, with much body and a strong flavor. A good red Graves is almost always slow to mature. The whites of the region are usually dry and rather watery, with a peculiar "rusty" taste; and with the exception of the champion of them all, Château Haut-Brion Blanc, they cannot be numbered among the most distinguished of France. Popular in their own land, comparatively few of them are exported.

North of the city we find the region of Médoc, the source of some of the most aristocratic and delicate red wines of the world— of which we shall say more later when we discuss what are known as the château-bottled wines of this particular region. To the south is the region of Sauternes, Barsac and Cérons. These latter areas produce white wines exclusively, most of which tend to be very sweet, what the French call *liquoreux,* perhaps best translated as "luscious." Two other famed regions of Bordeaux are St.-Émilion and Pomerol, which (although they lie on higher ground across the Dordogne River) also have soils that are predominantly gravel. St.-Émilion and Pomerol produce powerfully fragrant red wines that are now in great demand, bringing increasingly high prices.

Although the five regions mentioned above are the classic ones for Bordeaux, there are many other parts of the district that are responsible for good wines, both red and white, many of which are beginning to appear on foreign markets. Between the two rivers, for example, is a great pie-sliced area known as Entre-Deux-Mers (Between Two Seas). Along with its neighbors, Ste.-Croix-du-Mont, Loupiac and the Premières Côtes de Bordeaux, Entre-Deux-Mers produces mild white wines which—though not necessarily great, and as yet rarely seen outside of France—are both drinkable

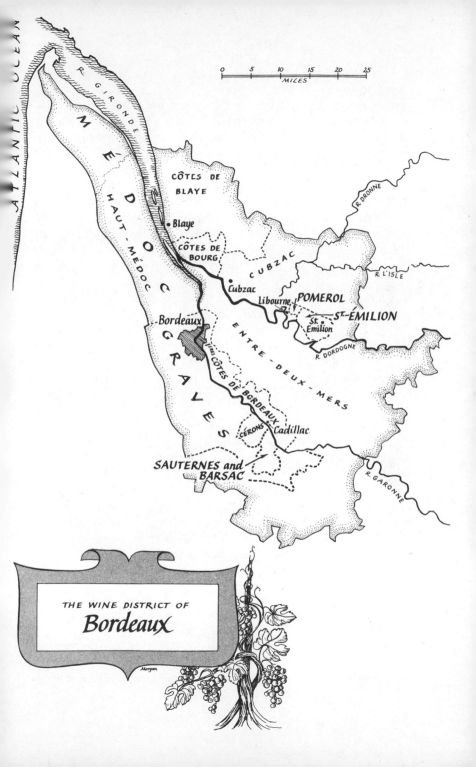

THE WINE DISTRICT OF
Bordeaux

and comparatively inexpensive. Other "unknowns" gradually emerging from obscurity are the excellent and also relatively inexpensive reds from the Côtes de Bourg and the Côtes de Blaye on the right bank of the turbulent Gironde, as well as those from the nearby Cubzac region with the quaint name of Cubzaguais—this latter at the moment meriting only the appellation of Bordeaux *Supérieur*. (See District Wines—Table A.)

In terms of labeling and identification, each of these regions, as well as the greater Bordeaux district itself,[7] has its own authorized system of *Appellations Contrôlées*, the official term we have already mentioned as being the consumer's basic guaranty of authenticity. What must be brought to the reader's attention here, however, is the fact that the Bordeaux district, viniculturally the largest of France, embraces nearly three dozen *Appellations Contrôlées*, all based theoretically on a sliding scale of quality, embodying the principle that the smaller the defined geographical area, the finer the wine. Hence wines (or blends) that are authorized to use the term *Appellation Contrôlée Bordeaux* only—the lowest in terms of quality—are not apt to be of great value. Superior wines, stemming from smaller geographical areas of Bordeaux, carry regional appellations *(Appellation Contrôlée Graves)*, and in the case of the finest —unblended wines—the name of the vineyard or château is added.[8]

Contrary to what one might think, a château in Bordeaux rarely means a castle, or even a manor house or an "estate," but simply an officially demarcated plantation of vines, with the buildings and equipment necessary to the production, storage and bottling of wine. With the finest wines of the Bordeaux district (unlike many other parts of France), it is the custom to make and bottle the wine at the vineyard itself, leading to the use of the term *Mise en Bouteilles au Château* (château-bottled)—a term which is usually both burned into the cork and printed on the label. Without words to this effect, a château-bottled wine may be a fake, something which an unscrupulous vintner has managed to put together in the privacy of his own cellar.[9]

---

[7] See Table A.

[8] Occasionally *Clos* or *Domaine* is substituted.

[9] One should be especially wary of wines labeled: *Mise en Bouteilles dans mes Caves* (or *dans nos Chais*)—bottled in our cellars. Hoping that the consumer will be so unsophisticated as to assume that the cellars *must* be at the vineyard itself, many a Bordeaux shipper has in this way profitably rid himself of many inferior admixtures and vintages.

THE BLENDS OR COMMON WINES

Throughout the Bordeaux district, where every nook and cranny of wine-producing land is a treasure-trove, there are more than three thousand officially authorized châteaux—far too many to be listed in a volume of this nature, even if all their wines merited mention. In the twin regions of St.-Émilion and Pomerol, for example, there are more than a thousand authorized vineyards alone. Fewer than half of these vineyards ever produce wines that are considered marketable with a château-bottled label; the balance, usually of quite mediocre quality, is sold in bulk to one of the numerous vintners in the cities of Bordeaux or Libourne, the port of the Dordogne, where it is blended with another wine (or wines), usually of the same year and from vineyards of the same region. Thus it is sold under what is known as a regional labeling and *Appellation Contrôlée.*

When these regional blends have been produced on the superior soils of the five classic regions—Haut-Médoc (upper Médoc, that part nearest to the city of Bordeaux), Graves, Sauternes (which includes Barsac), St.-Émilion and Pomerol—and their labels bear the names of honest and reliable merchants—they will almost always be of excellent value. This is especially valid today in view of the exorbitant prices being asked for the château-bottled wines with illustrious names. Again it must be emphasized that one of these regional wines is apt to be far better than any wine simply labeled *Appellation Contrôlée Bordeaux*—for under the law the latter *may* derive from any part of the entire Bordeaux district, and will in all probability be a blend of inferior wines that cannot be marketed otherwise. Since the quality (and labeling) of French wines is so inseparable from geography, one may be sure that if a wine of a good year has been produced on a famous piece of soil— whether it be a region, a subdivision of it or a specific vineyard— the vintner will have certainly seen to it that the label bore the highest allowable geographical appellation!

There is obviously little point in blending wines, except to stretch the qualities of a good one to improve a less good one. The origin of the Bordeaux blends, which also involves the derivation of the word "claret" (a term commonly used, especially in

England, for Bordeaux reds), has certain amusing aspects. In the twelfth century an English prince, Henry Plantagenet, descended from William the Conqueror, married Eleanor, the daughter of the French Duke of Aquitaine. When he succeeded to the throne he became not only King of England, but also ruler (by virtue of the marriage) of a large part of southwest France, including the Sénéchausée, or incorporated domain, of the city of Bordeaux.

In those days, it must be remembered, wine was rarely found far from its place of origin. People habitually drank local wines—just as they contented themselves with meat from their own farms and fish from the nearby sea or streams. Transportation of goods by land was both hazardous and expensive; each little walled town on the way demanded its toll, each turn of the road harbored a possible plundering brigand. Furthermore, the alcoholic content of the wine of that day was usually too low to warrant long, arduous land journeys, for even the strongest wine—unless, like Madeira or Sherry, it be fortified with spirits—can be joggled and shaken to the limit of its tolerance.

Thus, when wine moved at all, it usually followed the waterways. Alsatian and Rhine wines floated down the Rhine to the cities of northern Germany and thence across the Channel to England; the popes at Avignon were fortunate in being able to glut themselves on the rich reds of Burgundy, which came down the Saône and the Rhône. The court in Paris was less fortunate. It had to be satisfied with tart and undistinguished wines from nearby vineyards, and with those of Champagne (in that day a still wine) and Chablis (which arrived by the River Seine). Just as today many of us will drive fifty miles and back to have a good dinner and go to the theatre, in that day the rich and noble were impelled to journey hundreds of miles to drink the best wines of France, and frequently did. Even as late as the seventeenth century, a French king traveled all the way to St.-Émilion itself to sample the famous red wine he had never tasted, which, incidentally, he triumphantly pronounced *un doux nectar* (a charming nectar).

Once the tidal port of Bordeaux had become, under the Plantagenets, a part of the great seafaring nation of Britons, a new and vast outlet for Bordeaux wines was opened. The English had known a few wines—those of Champagne, the whites from Alsace and the precipitous hillsides of Germany, which had come to them across the Channel—and they were not long in demanding the stout red wines of England's newest province, of which so many travelers had talked. The voyage was not too long; the wines were cheap and strong and warming during the long damp winters, and made a fine variant for ale and mead. The only drawback—from the viewpoint of the Bordelais—was that the supply of good wine was limited. The superior wine the English demanded—the darkest and strongest—was only made, in that day as in this, in certain parts of the Graves peninsula and on the Haut-Pays (highlands) across the Dordogne. Throughout the rest of the territory under the control of the Sénéchausée, there was plenty of wine to be had, except that it was either white or—in the case of the reds—weak and watery, and all of it of a distinctly inferior nature.

History has not recorded the identity of the Frenchman who originally hit upon the practical idea of exploiting the English with a blend of the good and the less good, somehow persuading the gullible islanders that a fine Médoc or a lusty St.-Émilion, rendered milder and lighter by having been mixed with something else, would be an even more desirable drink than the original! All innovations, of course, need a name—preferably a catchy name, one which entices and excites the consumer and makes him think he's getting something new and different. The French called their new blend *clairet* (literally, something lighter than something else), and by virtue of some touch of marketing genius, the implication of *clairet* came also to imply something *better*. So successfully did this vogue for these new "lighter" wines catch on, that *clairet* not only became the British national drink but, even in Bordeaux itself, it got out of hand. Soon many owners of the great red-wine vineyards, not to be outdone by the blenders, took to planting white-wine grapes of their own and making their own superior *clairets*.[10]

Excessive blending, either for honest purposes or otherwise, always goes hand in hand with a demand exceeding the supply. Although, following the three-hundred-odd years of the English occupation of Bordeaux, the market for *clairet* considerably diminished and the Bordelais settled down to the making of great

[10] This is undoubtedly the origin of the white wines in the Graves vineyards, most of which have always produced red wines of far better quality. White wine is also made in the red-wine region of St.-Émilion, but of such an inferior grade that it is even debarred from the basic *Appellation Contrôlée Bordeaux*, and never exported.

wine once again, the very same situation arose in Burgundy in the first few decades of this century. For reasons which are not entirely apparent, the world's demand for a bottle labeled *Burgundy* suddenly became so great that adulteration and falsification proved to be—except with a very few vintners—positively irresistible. It was to combat this insidious practice that the French government finally stepped into the breach and appointed the *Comité National des Appellations d'Origine*—a task force to legalize and control the country's wine industry. This was the committee responsible for the *Appellations Contrôlées* laws and which—to protect the consumer—eventually graded and classified all the best wines of France. In the case of Bordeaux, as will be seen in Table A, the wines are divided into three geographical categories: 1) district wines; 2) regional wines and 3) château-bottled wines. If, in using this table, the reader continues to keep in mind the principle that the smaller the geographical area classified, the better the wine is considered to be, he should experience little trouble in assessing the potential quality of any Bordeaux wine from its label.

⤲ TABLE A   Appellations Contrôlées *of the* Bordeaux District

DISTRICT WINES

Appellation Contrôlée Bordeaux: A red, white or *rosé* wine from *anywhere* in the entire Bordeaux district. Usually blends. Often sold under trade or *monopole* names. (A Bordeaux *Supérieur* must by law have a slightly higher alcoholic content.)

REGIONAL WINES FROM SUPERIOR REGIONS
[FIVE PRINCIPAL (CLASSIC) REGIONS]

REDS

Appellations Contrôlées as follows:

MÉDOC (OR HAUT-MÉDOC).* Though the finest come from Haut-Médoc, the appellation is often shortened on labels to *Médoc*.

Subdivisions of Haut-Médoc (wines of which often use the subdivisional *Appellation Contrôlée* only) are:

Moulis	Listrac
Pauillac	St.-Julien
Margaux	St.-Estèphe

GRAVES‡

Côtes de Bourg
Côtes de Blaye
Néac

POMEROL

Lalande-de-Pomerol (Subdivision bordering Pomerol)

ST. ÉMILION

Subdivisions of St.-Émilion authorized to hyphenate their names with St.-Emilion are:

Lussac	Montagne
Puisseguin	St.-Georges
Parsac	Sables

Premières Côtes de Bordeaux

WHITES

SAUTERNES† (sweet)
  Barsac (sweet) A subdivision of Sauternes with the option to use its own *Appellation Contrôlée*
Cérons (generally sweet)

GRAVES‡ (dry; some can be very dry)
Loupiac (sweet)
Ste.-Croix-du-Mont (sweet)
Premières Côtes de Bordeaux (dry)

Other regions of Bordeaux entitled to their own *Appellations Contrôlées* are: Côtes-de-Fronsac, Côtes-Canon-Fronsac (red wines only), Entre-Deux-Mers, Côtes-de-Bordeaux-St.-Macaire (white wines only), Graves-de-Vayres, Ste.-Foy-Bordeaux (red and white).

CHÂTEAU-BOTTLED WINES (See Table B)

The finest traditionally come from Haut-Médoc, St.-Émilion, Sauternes (and their respective subdivisions), Pomerol and Graves.

NOTE: Many bottles of Bordeaux wines bear a seal with the initials *ADEB* (*Association pour le Développement de l'Exportation du Vin de Bordeaux*), indicating that the wine has been voluntarily submitted to a panel of Bordeaux experts before export. As a rule, this may be considered a mark of added quality.

* White and *rosé* wines of Haut-Médoc are only entitled to *Appellation Contrôlée Bordeaux.*

† Both the terms Haut-Sauternes and Haut-Barsac on a label are entirely meaningless. Likewise *Grand* (Grand Médoc, Grand St.-Julian, etc.) See footnote on page 14.

‡ A Graves *Supérieure*, like a Bordeaux *Supérieur*, requires a slightly higher alcoholic content.

THE CHÂTEAU WINES

Of all the wines of Bordeaux, the red wines of Haut-Médoc—
that part of the Médoc peninsula closest to the city—are considered
the finest and the most delicate, the aristocracy of clarets. By law,
Bordeaux reds may be made only from a blend of four or five
grapes, the principal two of which are the Cabernet-Sauvignon (a
grape we shall also meet in California and elsewhere) and its cousin
the Cabernet franc—with varying small proportions of the Merlot,
the Malbec, and the Petit Verdot, depending largely on the personal
formula of the vineyard owner. The soils of Haut-Médoc are
peculiarly well suited to the two Cabernets, and many producers
of this region use them to the exclusion of the others.

When sufficiently aged (eight or ten years is usually an ideal
minimum) the Médocs—they are paradoxically never spoken of as
Haut-Médocs, despite the fact that all the finest derive from this section of the greater Médoc area—possess that quality which connoisseurs call *finesse*. It would be futile to delve too deeply into their
comparative subtleties: the wine drinker's own palate must do that
by experimentation. But as one travels northward from the city
through the six official subdivisions of Haut-Médoc—Margaux
(Château Margaux), Listrac, Moulis (Château Chasse-Spleen), St.-
Julien (Châteaux Léoville-Lascases and Beychevelle), Pauillac (Châteaux Latour, Lafite-Rothschild and Mouton-Rothschild) and
St.-Estèphe (Château Cos-d'Estournel)—one will discover that the
wines of the southern subdivisions possess more delicacy and softness, while those made farther to the north, closer to the mouth of
the river, have more of what the French call *vinosité* (winyness).
These latter are sharp and bitter when young, and require far more
time for aging. A young château-bottled St.-Julien or St.-Estèphe,
for example, may be a very raw, unpalatable drink indeed.

The red wines of the Graves region—with the exception of the
celebrated Château Haut-Brion, which has always been classed
with the best—tend to be somewhat heavier and coarser than the
Médocs, and are characterized by a slight tang of mustiness which,
with many wine drinkers, usually becomes attractive only through
usage. The wines of the twin regions of Pomerol and St.-Émilion,

on the other hand, even though they are grown some twenty miles to the east, more resemble the Médocs than they do the Graves. And like red Burgundies, they have a distinctive floweryness and lightness about them (some people claim to smell violets and other exotic fragrances in them). Although St.-Émilions from the great vineyards may be aged to advantage for many years, the lesser ones from this region, as well as from Pomerol, are comparatively short-lived. Even the wine from the very best château of Pomerol, Château Pétrus, may be consumed and appreciated when ten years old, though it may not have reached its peak of perfection. The two traditionally best wines of St.-Émilion are Château Ausone and Château Cheval-Blanc. Unfortunately they are presently under-going a vogue that renders them almost prohibitively expensive.

The most celebrated white château wines of Bordeaux are the sweet Sauternes and Barsacs, the most famous of which is Château d'Yquem, a wine that in the original classification of Bordeaux wines in 1855 (see Table B) was singled out for the highest possible of titles, *Premier Grand Cru* (First Great Growth). These *liquoreux* wines made in Sauternes, Barsac and nearby Cérons—comparable to the sweet German *Trockenbeerenauslesen* and the syrupy Hungarian Tokay—owe their particular character to the presence of an indigenous mold or yeast known as the *Botrytis cineria*, called by the French the *pourriture noble* (noble rot). Again a part of nature's "packaging" of the wine grape, the *pourriture noble* manifests itself—though only in certain wine-producing parts of the world—as a grayish film that covers the skin of the grape when the latter has almost completely matured.[11] This extraordinary little organism grows tiny roots that pierce the skin, feeding on the liquid within and thus appreciably reducing the water content of the grape. In consequence, those grapes which have been attacked by it possess an abnormally high percentage of sugar—far more than is necessary for the natural yeasts to bring the wine to its maximum alcoholic limit—and the ensuing wine is

---

[11] The white wines of Sauternes, as with all Bordeaux whites, are a blend of three white grapes, the Sémillon, the Sauvignon (both sources of California dry white wines), and the Muscadelle.

thus left with a considerable quantity of residual sugar. It will be found that these *liquoreux* wines also have unusual body or thickness, for along with more sugar, they contain a higher proportion of glycerine than a dry wine does. And there is a subtle "nutty" flavor about them, imparted by the *pourriture noble* itself. Most people prefer to drink them at the end of a meal, with desserts.

At the Château d'Yquem, an imposing and handsome country establishment that is deserving of the name, there is a legendary tale of how, many generations ago, this vineyard—which, like its neighbors, once made only dry wine—came to produce sweet. In that day the grapes were never harvested without the express permission of the lord of the manor—and in the case of the Château d'Yquem, the lord happened at the time to be a gay blade who apparently preferred the salons and cotillions of Paris to the boredom of his country seat.

One particular autumn, as all the neighboring vineyards commenced the *vendange*, or harvest, the grapes of the Château d'Yquem had to be left on the vines. Frantic appeals were sent to Paris; one thinks of the old peasants wringing their hands, of the priest initiating special prayers. But to no avail: the young noble had found an undeniable attraction—or possibly two. Finally, weeks later, a cloud of dust appeared on the road, the young lord rode heavily into the courtyard and gave the seemingly futile order. In those days orders were orders—even if given by a love-smitten young madman. The peasants moved obediently to the vineyards and commenced the seemingly futile task of picking the rotten grapes—and thus was born the greatest sweet wine of all France! Nowadays the grapes in Sauternes are no longer harvested in such a hurry, but bunch by bunch—or even one by one with scissors—as they reach the desired degree of sticky sweetness brought about by the predatory *pourriture*.

Wine drinkers these days seem not to have either the time or taste for sweet dessert wines, especially the expensive imported ones, thus many of the vineyards of Sauternes and Barsac are returning once again to the production of dry wines—those made from grapes before the *pourriture* has settled on them. (The Château d'Yquem itself now makes and markets an experimental dry

white called Château Y.) This renders them comparable to—
though not necessarily any better than—the white wines of nearby
Graves, which have always been dry. As we have said, the whites of
Graves are, in the opinion of most connoisseurs, a rather undistinguished lot—as a certain writer of the last century put it: "Not
very well endowed." Two of the best and most typical are Château
Olivier and Château Carbonnieux. Château Haut-Brion Blanc, one
of the greatest wines in the world, is in a class by itself. It is neither
dry nor sweet, possesses great character all its own—and is nearly
impossible to obtain!

Some other good white wines of the Bordeaux district come from
the regions of Loupiac and Ste.-Croix-du-Mont, and from the
vicinity of the village of Cadillac, across the Garonne in the region
called Premières Côtes de Bordeaux.

All these Bordeaux whites are ready to drink when they are two
or three years old, although the sweeter ones, such as the Sauternes
and Barsacs, will improve slightly in the bottle over a period of
ten or fifteen years. The reader should be warned, however, that
there is always a danger that with too much age these latter will
become what is known as *maderizé*, a form of oxidation to which
all white wines—sweet or dry—are susceptible after a certain time.
The term *maderizé* is an entirely literal one: the wine turns the
color of Madeira, and takes on a bitter, acrid taste. The best rule of
thumb: drink most French white wines when relatively young.

A list of the best-known château-bottled wines of Bordeaux,
may be found in Table B.[12] These are known as the *Grands Crus
Classés* (Important Classified Growths), and in the case of seventy-
odd-top vineyards of Haut-Médoc[13] and about twenty of Sauternes,
the gradings are based on an official classification that traces back to
1855. It is a revealing sidelight that the judges, who more than a
century ago picked these ninety-odd wines from among many
hundreds of others, must have been on the soundest ground—for to
this day French officialdom has never seen fit to alter the original
judgment on these premium vineyards (despite the agitation of many

[12] One should remember that, to be authentic, each of their labels must not
only bear the *Appellation Contrôlée* of the appropriate, authorized regional area
(See Table A), but also the vineyard name (*Château, Clos, Domaine*, etc.).

[13] Including Château Haut-Brion in Graves.

a competitive vineyard owner). Over the years some have gone out of existence, some others are currently under the shadow of poor management—and certain others yet, as are indicated in the listing, by virtue of changes in management and vinicultural techniques have risen in stature and passed into another category of excellence. Yet the 1855 list stands—as a monument to the judgment of the men who made it, and to the truth that the best wine essentially derives from the most appropriate soils and grapes. Cuttings from Bordeaux have been carried all over the world and grown in every type of soil and under every conceivable condition—but at no place on the face of the globe has any vintner ever been able to reproduce, or duplicate with any crowning success, that exact character and flavor of the wines from the Graves peninsula and the Haut-Pays.

Within the last two decades (many of the finest red and, as we have pointed out, the best of the sweet white wines of Bordeaux are capable of this span of years) the best vintages have been 1943, 1945, 1947, 1949, 1952, 1953, 1955, 1957, 1958, 1959, 1961, 1962 and 1964.

SUMMARY

Under the *Appellations Contrôlées* laws, Bordeaux wines are labeled in three general grades, in this order of excellence: 1) *Bordeaux*, which may be a wine (or blend of wines) from any part of the entire district; 2) regional or subregional, usually blends (those considered best come from Haut-Médoc, St.-Émilion, Sauternes (and their subdivisions), Graves and Pomerol and 3) château wines, stemming from officially recognized and classified vineyards. Of the reds, Haut-Médoc produces the finest (the aristocracy), those of Graves are somewhat heavier and coarser, the St.-Émilions and Pomerols are lighter and more flowery, more like red Burgundies. Graves whites are dry and slightly watery, often lacking in distinguished tastes; the classic Sauternes and Barsacs are sweet wines to drink with desserts.

~§ TABLE B　*Châteaux-Bottled Wines of Bordeaux*

PRINCIPAL CLASSIFIED RED WINES OF HAUT-MÉDOC

(Official classification, unchanged since 1855)

1.
(Premiers Crus)

Château Lafite-Rothschild	Château Latour
Château Margaux	Château Haut-Brion
	(see Graves)

2.
(Deuxièmes Crus)

*Château Mouton-Rothschild	Château Léoville-Lascases
Château Rausan-Ségla	Château Léoville-Poyferré
Château Rauzan-Gassies	Château Léoville-Barton
Château Durfort-Vivens	Château Cos-d'Estournel
Château Lascombes	Château Ducru-Beaucaillou
Château Gruaud-Larose	Château Montrose
Château Brane-Cantenac	Château Pichon-Longueville
Château Pichon-Longueville	(Countesse de Lalande)
(Baron de Pichon)	

3.
(Troisièmes Crus)

Château Cantenac-Brown	Château Giscours
Château Palmer	Château Kirwan
Château Grand La Lagune	Château d'Issan
Château Calon-Ségur	Château Lagrange
Château Ferrière	Château Langoa-Barton
Château Marquis d'Alesme-	Château Malescot-St.-Exupéry
Becker	Château Boyd-Cantenac

4.
(Quatrièmes Crus)

Château Gloria
Château St.-Pierre
  (formerly Château St.-Pierre-
  Sevaistre)
*Château Branaire-Ducru
*Château Talbot
Château Duhart-Milon
Château La Tour-Carnet

Château Pouget
Château Rochet
  (formerly Château Lafont-
  Rochet)
*Château Beychevelle
Château Prieuré-Lichine
Château Marquis de Terme

5.
(Cinquièmes Crus)

Château Pontet-Canet
*Château Batailley
*Château Grand-Puy-Lacoste
*Château Grand-Puy-Ducasse
*Château Lynch-Bages
Château Lynch-Moussas
Château Camensac
Château Cos-Labory
Château Clerc-Milon

Château Dauzac
*Château Mouton-Baron Philippe
Château Le (du) Tertre
Château Haut-Bages-Libéral
Château Pédesclaux
Château Belgrave
Château Croizet-Bages
*Château Cantemerle
Château Haut-Batailley

6.
(Crus Exceptionnels et Bourgeois)

Château Villegeorge
*Château Angludet
Château La Couronne
Château Moulin-Riche
*Château Capbern
*Château Dutruch-Lambert
*Château Fourcas-Dupré
*Château Le Boscq
*Château Meyney
*Château Les-Ormes-de-Pez
*Château Paveil-de-Luze

*Château Chasse-Spleen
*Château Poujeaux-Theil
Château Bel-Air-Marquis-
  d'Aligre
*Château Fourcas-Hostein
*Cru Gressier-Grand Poujeaux
*Château Lanessan
*Château de Pez
*Château Phélan-Ségur
*Château La Tour-de-Mons
*Château Sénéjac

---

* Denotes a wine which in the opinion of most experts is better than indicated by its above position on the list.

PRINCIPAL CLASSIFIED WINES OF GRAVES

(R) red wine only. (W) white wine only.

1.

(Premier Grand Cru)

Château Haut-Brion

2.

(Grands Crus Classés)

Château La Mission-Haut-Brion (R)
Château (Domaine de) Chevalier
Château Bouscaut
Château Fieuzal (R)
Château Malartic-Lagravière
Château Latour-Martillac (R)
Château Haut-Bailly (R)

Château Carbonnieux
Château Olivier
Château La Tour-Haut-Brion (R)
Château Pape Clément (R)
Château Smith-Haut-Lafitte (R)
Château Laville-Haut-Brion (W)
Château Couhins (W)

3.

(Crus Supérieurs Principaux)

Château Baret
Château Brown
Château Cabannieux (W)
Château Carmes-Haut-Brion (R)
Domaine de Grandmaison (W)
Château de Hilde (R)
Château Haut-Gardere (W)
Château Le Désert (W)

Château Lagarde (R)
Château Malleprat (W)
Château Le Pape
Château de Respide
Château de Tuquet
Château Virilade (W)

Clos du Roy (R)
Château Couhins (R)
Château de la Brede (W)

Château Ferran (W)
Château Ferrande (W)
Château Gazin (W)
Château Limbourg (R)
Château La Louvière
Château Larrivet-Haut-Brion (R)
Château Moulerens (R)
Château Poumey
Château La Tour (W)
Château Valoux (R)

PRINCIPAL CLASSIFIED RED WINES OF ST.-ÉMILION

1.

(*Premiers Grands Crus*)

Château Ausone   Château Cheval-Blanc

2.

(*Grands Crus*)

Château Beauséjour-Lagarosse   Château Beauséjour-Fagouet
Clos Fourtet   Château Belair
Château Figeac   Château Canon
Château La Gaffelière Naudes   Château Magdelaine
Château Pavie   Château Trottevieille
Château Ripeau   Château Trimoulet

PRINCIPAL RED WINES OF POMEROL

(Unofficial classification by the Pomerol Wine Growers' Syndicate)

1.

(*Grands Premiers Crus*)

Château Pétrus

Château Certan   Vieux Château Certan

2.

(*Premiers Crus*)

Cru l'Évangile   Château Nénin
Château Beauregard   Château Petit-Village
Château Clinet   Le Clos Lacombe
Château Lafleur   Le Clos de l'Église
Château La Commanderie   Clos du Clocher
Château Gazin   (Château) Certan-Sauteloup
Château Le-Gay-et-La-Fleur   Château Trotanov
Château Guillot

PRINCIPAL CLASSIFIED WHITE WINES OF SAUTERNES (AND BARSAC)

1.

(Premier Grand Cru)

Château d'Yquem

2.

(Premiers Crus)

Château Giraud
Château La Tour Blanche
Château Lafaurie-Peyraguey
Château Rayne-Vigneau
Château Rabaud-Promis
Château Sigalas-Rabaud

Château Haut-Peyraguey
Château Coutet (Barsac)
Château Climens (Barsac)
Château de Suduiraut
Château Rieussec

3.

(Deuxièmes Crus)

Château Filhot
Château d'Arche
Château Lamothe
Château d'Arche-Lafaurie
Château Caillou (Barsac)
Château Suau (Barsac)
Château Nairac (Barsac)

Château Doisy-Védrines (Barsac)
Château Doisy-Daëne (Barsac)
Château Doisy-Dubroca (Barsac)
Château de Myrat (Barsac)
Château Broustet (Barsac)
Château de Malle
Château Romer

BURGUNDY:
WINES OF AN ANCIENT DUKEDOM

No real wine lover could praise the wines of Bordeaux without including, in the same breath, those of Burgundy. The wines of these two districts, quite different in character, are without doubt the finest in France. About this there has never been any question.

Burgundy produces both red and white wines, but many people think of Burgundy only as a red wine—just as they think of Bur-

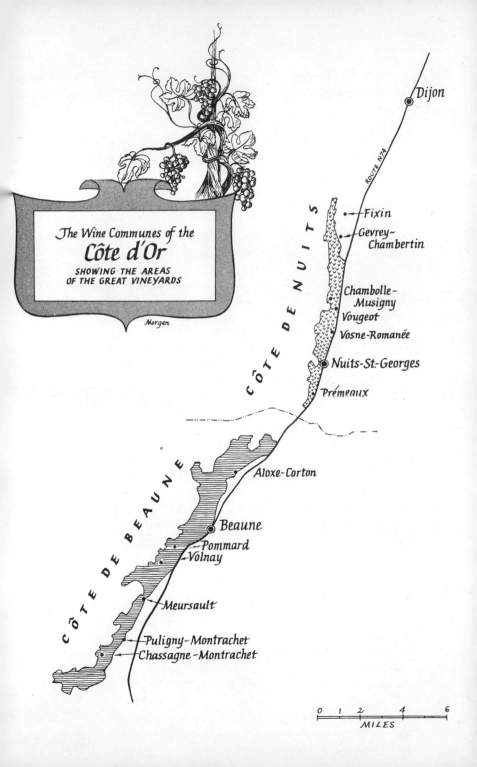

The Wine Communes of the
Côte d'Or
SHOWING THE AREAS
OF THE GREAT VINEYARDS

Morgan

Dijon

ROUTE N74

CÔTE DE NUITS

Fixin
Gevrey-
Chambertin

Chambolle-
Musigny
Vougeot
Vosne-Romanée
Nuits-St-Georges
Prémeaux

CÔTE DE BEAUNE

Aloxe-Corton

Beaune
Pommard
Volnay

Meursault

Puligny-Montrachet
Chassagne-Montrachet

0 1 2   4   6
MILES

gundy as a red color with a slightly purplish tinge. It is true that the traditionally great vineyards of Burgundy, many of which have existed since Roman times, are predominantly devoted to red rather than to white wines—but when one thinks of fabulous ruby-colored wines such as Chambertin and Clos de Vougeot, one should never discount the charm and power of those rare white vintages of Corton-Charlemagne and Montrachet.

Closely packed into a tight little ribbon, the greatest vineyards of Burgundy stretch southward for approximately thirty miles from the city of Dijon, almost in the center of France. This is Burgundy proper, known as the Côte d'Or, in the fifteenth century the epicenter of a little duchy which, during the aggressive reign of its aptly named ruler, Charles the Bold, came near to becoming the epicenter of the French nation. Today Dijon might well hold the position of Paris, except that like all power seekers, Charles spread himself too thin, drove his people into too many debilitating wars and was eventually unseated by Louis XI, a crafty little man from the west who planned his wars and ran his country while riding around on a donkey and quietly chatting with the common people.

Nowadays Burgundy (the French term is *Bourgogne*) is more a name than a place. Viniculturally speaking, the term is used for almost all the wines made in central France, from Paris to the Rhône. This includes the region of Chablis in the north, the home of very dry white wines—classics with seafoods; the Côte d'Or itself, producing both reds and whites; and the scattered vineyards known as Southern Burgundy, split into three regions called the Chalonnaise, the Mâconnais and the Beaujolais.

There are so many vinicultural differences between Bordeaux and Burgundy that it seems best to begin by disposing of the major ones. To begin with, whereas the wines of Bordeaux are blends or mixtures of several grapes, a fine Burgundy is invariably made from one prescribed grape alone. In fact, in all of greater Burgundy, only three grapes are officially authorized for the better wines. These are the white Chardonnay (sometimes colloquially known as the Pinot blanc); the red Pinot noir; and the Gamay, the grape responsible for the delicious, fruity red wines of Beaujolais.

Again in contrast to Bordeaux, where the vineyards (châteaux) are relatively large and usually owned by a single individual, Burgundian vineyards are minuscule in size—sometimes only a few acres—and oftentimes subdivided among dozens of owners. Many of these owner-producers may only own a few rows of vines. Originally parts of larger tracts belonging, in many instances, to the Church, their subdivision took place during the French Revolution, when for *le bien national* (the national good), the property of the clergy, and of the high and mighty, was confiscated by the state and divided among the masses. The châteaux of Bordeaux miraculously escaped this fate; but in Burgundy and many other parts of France, the *bien national* created anything but an ideal situation. Nowadays the owner of a few rows of vines in a great and famous vineyard of the Côte d'Or may make his wine very differently from the owner of the next few rows; yet the vineyard name on the label—the wine drinker's logical guide to quality among Burgundies—remains the same.

Once again, unlike the usual practice in Bordeaux, Burgundian vintners usually make their wines away from the vineyard, in the privacy of their own cellars. Obviously the government inspectors cannot be everywhere at the same time—which is why Burgundies can be the most variable wines in the world.

These cellar-bottled wines of Burgundy are often known as "estate-bottled," and their labels will generally bear words such as *Mise en Bouteille au Domaine* or *Mise à la Propriété* (bottled on the property). The point to be emphasized is that estate-bottled is by no means comparable to the Bordeaux term of château-bottled, and no real insurance of a wine's quality. Given the name of the vineyard, the wine drinker must also know the names of reputable vintners and importers, or be guided by a conscientious and knowledgeable dealer. For this reason—although the reader will readily understand that it does not come within the actual scope of this volume to give all the names of all the best vintners and bottlers in France—Table F, somewhat farther along in these pages, is a partial list of reputable vintners *(négociants)* for the Côte d'Or itself.

CHABLIS

The white, delicate and extremely dry, "flinty" wines of Chablis (the northernmost region of modern Burgundy) have for a great many generations been the world's favorite accompaniment to seafood. They are all made in a small region lying about a hundred miles southeast of Paris, the grapes being grown on chalky slopes drained by the placid little River Serein—the French word for serene. It was by virtue of this little stream, which turns into the larger Yonne, and thence into the Seine, that the wines of Chablis were among the first to reach the French court from any distance. Indeed, a few of them must even have been allowed to slip through Paris and make their way across the Channel, for it is a matter of record that as early as 1212, King John of England had tasted them, and was negotiating for a supply of his own. In fact, Chablis vies with the still wines of Champagne for the honor of being the first French wine to be exported in any quantity.

As has so often been the case with the great wines of the world, it is to the Church that the basic credit must be given for Chablis. History reveals a group of Cistercian monks busily experimenting around the vineyards of Chablis and its two adjacent towns, Auxerre and Tonnerre, in the early part of the twelfth century, trying out one grape after another, searching diligently for the best soils and exposures. And while there is ample evidence that over the centuries wines of many localities had radically changed, usually for the better, in Chablis the Cistercians evidently established, some eight hundred years ago, a lasting prototype. A description of Chablis written by a traveling monk in 1280 is, remarkably enough, almost as valid today as it was then: "A white wine, sometimes golden, which has aroma and body, an exquisite, generous savor, and fills the heart with joyous assurance." Had he added the word "dry" and perhaps noted that Chablis's light goldenness is (to use the words of another thirteenth-century account) like "the color of spring water in sunlight"—one could not better describe it.

Chablis is produced under the most trying circumstances, and unfortunately, so great is the world's demand for it (estimated at about ten times the supply) that a vast quantity of wine so labeled is either adulterated with other wines and too poor to drink, or not Chablis at all. Taken together, all the vineyards producing wine within the four grades allowed by the *Appellations Contrôlées* of Chablis amount to considerably less than a thousand acres, which acreage is diminishing every year. Thus good Chablis is logically both rare and expensive. Among other adversities, the region itself is just barely south of the northernmost growing limit for the wine grape, and—about every five years out of ten—is beset by killing frosts or other ravages of nature. Even so, in many of the good years, much of the crop is lost by frost. And as though this were not enough to plague the vintners, the chalky hillsides do not adapt themselves to mechanization, and there is a shortage of labor!

Nonetheless, always bearing their expense in mind, it must be said that wines from any of the eight *Grand Cru* and the twenty-four *Premier Cru* vineyards, all of superior quality, may be numbered among the finest and driest wines of France. There is nothing better with lobster or oysters, clams or even the menial halibut! But the reader must be warned that the wines of the two lower appellations—*Petit Chablis* and *Chablis*—may well be weak and acid, and will more often than not constitute a bitter disappointment, especially in view of the price one must pay. Before buying them, one should look well to the name of the bottler and to the reputation of the importer—and perhaps end by settling for another type of dry wine. In its price class, there is no more adulterated and/or faked wine in all of France.

The name Chablis, too, is not alone in having been appropriated by almost every other white wine-producing country of the world. It is well always to remember that there is no relationship. Only on the chalky banks of the Serein—part of the geological Kimmeridgian stratum which manifests itself again in the Cliffs of Dover—does the Chardonnay grape produce this flawless type of white Burgundy, and only then in the best vineyards and at the hands of the best producers. Most imitation Chablis is anything but "bone dry." Spanish "Chablis," for example, from the Rioja district, may be a good wine, but no more resembles its French namesake than Bourbon is reminiscent of Crème de Menthe. South American and Australian "Chablis" are even more nondescript. California "Chablis" (never made from the Chardonnay) is something that is best described as merely white and light. This is not to say it cannot be a pleasant wine which is usually far more palatable than a bad version of its original French counterpart.

Table C gives the eight *Grands Crus* (Important Growths) and the twenty-four *Premiers Crus* (First Growths) of Chablis, each category being entitled to its own authorized *Appellation Con-*

trôlée. As we have mentioned, within the two lower official classifications one should choose carefully: the name of a reliable grower is of paramount importance. Good recent years for Chablis are 1952, 1953, 1955, 1958, 1959, 1961 and 1962—and the Chablis region is perhaps the sole exception to our own favorite rule that slavery to vintage charts is a form of abject foolishness.

⤷ **TABLE C**   *The Two First Crus of Chablis*

Grands Crus

Blanchots	Vaudésir
Les Clos	Bougros
Grenouilles	La Moutonne
Valmur	Les Preuses

Premiers Crus

Beauroy (Boroy)	Montée de Tonnerre
Beugnon(s)	Montmains
Butteaux	Pied d'Aloup
Chapelots	Séchet
Châtains	Roncières
Côte de Fontenay	Troëme (Troêne)
Côte de Léchet	Vaillons
Les Forêts	Vaupulent
Fourchaume	Vaucoupin
Les Lys	Vaulorent
Melinots	Vosgros
Mont-de-Milieu	Vogiros (Vaugiraud)

THE CÔTE D'OR

Just south of Dijon, a city now chiefly famous for its powerful mustard and Cassis, a syrupy liqueur made from black currants, there begins the little region called the Côte d'Or—the Slope of Gold. Its glamorous name should provoke the image of some sparkling cove on the Riviera, or perhaps a buttercup-carpeted valley high in the Alps—but such is simply not the case. The Slope of Gold is, in truth, an undeniably drear, unassuming range of low hills, paralleled (and certainly not enhanced) by a trunk railroad and the busy highway from Paris to the Mediterranean. Its limestone soil is filled with rocks and boulders, and far too poor for growing anything but the wine grape, its little villages—whose famous names are seen in wineshops the world over—are by no means among the most charming of France.

The vineyards themselves are slightly elevated above the valley floor, exposed to the southeast and protected by hills to the west, and concentrated into a narrow ribbon of land that is barely thirty miles long and less than half a mile wide at its broadest. Midway between Dijon and the ancient fortress city of Beaune, this undulating little ribbon almost completely vanishes, like some underground river. An ugly quarry appears, the countryside takes on an almost commercial aspect, and the ribbon is hardly seen again for almost two miles. North of this break, the Côte d'Or has the subdivisional name of the Côte de Nuits; the southern half, containing the city of Beaune, is known as the Côte de Beaune.

The wines of the Côte de Nuits, which include the greatest Burgundies, are nearly all red. They are sturdier and tend to live longer than those of the Côte de Beaune. Although the term is almost never seen on a label, the twenty-odd finest have been awarded the official title of *Grand Cru*,[14] these latter carrying the right to use on labels the words *Appellation Contrôlée* as applied specifically to the vineyard itself (see Table D). The next best wines are known as *Premiers Crus*. Their labels not only bear the vineyard name (supplemented sometimes with the term *Premier Cru*),[15] but also the *Appellation Contrôlée* of the town or commune from which they come.

Unfortunately, a hidden danger lurks in many of these communal names of the Côte d'Or, which the unknowing reader should be made aware of for his own protection. Toward the end of the last

[14] Previous to the advent of the *Appellations Contrôlées*, the finest vineyards of the Côte d'Or were called *Têtes de Cuvée*. The term is sometimes still seen on labels.
[15] A Chablis or Côte d'Or label bearing the words *Premier Cru* without a vineyard name usually means a blend of wines from *Premiers Crus* vineyards.

century—without doubt for the purpose of selling more inferior wine at better prices—many of the communes of the Côte d'Or adopted the disturbing practice of hyphenating the name of the commune with that of its most famous vineyard. Thus, for example, Gevrey (the commune) was married to Chambertin (among the most celebrated vineyards of the entire Côte d'Or), and officially became Gevrey-Chambertin; Chambolle took on the name of its most illustrious wine, Musigny, to become known thenceforth as Chambolle-Musigny. And since the great white vineyard of the Côte de Beaune, Montrachet, was spread between the two communes of Puligny and Chassagne, both claimed it. Today they are Puligny-Montrachet and Chassagne-Montrachet.

The practice, which is comparable to calling *all* Milwaukee beer Milwaukee-Schlitz, has no doubt been an economic boon to the Côte d'Or; but the wine drinker should never forget that a bottle simply labeled Chassagne-Montrachet or Gevrey-Chambertin is only a wine—and often a quite common one—from any vineyard within one of these two communes; or a blend of wines from two or more vineyards within the same commune. In any case it is certainly neither a true Chambertin nor a bona fide Montrachet, nor even one of the other several *Grands Crus* from vineyards that are officially entitled to hyphenate their names with those of the two greatest (see Table D).

Going south from Dijon, the first cluster of *Grands Crus* vineyards one meets are those of Gevrey-Chambertin. These include the famed Chambertin and its twin, the Clos de Bèze, and the other seven nearby vineyards whose wines are so excellent that they are authorized to hyphenate their names with the parent vineyard of Chambertin and use their own individual *Appellation Contrôlée*. We repeat—do not fall into the trap of confusing them with a communal wine simply named Gevrey-Chambertin! Chambertin, so goes the traditional story, was once a field planted to turnips, adjacent to the great vineyard belonging to the Abbey of Bèze. So excellent were the wines of the Abbey that a rival religious order finally could stand it no longer and subsidized the peasant owner of the turnip patch to rip up his crop and plant vines. This peasant was named Bertin—thus the vineyard acquired the name of Champ de Bertin (Bertin's field).

Wines of the Chambertin cluster are dark and heavy, with a reputation for aging comparable to the Médocs of Bordeaux, although this is not par for the average red Burgundy. Over the ages the Chambertins have been the favorites of many an illustrious person. Napoleon is said to have allowed nothing else on his table, and to have taken an ample supply to Russia with him during the ill-fated campaign of 1812. As we have already warned, each of these *Grands Crus* vineyards, like most of the Côte d'Or, is divided among many growers, resulting in wines of variable quality. When made by a conscientious vintner, there are few finer red Burgundies; yet even the more poorly made ones are hard to find, and expensive. Alternately, we recommend the *Grands Crus* wines of the adjacent commune, Morey-St.-Denis, the best of which are Clos de Tart, Clos de la Roche, and the Clos St.-Denis; as well as some of the other excellent *Premiers Crus* wines listed in Table D.

All Burgundies from the Côte d'Or are noted for their almost overpowering, though entirely attractive, fragrances—aromas which carry overtones of more than just wine. Some people relate these overtones and fragrances to raspberries, violets and even truffles—and in the case of the white Montrachet, the term often used by the experts is beeswax. The red wines of the next three communes—Chambolle-Musigny, Vougeot, and Vosne-Romanée—are the most fragrant of the whole Côte d'Or. Red Musigny[16] is indeed redolent of raspberries; nor does it take a veteran to spot the fragrance of violets wafting from a glass of well-made Clos de Vougeot.

Almost the entire commune of Vougeot is taken up by the hundred-and-thirty-acre Clos, one of the Côte d'Or's largest vineyards. Planted in the twelfth century by Cistercian monks, whose noble monastery still stands amid the rows of vines as the headquarters of a distinguished organization of Burgundian vintners (*the Confrérie des Chevaliers du Tastevin*), no wines on the whole Côte d'Or have been more praised in days gone by than the flowery ones of this vineyard. Its glories have been sung by Stendhal and Voltaire, by popes and kings and generals; in fact, to this day the vineyard is still honored by passing regiments, for whom it has become customary to halt and present arms. Regrettably, the *bien national*

---

[16] The vineyard is also the source of one of France's finest and rarest white wines, Musigny Blanc.

wrought more than just the usual harm to the Clos de Vougeot—for even this sacrosanct ground was not spared the revolutionary auctioneer's hammer—and the Clos is now owned by more than four dozen owners, many of whom simply fall back or capitalize on its famous name. Thus the wine drinker should look carefully for the name of a reputable *négociant* on a label of Clos de Vougeot. A small section of the Clos is devoted to the production of an excellent white wine—Clos Blanc de Vougeot, happily the monopoly of a superior vintner.

Whereas the lore of the Clos de Vougeot captures the inherent sentiment of the entire French nation, the most glamorous vineyards of the Côte d'Or are to be found in the next commune of Vosne-Romanée. Though in our opinion (and in many another), its wines are nowadays considerably overrated and certainly shockingly overpriced, the fact remains that the tiny four-acre vineyard of Romanée-Conti has probably been coveted over the years by more powerful and colorful personalities than any other plot of land on the surface of the earth. Originally the site of a Roman camp (hence the name Romanée), this little vineyard and its four *Grands Crus* neighbors—La Romanée, La Tâche, Richebourg and Romanée-St.-Vivant—once all simply known as Romanée, have been squabbled over and jockeyed for by more princes and kings (including their mistresses), churchmen, diplomats and fortune seekers than bears recounting. A comparatively recent owner in this long line, the Prince de Conti, once an adviser to Louis XV, sagely saw to it that the most precious four-acre section of the original Romanée should forever perpetuate his name. Having stolen it from under the very nose of Madame de Pompadour, the king's mistress, he promptly hyphenated its name to his. Today the Romanées are safely in the hands of an ultra-conservative syndicate.

All the wines of Vosne-Romanée are fragrant and light-colored, with a unique softness about them. A phrase coined for them two hundred years ago by one of the Prince de Conti's friends should require no amendment: "Bottled velvet and satin." To some degree the description holds—yet the wines of this commune are not as well made today as they once were, and almost comparable wines may be found, at more reasonable prices, from the adjacent commune of Flagey-Échézeaux, the latter being such a tongue-twister to the average foreigner that it is thought to be responsible for the relatively small popularity of its wines outside of France. One may take comfort, however, in the probability that one's wine dealer won't know how to pronounce the word either!

Rather inexplicably, none of the excellent vineyards of the two southernmost communes of the Côte de Nuits—Nuits-St.-Georges and Prémeaux[17]—have been given official *Grand Cru* status, even though traditionally many of them are numbered among the finest red Burgundies—the best being traditional *Têtes de Cuvée*. The vineyards here are close to being the oldest of the Côte d'Or, and their grapes have a way of ripening earlier, thus containing more natural sugar than those of many other parts of the region, and resulting in wines that have an unusual degree of mellowness. This also often renders them less subject to the sanctioned, though not always enhancing practice known as *chaptalization*—the adding, especially in a poor year, of sufficient sugar to the fermenting grapes to attain the required amount of alcohol.

Between the two communes there are almost four dozen *Premiers Crus* vineyards, nearly all of which are of outstanding excellence. Among the best in Nuits-St.-Georges are Les St.-Georges, Les Cailles, Les Vaucrains and Les Porrets; and in Prémeaux, the Clos de la Maréchale, Les Didiers and Les Corvées. Nor is a mere communal Nuits-St.-Georges something to be overlooked if it comes from a good vintner. It will usually be of excellent value and quality.

The first commune for great wines on the Côte de Beaune is Aloxe-Corton, the source of the red Corton (often seen as Le Corton), as well as the equally prized Corton-Charlemagne, a delightful and expensive dry white wine. The Emperor Charlemagne once owned this vineyard, which should be indicative of its traditional greatness; Voltaire is said to have been so fond of the heavy-bodied Corton (as well as so parsimonious) that he drank it himself while providing ordinary Beaujolais for his guests at the same meal. As will be observed in Table D, many vineyards of the commune, such as Les Bressandes and Le Clos du Roi, hyphen-

---

[17] Both are entitled to the *Appellation Contrôlée* of Nuits-St.-Georges, although one often sees the term: Nuits-St.-Georges-Prémeaux.

ate their names with the great Corton—an authorized mark of added quality. Another of Corton's excellent reds is the wine called Château Grancey or Corton-Grancey which, though an officially unclassified wine, is produced by one of the Côte d'Or's outstanding growers, Louis Latour.

South of Aloxe-Corton lies the large wine-producing commune of the Côte d'Or—Beaune.[18] Here, a bit like a boa constrictor which has just devoured a rabbit, our thin ribbon of vineyards has acquired an unproportionate bulge. In the bulge's center lies the medieval city of Beaune itself, the lovely wine capital of the Côte d'Or, flanked by walls and mammoth bastions which are nowadays used as wine cellars. Perhaps the best one-word description of the wines of Beaune is "uncomplicated." One will find them earthy—and many people refer to them as "men's wines," meaning they may be consumed in gulps and swallows, without lingering too long over refinements and flowery aromas. The Beaunes are great favorites with the Burgundians themselves, who have a traditional saying about them: "There are no bad wines in Beaune." Like the communal wines of Nuits-St.-Georges to the north, the blends of this commune generally rank a notch or two above many of their communal competitors—though in this connection it is well to remember that *Appellation Contrôlée Beaune* on a label indicates a far better standard than a *Côte-de-Beaune* or a *Côte-de-Beaune-Villages*. These latter special appellations apply to wines from vineyards further afield than the commune of Beaune itself, and wines so labeled are more often than not only a step or two away from *ordinaires*.

The city of Beaune, as picturesque as any in France, also houses a celebrated semicharitable institution, the Hospice de Beaune, a hospital and almshouse that functions in a lovely fifteenth-century Gothic building, and is supported almost entirely by the proceeds of its vineyards. Founded in 1443 by Nicolas Rollin, chancellor of the Duchy of Burgundy, and his wife, Guigone de Salins, over the years it has become the recipient of more than two dozen vineyards scattered across the Côte de Beaune. Among other duties, Rollin was the tax collector thereabouts, which led to the facetious remark of the then king of France to the effect that, since Rollin had taken

---

[18] With one exception, an outstandingly fragrant wine known as Clos des Mouches Blanc, all the best wines of Beaune are red.

so much money away from so many people, it was only proper and fitting that he return some of it.

The wines of the Hospice, which are known as *Cuvées*, are named after the donor of each particular vineyard, and carry the *Appellation Contrôlée* of the commune in which they are produced. Though not all of equal quality, their production is at least under a single supervision, a rare and happy circumstance in the Côte d'Or. Some of the best vineyards belonging to the Hospice—which produces both reds and whites—are Nicolas Rollin, Guigone de Salins, Dr. Peste and Gauvain. Every mid-November the whole town turns out for a three-day wine *fête*, centering on one of the most dramatic auctions in France. This is when the casks of the Hospice are sold, one by one, to the highest bidder. The bidding on each cask ends not by the fall of any auctioneer's hammer, but when a flickering taper has burnt to its end. Wine buyers from all over the world attend, and careful attention is given to the prices paid, since they are always indicative of the prices Burgundies will bring for that particular year.

Below Beaune are the twin communes of Volnay and Pommard, producing red wines that are usually light in color, and more tart and fruity than many other reds of the Côte d'Or. The fame of Volnay and Pommard is said to have been spread because their names—like their delightful and potable wines—slip so smoothly across the tongue and therefore present no pronounciation problem to the foreigner. A more plausible explanation involves the fact that in the seventeenth century this little section of the Côte d'Or was one of the strongholds of the Protestant Huguenots. Following the revocation of the Edict of Nantes, many citizens of Pommard and Volnay were forced to flee France. Wherever they settled they demanded their native wines, and soon the outside world, too, came to appreciate the virtues of these simple, unassuming vintages.

Until the advent of the *Appellations Contrôlées* laws in 1936, perhaps only Chablis—among French wines—was more tampered with or adulterated than Pommard and Volnay. As we have mentioned, tampering or extreme practices of blending are nearly always the result of a demand exceeding a supply—and it so happens that the wines of both Pommard and Volnay were the first Burgundies to attain popular world appeal, thus creating a demand.

Yet there was another factor to cause the shortage itself, one that pertained not only to all other Burgundies, but also to the wines of all the Old World. In the 1870's and 1880's an American vine louse, or aphid, brought accidently to England on experimental cuttings, leaped the Channel and spread like wildfire through the vineyards of Bordeaux and Burgundy, and thence throughout the rest of Europe. Only two spots on the entire continent, in fact, the remote Rioja district of Spain and the sandy Colares vineyards on the coast of Portugal, were not seriously affected—and even the good fortune of the Rioja lasted only a few decades. Known as the *phylloxera*, this insidious little organism, which attacked the roots of the vines and thus could not be reached or affected by chemicals or any known insecticides, had its origin among the native grapes of the eastern United States, which over the years had become resistant to it. Its effect on the other side of the Atlantic was almost catastrophic. The vines withered and died like flies under D.D.T.; wine production all over Europe fell to a mere trickle, and it was many years before the problem was solved by importing impervious wild-grape roots from the upper Mississippi-Missouri watershed to be used as grafting stock.

With the introduction of new root stock, European vineyards were on the road to revival—but at this juncture the vintners of the Côte d'Or made a serious error. Instead of grafting with their traditional Pinot noir, many of them gave in to temptation and used another red-wine grape called the Gamay—hardier than the Pinot, and a comparatively prolific producer. On certain soils, such as the Beaujolais region of Southern Burgundy, the Gamay makes delicious (though hardly great) wine—but not a Burgundy as the world knew and demanded it from the Côte d'Or at the turn of the century. Between the *phylloxera* and the Gamay the shortage of good Burgundy reached a low from which it did not recover for almost sixty years. Finally banned by the *Appellations Contrôlées* laws from all the best vineyards, the juices of the Gamay are now only to be found in Beaujolais and in those pedestrian regional Burgundies with the *Appellations Contrôlées* of *Bourgogne Ordinaire* or *Bourgogne Passe-Tous-Grains*, both authorized blends of the Pinot noir and the Gamay.[19]

[19] The Gamay also has a white cousin, the Aligoté, used (with or without the Chardonnay) for a wine officially classified as *Bourgogne Aligoté*. At its best,

The southernmost vineyards of the Côte de Beaune are predominantly devoted to white wines, and situated chiefly in the communes of Meursault, Puligny-Montrachet and Chassagne-Montrachet. As has already been mentioned, the great Montrachet vineyard is shared by both the latter communes. Along with Bordeaux's Château d'Yquem, the wine of this eighteen-acre plot (owned by almost as many owners) is one of the most highly prized whites of France. Fairly dry, with a highly distinctive flavor and bouquet all its own, it is the color of gold, and needless to say, extremely difficult to come by. Even though one may not like it, one will hardly fail to understand why over the ages the great and the powerful have always coveted and praised it. Rabelais called it "divine," Dumas once said that it should be drunk "only while kneeling." When well made, Montrachet is the quintessence of the Chardonnay. Wines from the four neighboring *Grands Crus* vineyards that are allowed to hyphenate their names to Montrachet (see Table D) are of nearly the same quality, and less scarce. Also to be recommended are the *Premiers Crus* vineyards of these three communes, wines from which are usually considerably easier on the pocketbook.

The white wines from the commune of Meursault, to the north, are stronger in taste, less delicate, usually a little less dry than the Montrachets. Only a few of them are seen away from their own land, though their popularity in France itself is extremely high. Among the best are Les Perrières (or Clos des Perrières), Les Genevrières, La Goutte d'Or (a favorite with foreigners) and Les Charmes.[20] Excellent red wines, too, are made in Meursault, Puligny and Chassagne, as well as in Santenay, the southernmost commune of the Côte d'Or. *Premiers Crus* wines from these latter communes are almost always excellent buys, and they are apt to be sturdy and long-lived—comparable to those of the northern vineyards of Gevrey-Chambertin and Morey-St.-Denis.

Since no wine lover will necessarily wish to drink the *Grands* and *Premiers Crus* exclusively, no one should overlook the Burgundian equals of the regional wines of Bordeaux—in this case

---

Bourgogne Aligoté is not a very palatable drink. It is never produced in the best white-wine vineyards of the Côte d'Or, which are restricted to one grape only, the Chardonnay.

[20] Many of these vineyards commonly hyphenate their names with Meursault: such as Meursault-Charmes, Meursault-Genevrières, etc.

known as communal wines. These latter are often of a very high quality when made or endorsed by a good producer. Usually (though not invariably) blends from two or more *Premiers Crus* vineyards, they are simply called Gevrey-Chambertin, Meursault, Pommard, Chassagne-Montrachet, and so forth. We have already mentioned those of Nuits-St.-Georges and Beaune as being exceptional. Reputable producers are of course a requisite; thus we once again refer the uninitiated reader to Table F, listing some of the better-known vintners (*négociants*) of the Côte d'Or. We only caution that this list is neither complete nor exhaustive.

The best recent years for Burgundies, red and white, were 1952, 1953, 1955, 1957 (also 1958 for Chablis), 1959, 1961, 1962, 1964 and 1966. Occasionally, as we have pointed out, fine wines were made in the intervening years, which wine drinkers will eventually discover after sufficient experimentation. White Burgundies are usually ready for drinking at two or three years of age, whereas most of the *Grands Crus* and *Premiers Crus* reds should be allowed at least a couple of years longer. The traditionally great reds from the northern part of the Côte d'Or have been known to live and improve in the bottle for many years, and it is a crime to drink a well-made Chambertin before it has been allowed eight or ten years to come into its own. Yet, in this very connection, it is unfortunately the case that over all of France—and Burgundy is no exception—the practice to make red wines so that they will mature early and thus "move" faster to the markets of the world is on the increase. Generally speaking, this involves an abandonment of the traditional techniques of making red wine by leaving the stalks, or other tannin-making elements, to ferment with the juice. Tannin adds flavor and long-lasting qualities to the wine, and every good vintner knows that any short-cut method reduces the quality of his product. Yet commerce is commerce, and it will be a long time, if ever, before the pendulum swings back. A bottle of well-aged red Burgundy—harsh, tannic and acid when young, showing a healthy dosage of dregs when aged to softness and charm—is nowadays more of a rarity than a rule.

(Entitled to a vineyard *Appellation Contrôlée*)

CÔTE DE NUITS*

(Le) Chambertin	Clos de la Roche
Chambertin-Clos de Bèze	Clos St.-Denis
Latricières-Chambertin	(Le) Musigny*
Mazys-Chambertin (Mazis)	Clos de Vougeot
Mazoyères-Chambertin	Grands Échézeaux (and Échézeaux)
Ruchottes-Chambertin	eaux)
Chapelle-Chambertin	Romanée-Conti
Charmes-Chambertin	La Romanée
Griotte-Chambertin	La Tâche
Clos de Tart	Richebourg
Bonnes-Mares	Romanée-St.-Vivant

CÔTE DE BEAUNE†

Corton†	Bâtard-Montrachet
Corton-Charlemagne	Chevalier-Montrachet
Charlemagne	Bienvenues-Bâtard-Montrachet
(Le) Montrachet	Criots-Bâtard-Montrachet

PRINCIPAL PREMIERS CRUS

(Vineyards entitled to the *Appellation Contrôlée* of their own particular commune. Labels need not bear the words *Premier Cru*).

Commune	*Vineyard*
	CÔTE DE NUITS——RED WINES
Fixin	Clos de la Perrière
	Clos du Chapitre
	Les Hervelets

---

* All listed wines are red, with the exception of Musigny, which vineyard also produces a rare, expensive white (Musigny Blanc).

† All listed wines are white, with the exception of Corton, which may be either red or white (Corton Blanc).

Commune	Vineyard
Gevrey-Chambertin	Clos de Ruchottes
	Clos St.-Jacques
	Varoilles
	Fouchère
	Estournelles (or Étournelles)
	Cazatiers
	Les Combottes
Morey-St.-Denis	Clos des Lambrays
	Calouère
	Les Charnières
Chambolle-Musigny	Les Amoureuses
	Les Baudes
	Les Charmes
	La Combe d'Orveau
Vougeot	Les Petits-Vougeot
	Le Cras
	Clos de la Perrière
Flagey-Échézeaux	Les Beaumonts (Beaux-Monts)
	Champs-Traversin
	Clos St.-Denis
	Les Cruots (or Vignes-Blanches)
	Les Rouges-du-Bas
	Les Poulaillières
	Les Loachausses
	Les Quartiers-de-Nuits
	Les Treux
	En Orveaux
	Les Échézeaux-de-Dessus
Vosne-Romanée	Les Beaumonts (Beaux-Monts)
	Les Gaudichots
	Les Malconsorts (Clos Frantin)
	La Grande Rue
	Les Suchots (Grands Suchots)
	Aux Brûlées
	Les Reignots
	Clos des Réas
	Les Petits-Monts
	Les Chaumes

Commune	*Vineyard*
Nuits-St.-Georges	Les St.-Georges
	Les Baudots
	Les Cailles
	Les Porrets
	Les Pruliers
	Les Vaucrains
	Les Cras
	Les (Aux) Murgers
	Les Thorey (Clos de Thorey)
Nuits-St.-Georges-Prémeaux	Clos de la Maréchale
	Les Didiers-St.-Georges
	Clos des Forêts-St.-Georges
	Les Corvées (Les Corvées-Paget)
	Le Clos St.-Marc
	Clos des Argillières
	Clos Arlot (d'Arlot)
	Les Perdrix

CÔTE DE NUITS——WHITE WINES

Fixin	Clos de la Perrière Blanc
Morey-St.-Denis	Mont-Luisants Blanc
Vougeot	Clos Blanc de Vougeot
Nuits-St.-Georges	La Perrière
Prémeaux (Nuits-St.-Georges)	Clos Arlot (d'Arlot) Blanc

CÔTE DE BEAUNE——RED WINES

Pernand-Vergelesses	Ile-des-Vergelesses
	Les Basses-Vergelesses
Aloxe-Corton	Corton-Bressandes
	Corton-Clos du Roi
	Corton-(Les) Renardes
	Corton-Chaumes
	Corton-Maréchaudes
	Corton-Vigne-au-Saint
	Corton-(Les) Perrières
	Corton-(Les) Grèves
	Corton-Pauland

Commune	*Vineyard*
Aloxe-Corton (*Cont.*)	Corton-(Les) Meix
	Corton-(Les) Pougets
	Corton-Vergennes
Savigny-lès-Beaune	Les Vergelesses
	Les Marconnets
	Les Jarrons
Beaune	Les Grèves (Grèves de l'Enfant Jésus)
	Les Fèves
	Les Marconnets
	Les Bressandes
	Le Clos des Mouches
	Le Clos de la Mousse
	Le Cras
	Les Champs-Pimonts
	Les Cent-Vignes
Pommard	Les Épenots (Épenaux) (Grands Épenots)
	Les Rugiens-Bas
	Le Clos Blanc
Volnay	Les Angles
	Les Caillerets
	Les Champans
	Les Fremiets
	Santenots (Volnay-Santenots)
	Les Petures
	Clos des Chênes
	Clos des Ducs
Auxey-Duresses	Les Duresses
	Le Bas-des-Duresses
	Les Bretterins
	Les Écusseaux
	Les Grands-Champs
	Les Reugnes
	Clos du Val
Puligny-Montrachet	Le Cailleret
	Clavoillons

Commune	*Vineyard*
Chassagne-Montrachet	Le Clos St.-Jean-Morgeot Morgeot Clos de la Boudriotte (La Boudriotte) La Romanée
Meursault	Les Cras

CÔTE DE BEAUNE——WHITE WINES

Beaune	Clos des Mouches Blanc
Meursault	Clos des Perrières (Les) Perrières (Les) Genevrières (La) Goutte d'Or (Les) Charmes (Les) Santenots (Les) Bouchères La Pièce-sous-le-Bois Sous-le-Dos-d'Âne
Puligny-Montrachet	Le Cailleret Les Combettes Hameau de Blagny Blanc Le Champ-Canet Les Pucelles Les Chalumeaux
Chassagne-Montrachet	Les Ruchottes Morgeot La Maltroie (Château de)

SOUTHERN BURGUNDY AND THE BEAUJOLAIS

Just south of the Côte d'Or, on the River Saône, one comes to the quaint wine town of Chalon. Here begins the region known— for want of a more appropriate term—as Southern Burgundy, embracing three subdivisions: the Côte Chalonnaise, the Mâconnais (thirty-five miles further south) and the Beaujolais. In the sense of the Côte d'Or and Bordeaux, there are no truly great wines made in Southern Burgundy—but the red wines of Mercurey and

Givry of the Côte Chalonnaise and the white Pouilly-Fuissé from the Mâconnais are unquestionably ones of much distinction. Pouilly-Fuissé and its two plainer sisters, Pouilly-Loché and Pouilly-Vinzelles—all moderately dry, with a "flintiness" akin to Chablis and the characteristically pungent aroma imparted by the Chardonnay grape—rank extremely high among wine drinkers the world over.

The Côte Chalonnaise covers four officially recognized wine-producing communes: Rully, Givry, Mercurey and Montagny. As in the Côte d'Or, the finest wines are made from the red Pinot noir and the white Chardonnay, though a subtle difference in the soil produces lighter and shorter-lived—and somewhat coarser—wines than those from the Slope of Gold. In view of the prices often asked for the nobility of the Côte d'Or, these are good, solid wines that should not be overlooked or thought of as mere upstarts. In Mercurey, once a Roman settlement, the vineyards are said to antedate even the Romans themselves. Rully and Montagny are famous for their exceptionally light-bodied whites. In all four communes certain exceptional vineyards have been awarded a *Premier Cru* status, and are thereby allowed to print the vineyard name on their labels (with or without the words *Premier Cru*, as in the Côte d'Or). Unfortunately, not too many wines of the Côte Chalonnaise are nowadays seen outside of France, but this is a situation which may soon be remedied by economic factors.

Pouilly-Fuissé is far and away the finest and best-known white wine region of Southern Burgundy. Regrettably, because of the great demand for it, more and more of the wine is being shipped as a blend, simply under the generic name of Pouilly-Fuissé. As in the Côte Chalonnaise, certain vineyards in the Pouilly-Fuissé region may market their wines under their own names, giving them, in this case, a quasi-*Premier Cru* status. A list of some of the best of these vineyards appears in Table E—in almost every case one will find that a Pouilly-Fuissé from a bona fide vineyard is vastly superior to one not so labeled. The wines of Pouilly-Loché and Pouilly-Vinzelles do not have authorized vineyard names. Generally made by cooperatives, they are never the qualitative equals of Pouilly-Fuissé.

Other whites of the Mâconnais, similar in type to Pouilly-Fuissé, come from the communes of Viré, Lugny, Clessé and Chardonnay (the legendary birthplace of the Chardonnay grape). Wines from these four communes usually have the name Mâcon hyphenated to their own; once again, vineyard names are anything but superfluous. The reds of Mâcon are usually made from a blend of the Gamay and the Pinot noir; and may be considered in the same qualitative class as the *ordinaires* of Beaujolais. A Mâcon *Supérieur*, like a Bordeaux *Supérieur*, is required by law to contain a small additional amount of alcohol.

Most purists rebel at calling the joyous, thirst-quenching Beaujolais—the "toast" of Lyon and the avowed favorite of all France— a Burgundy, and not without good reason. Both grape and soil are totally foreign to the Côte d'Or. About five miles south of the city of Mâcon, bordering the vineyards of Pouilly-Fuissé, the soil changes abruptly to a granite base, and the fermented juice of the otherwise frowned-upon Gamay loses the metallic harshness that it nearly always manifests elsewhere, and becomes something entirely delicious and satisfying. A few white and *rosé* wines of no particular merit are made in the Beaujolais region, but this is predominantly a red-wine region. The latter wines are probably the fruitiest and most refreshing in the world—and to be numbered among the few reds which actually taste better at a cool cellar temperature. Most of them are better when young than when aged, and they are not consumed in sips—but in gulps! Enormous quantities are imbibed every year in the nearby city of Lyon, most of it at an age so tender that it has never merited the honor of a bottle.

Given the amount of Beaujolais that is patently consumed throughout France itself, as well as its omnipresence on the shelves of nearly every wineshop in the world, it goes without saying that there are many more bottles labeled *Beaujolais* than can possibly be produced in a restricted area of central France barely covering thirty-five square miles. Thus it is advisable to heed the nine official geographical superior *Appellations Contrôlées* of the region (see Table E), bearing in mind that an authorized vineyard name on a label—emphatically not meaning a trade name—will almost always mean a better bottle. Of these nine *Appellations*, perhaps Moulin-à-Vent, Fleurie and St.-Amour have the highest reputations. Their wines are noted for bouquet and comparative softness, and the better ones will actually improve with a few years in the bottle—although most Frenchmen will tell you this is a criminal waste of time and storage space!

Two other popular Beaujolais—more favorites of the French than of foreigners—have the subregional *Appellations Contrôlées* of Brouilly and Côte de Brouilly, wines which are stronger in taste and less delicate than many of their neighbors. Once again, a Beaujolais *Supérieur* is slightly more alcoholic than one simply labeled Beaujolais, though not necessarily any better; wines with the appellation of *Beaujolais-Villages* are communal wines, coming from any one of the thirty-five villages of the region. Although they are the *ordinaires* of the lot, some of these will be found to be extremely good.

Vintage years in Beaujolais are of relatively little significance, although 1959, 1961, 1962 and 1964 produced wines better than most; those for the balance of the vineyards of Southern Burgundy may, in general, be considered the same as for the Côte d'Or (see p. 54).

SUMMARY

Because of a demand far exceeding the supply, few wines are more faked or adulterated (or of poorer quality or more overpriced) than white Chablis. The two top classifications, *Grand Cru* and *Premier Cru*, are always expensive—but at least reliable. Other wines labeled *Petit Chablis* or simply *Chablis* should be approached with suspicion. They will nearly always be overpriced for what they are. California and Spanish "Chablis" are not even good imitations. They would do better on the markets of the world with other names.

The Côte d'Or (traditional Burgundy) produces fragrant reds and medium-dry whites that are the qualitative equals of Bordeaux wines. Reds from the northernmost sections (Gevrey-Chambertin, Chambolle-Musigny, etc.) are the finest and require more years (eight to ten) to mature; most of the best whites stem from the southernmost communes of Meursault, Puligny-Montrachet and Chassagne-Montrachet, and may be consumed when three years old. Since most Côte d'Or vineyards are divided among many owners, each making his own wine, the name of a reliable producer on a bottle is of paramount importance (see Table F). And because many communes have hyphenated their names with that of their best vineyard, many a wine drinker is led to mistake an ordinary communal wine or blend for a wine from one of the great vineyards. Example: Gevrey-Chambertin, though it may be of good value, is not from the great Chambertin vineyard, but usually a blend from one or more vineyards of the commune of Gevrey. The best-known wines of Southern Burgundy are medium-dry white Pouilly-Fuissé and lusty red Beaujolais. Terms on labels of these wines, such as *Grand Cru* or *Premier Cru*, have no meaning—but a vineyard name (as well as, in the case of Beaujolais wines, one of the nine superior geographical *Appellations Contrôlées*) should be indicative of the best.

CÔTE CHALONNAISE——RED WINES

Commune (or Appellation Contrôlée)	*Vineyard*
Rully	La Fosse
	Marisou
Mercurey	Clos du Roi
	Clos de l'Évêque
	Clos Marcilly
Givry	Clos St.-Pierre
	Clos St.-Paul
	Cellier aux Moines

BEAUJOLAIS——RED WINES

St.-Amour	Champ Grillé
	Château de St.-Amour
Juliénas	Château des Capitans (Les Capitans)
	Les Mouilles
Fleurie	Clos de la Roilette
	La Madonne
	Le Vivier
Moulin-à-Vent	Les Carquelins
	Le Moulin-à-Vent
	Les Burdelines
Chénas	La Rochelle
	Les Caves
	Les Vérillats
Chiroubles	Le Moulin
	Bel Air

Morgon	Château de Bellevue
Brouilly	Les Bussières
Côte de Brouilly	Le Pavé

CÔTE CHALONNAISE———WHITE WINES

Rully	Raclot
Mercurey	Clos de Petit Clou
Givrey	Champs Pourot
Montagny	Vieux Château

MÂCONNAIS———WHITE WINES

Pouilly-Fuissé
Les Chailloux
Les Bouthières
Les Prâs
La Frérie (Frairie)
Château Fuissé
Château Pouilly
Les Perrières
Les Brûlets
Les Crays
Les Chanrue
Les Chevrières
Les Vignes-Blanches

(Other *Appellations Contrôlées* for white wines of the Mâconnais include Pouilly-Loché and Pouilly-Vinzelles; Chardonnay and Viré, usually hyphenated with Mâcon, which latter is also entitled to its own *Appellation Contrôlée* and is the source of some excellent whites.)

NOTE: *Grand* or *Premier Cru* or *Tête de Curée* on labels of any wines from Pouilly-Fuissé or other parts of the Mâconnais or the Beaujolais are entirely meaningless, and should be viewed with suspicion. *Premier Cru* vineyards are, however, autororized for the Côte Chalonnaise and are indicative of officially recognized quality. (See page 14).

D'Angerville, J., Marquis
Bavard, Joseph
Bouchard, Père et Fils
Buisson-Larue, Mme.
Camus, Leon
Cavin, Roger
Clair-Däu
de Courcel, B., Mme.
Damoy, Pierre
Domaine Leflaive
Domaine de la Romanée-Conti
Drouhin, Joseph
Engel, René
Faiveley, J.
Fleurot-Larose
Gouges, Henri
Grivault, A.
Gros, Louis
Jaboulet-Vercherre, U. G.
Jadot, Louis
de Laguiche, Marquis
LaMarche, Henri
Lamblin et Fils
Latour, Louis
Lequin-Roussot
L'Héritier-Guyot
Long-Depaquit (Chablis)

Maire et Fils
Matrot, Joseph
Maufoux, Pierre
de Mérode, Prince
Moillard, J.
Moillard-Grivot
Monnot, Julien
de Moucheron, Comte
Mugneret, E.
Mugnier, F.
Noëllat, Vve.
Poirier, Louis
Ponsot, H.
Poupon, P.
Prieur, Jacques
Ramonet, Claude
Ramonet, Pru'hon
Rémy, J. H.
Ropiteau Frères
Ropiteau, Maurice
Ropiteau-Mignon
Rousseau, Armand
Thénard, Baron
Thévenin, Roland
Viénot, Charles
de Vogüé, Comte Georges
Yard, Georges

THE RHÔNE VALLEY AND PROVENCE

THE "CLASSIC GROWTHS"

From its headwaters high in the glaciers of the Swiss Alps, beside the perilous Simplon Pass forged by Napoleon as a military and trade route to Italy, the Rhône drops swiftly into the crescent-shaped Lake of Geneva, thence meanders in undulating curves across France until—just above the city of Lyon—it turns abruptly and flows hurriedly toward the Mediterranean. Many of Switzerland's better vineyards border the upper reaches of the Rhône and the shores of the Lake of Geneva—but we are concerned here with those wines which are produced along the Rhône's one-hundred-and-fifty-mile stretch as it rushes from Lyon to the river's delta near Marseille, the Bouches-du-Rhône.

This stretch of the Rhône Valley is a source of great quantities of wines—a vast majority of them coarse and unappealing, wines that usually shed their individual identities in the carafes of the small bars and *bistros* of France, having been blended with something even less distinguished from Algeria, Tunisia or Greece. In the midst of this vinicultural sea, however, one comes across four or five isolated atolls of vineyards that have produced superior wines since Roman times, and in some instances even before. These are known as the "classic growths" of the Rhône. The first of them is to be found about fifteen miles downstream from Lyon, across from the town of Vienne. Here, nestled along the steep slopes of a sheltered, sun-baked arena—a natural little hothouse—is a handful of appallingly rocky, terraced vineyards called the Côte Rôtie (Roasted Slope). The Côte Rôtie has two integral parts, known respectively as the Côte Blonde and the Côte Brune, a nomenclature literally based on the differences in color of their respective soils—yet, as one might imagine, the source of inevitable bar-room jokes concerning the relative merits of blondes and brunettes. As opposed to that from the Côte Blonde, wine from the Côte Brune is reputed to have superior lasting qualities. Be that as it may, nowadays most bottles of Côte Rôtie will be a blend of both. Vineyard names, though authorized, are rare.

The wines or the Côte Rôtie, of a deep red color, are made predominantly from the Syrah grape—a plant thought to be of Persian origin which, in France, is now unique to this section of the Rhône Valley. Offensively harsh when young, with sufficient age they develop a rich, velvet, highly perfumed and distinguished quality. They also have the reputation of living in the bottle for an unusually long time. Vienne was once a Roman town, but the vineyards are thought to be older yet, and to have been planted by the Greeks in 500 B.C., shortly after the original plantings near Marseille. Pliny the Younger, seemingly praising the wines of Vienne in the first century A.D., described them as "pitchy"—even now a fair description for improperly aged wines made from the Syrah grape. Nearly seventeen hundred years later another avid vinophile, Thomas Jefferson, touring the vineyards of France on a donkey, also admired these wines, and noted in his diary that they possessed "a quality which keeps well, bears transportation and cannot be drunk under four years."[21]

Just south of the Côte Rôtie are grown the white wines bearing the two *Appellations Contrôlées* of Condrieu and Château Grillet. Here again the vineyards are on abrupt, terraced slopes, and the finely fragrant wines are produced at great expense. The wine of Château Grillet, a minuscule two-and-one-half acre vineyard with its own *Appellation Contrôlée* (giving it, in effect, a *Grand Cru* status), is nearly impossible to come by except in the best restaurant of Vienne itself, and is considered by many experts to be one of the greatest and most individualistic dry white wines of France, ranking with the Côte d'Or's Montrachets and Corton-Charlemagne and Musigny Blanc. The grape used exclusively for both the wines of Condrieu and Château Grillet is the Voignier, a vine strictly indigenous to this particular little pocket of the Rhône, used nowhere else in France. Château Grillet, incidentally, is one of several French white wines that have a way of becoming seasonally *pétillant*—that is, inexplicably undergoing, of their own accord, a secondary fermentation in the bottle which makes them slightly prickly on the tongue, though only at one season of the year, the spring. We shall have more to say about this rather spooky phenomenon—a subject which is anathema to the scientific logic of wine chemists—when we come to Champagne.

The next cluster of classic growths is to be found, once again downstream, near the busy town of Valence. These are the red and white wines bearing the *Appellation Contrôlée* of either Hermitage or Croze-Hermitage, the former being the nobility of the two. The vineyards of Hermitage (sometimes seen on labels as L'Hermitage or L'Ermitage, and not to be confused with a Swiss wine called Ermitage) are spread over the top of a loaf-

---

[21] *Papers of Thomas Jefferson*, XI (Princeton University Press, 1955).

shaped hill known locally as the Hill of the Hermit. It owes its name—so the story goes—to a thirteenth-century Crusader who, returning one day from the wars, knelt in exhaustion at a nearby shrine, where he received a vision instructing him to remain on the hilltop for the balance of his life, living in the service of his Lord.

A well-aged Hermitage, especially a red, is expensive, and unquestionably the finest red wine of the Rhône. The acreage of the vineyards is small, only a few hundred acres of flinty, stony and shallow soil lying on top of bedrock—and manifestly useless for growing anything but the wine grape. The roots of the vines penetrate the cracks and fissures of the rock for their moisture. As in the Côte Rôtie to the north, the Syrah grape is used for the red wines. These are usually a blend from several vineyards (locally called *mas*) found in different sections of the hill. Strong wines, dark and with a deep purple hue, they accumulate an appreciable sediment, and improve tremendously in the bottle for several decades. A hundred and fifty years ago Hermitages were often used to lend color to and otherwise strengthen weaker wines. White Hermitage is dry but exceptionally mellow, charmingly honey-colored and possessing even more prodigious lasting qualities than its red counterpart. Some of them will live for fifty years.

Surrounding the Hill of the Hermit is the *Appellation Contrôlée* area of Croze-Hermitage, the source of wines of somewhat lesser quality. One of the whites, which goes by the name of *Chante-Alouette*, is especially popular outside of France. Also near Valence and across the river are the communes of St.-Joseph and Cornas, both founts of good red wines, likewise made from the Syrah. St.-Péray, another neighboring commune, is noted for its sparkling whites, manufactured by a process which resembles that used for Champagne, and which local vintners claim antedates the Champagne process itself.

In English-speaking countries undoubtedly the most popular and well-known Rhône red wine is Châteauneuf-du-Pape, another of the "classic growths." When, in the fourteenth century, the papacy moved from Rome to the fortress city of Avignon on the Rhône, the first pope to preside in the Church's new headquarters was a Frenchman, Clement V, a native of Bordeaux. Although the papal

court is known to have been especially partial to the good wines of
Beaune—in fact, the proximity of the Côte d'Or to Avignon is
often said to have been in part responsible for the court's tardiness
in moving back to Rome—under its fond eye the local wines of
Avignon were brought to a degree of perfection they have held
ever since. Red Châteauneuf-du-Pape is a wine of great warmth,
with much the same richness of flavor and deep purple hue as
Hermitage. One of the strongest red wines in France, with a minimum alcoholic content of 12 per cent (which it often exceeds),
it is traditionally made from as many as twelve varieties of grape,
though unfortunately the tendency of many of the vintners today
is to restrict it to two or three, or even just one: the Grenache[22]—a
part of the lamentable contemporary trend to market wines as
soon as possible.

Châteauneuf-du-Pape appears to have been almost entirely unknown throughout France until Napoleonic days, when it was
arrestingly brought to the attention of Paris by the antics of one
of its growers. This was a certain venerable noble, the Marquis de
la Nerthe, whose vineyard to this day still bears his name and continues to be one of the finest of the region. Famed at the French
court as a ladies' man, *bon viveur* and wit, the marquis was once
asked how, in his so advanced years, he managed to maintain
such astounding health and vigor amid a life of such frivolity, not
to say debauchery. Nearly every Frenchman is a born promoter;
the Marquis replied, of course, that his elixir was the wine of his
own vineyard on the Rhône. Châteauneuf-du-Pape was not long
in becoming the most popular wine at court, and to this day it is
not unusual to hear the old wives' tale that it contains effective
aphrodisiacal and medicinal elements.

White Châteauneuf-du-Pape is a pleasantly dry, if somewhat
unfragrant, wine—and no serious rival to the honey-colored whites
of Hermitage, or to Château Grillet and Condrieu. A far better
local white, when one can find it, comes from the nearby commune of Gigondas.

Vineyard names on labels of Châteauneuf-du-Pape are as significant as those of Pouilly-Fuissé, especially in the case of the

---

[22] Other traditional grapes include the Syrah, the Clairette, the Mourvèdre, the
Picpoul and the Terret noir.

reds: wines from officially recognized vineyards are well worth the extra dollars and cents one has to pay. To be at their best, they should be *at least* four or five years old. Again, the reader must be reminded of that convenient loophole in French law which allows a vintner of one district to appropriate the qualitative terminology of another, it being peculiarly applicable to these wines from the Rhône. Many a Rhône wine can be a "great" wine—yet no vineyard along the entire Rhône Valley is officially authorized to place the terms *Grand Cru, Premier Cru* or *Grand Vin* on its labels. Such is, regrettably, a fairly common practice and the words *Premier Cru* on a Rhône label (which do have official significance for a wine from the Côte d'Or or Chablis) should constitute grounds for suspicion of the integrity of the bottler and the intrinsic value of the wine.

Rosés *and the Wines of Provence*

Although some of them are classified as Rhône wines, the finest *rosé* (pink) wines of France are traditionally associated with Provence, the ancient province which borders the shores of the Mediterranean from the Rhône delta to Italy. The best of them come from the twin communes of Tavel and Lirac, lying in the hills a few miles west of Avignon. Here, away from the river, one finds a bleak and sinister countryside. The vineyards look baked and parched—almost no other vegetation seems to exist. Gazing over the landscape one thinks of Keats: "The sedge is withered from the lake, and no birds sing." In winter the two winds that alternately plague this whole Mediterranean area, the nerve-wracking mistral from the north and the stifling desert-born sirocco from the south, course by—unheedful of all in their path. It does not seem to be a fit place for man—but the wine grape thrives.

Rosé wines are produced by several methods. The first is the obvious simple mixture of red and white wines. In some parts of France this mediocrity is called *vin gris* (gray wine). It rarely results in a more potable drink than a straight white wine tinted with a bit of red cochineal coloring—a method sometimes used to make inexpensive "pink" Champagnes and other sparkling wines. Another procedure is the use of red-skinned grapes with white juice, withdrawing the skins from the juice as soon as the desired degree of color is attained. In Tavel and Lirac both red- and white-wine grapes are utilized in the "crush," and all the grapes are withdrawn when the *mélange* has reached the wished-for pinkish tint. The subsequent fermentation is then the same as for white wines, without benefit of skins and stalks.

In this part of the Rhône, the predominant grape for *rosés* is the Grenache, a prolific red grape also used for *rosés* in California, for red wines in Portugal and Spain, as part of the traditional combination for Châteauneuf-du-Pape, and for many another. The *rosés* of Tavel and Lirac, considered by most authorities to be the best of their kind in France, are sharp and (for a *rosé*) unusually "winy" in character, with a higher alcoholic content than the average French white wine. They are noted for keeping well in the bottle—though they do not necessarily improve there over the years. Although it should be pointed out that there is no such thing as a "great" *rosé*, they have their many uses. On hot summer days they can be refreshing, and they hold a distinct overall advantage in that they combine with almost any food. Furthermore, they are usually preferred by novice wine drinkers.

Although Tavel has been for many generations the most widely known *rosé* wine of France, in our opinion the wines of Lirac— even alcoholically stronger yet—are the softer and more delicate. Here are wines made with infinite care, and the vintners of Lirac have an additional, self-imposed standard by which every wine must run the gauntlet of a local tasting committee before it is entitled to the *Appellation Contrôlée*.

Farther south, along the shores of the Mediterranean and in the lovely foothills of the Alpes-Maritimes behind, are the sources of many other good *rosés*, along with scatterings of reds and whites. At Cassis, a quaint fishing village just east of Marseille (the name should not be confused with the black currant liqueur made in Dijon), dry and refreshing whites and *rosés* are made—wines which, although they do not always travel too successfully, are famous far from the shores of France. The nearby village of Bandol produces an excellent red, as well as a passable *rosé*; other good whites and *rosés* are made at Bellet, near Nice, and in the area of

La Palette near the breathtakingly beautiful, ancient city of Aix-en-Provence.

The wines of Cassis, Bandol, Bellet and La Palette are entitled to their own *Appellations Contrôlées*—but many of the other wines of Provence and the Mediterranean will bear another appellation: *V.D.Q.S.*, standing for *Vins Délimités de Qualité Supérieure* (Wines of Superior Quality from Delimited Areas). *V.D.Q.S.* wines, although they do not have the ranking of the *Appellations Contrôlées* wines, and their vineyards are not always subject to the same strict regulations, are many of them nonetheless excellent. The *V.D.Q.S.* designation was invented in order to promote relatively unknown local wines of France, and although those presently exported are largely *rosés*, there is good reason to believe that many others will soon be seen in foreign markets. Certain of the traditional vineyards of Provence have been granted the right to the words *Cru Classé* (See Table G).

As in the Beaujolais, vintage years in the Rhône and Provence are actually of minor significance, although it should be mentioned —for the Rhône itself—that the two outstanding years of the past decade have been 1955 and 1961.

SUMMARY

The "classic growths" of the Rhône Valley are predominantly red, the principal ones being Côte Rôtie, Hermitage and Château-neuf-du-Pape. Sturdy and usually dark in color, they require at least four to five years in the bottle, preferably more, before approaching mellowness. White Hermitage and Château Grillet are the outstanding whites.

Vineyard names on labels of all Rhône wines are to be preferred, but not always easy to find outside of France.

Vintage years for the Rhône are of minor importance, although the exceptional ones in the past decade have been 1955 and 1961. The terms *Grand Cru, Premier Cru*, etc., are not prescribed by law, and wines so labeled can only reflect on the integrity of the vintner, who can only be banking on the ignorance of the public.

The traditionally best *rosé* (pink) wines of France are from the two communes of Tavel and Lirac, near Avignon on the lower Rhône. But many a pleasant, less "winy" *rosé* is made in Provence, to the south. Most of these do not have *Appellations Contrôlées*, but bear instead the initials *V.D.Q.S.* Some traditional vineyards of Provence are entitled to the term *Cru Classé*, an added guaranty of quality (See Table G).

Principal Wines of the Rhône and Provence

REDS

Appellation Contrôlée	*Vineyard*
Côte Rôtie*	La Brocarde
	Les Chaveroches
	Grande Plantée
	Tharamont-de-Gron
Hermitage*	L'Ermite
	La Sizeranne
	La Chapelle
	Burge
	Columbiers
	Le Méal
Cornas	Chambon
	Le Moulin
	Pied la Vigne
Châteauneuf-du-Pape	Château Fortia (Fortiasse)
	Château de la Nerthe
	Château des Fines-Roches
	Domaine de Mont-Redon
	Château de la Gardine
	Domaine de Nalis (Nalys)

WHITES

Appellation Contrôlée	*Vineyard*
Château Grillet	Château Grillet
Condrieu	Chéry
	Basamon
	Côte Chatillon
Hermitage	Mûrets
	La Chapelle
	Beaumes

---

* Côte Rôtie and Hermitage wines are usually blends from different vineyards, and are infrequently labeled with an individual vineyard name.

St.-Péray	Coteau Gaillard
Châteauneuf-du-Pape	Château Rayas
	Mont-Redon
	Domaine de Nalis (Nalys)

NOTE: Although vineyard names are less often seen on labels of wines from the Rhône than from other parts of France, they definitely indicate a mark of quality. Such wines are almost invariably worth the higher prices they bring.

ROSÉS (RHÔNE AND PROVENCE)

Appellation Contrôlée	*Vineyard*
Tavel	Château d'Aquéria
	Clos de Vaucroze
Lirac	Château de Segriès
Cassis	Marseille
	La Treille
La Palette	Domaine de Moulières
Bandol*	
Bellet*	Château de Cremat

V.D.Q.S. *(Commune)*	*Vineyard*
Taradeau	†Château de St.-Martin
	†Château de Selle
Croix Valmer	†Domaine de la Croix
Les Arcs	†Château de Ste.-Roseline
Bormes	†Domaine du Noyer
Cogolin	†Domaine de St.-Maur
Gassin	†Domaine de Minuty
La Garde	†Clos de la Bastide Verte
La Londe	†Clos Mireille
	†Domaine du Galoupet
Lorgues	†Domaine de Castel Roubine
La Motte	†Domaine de Jos d'Esclans
Pignans	†Domaine de Rimauresq
La Valette	†Domaine de Moulières

---

* Vineyard names of Bandol and Bellet rarely appear on labels.
† *Crus Classés* of Côtes de Provence (*V.D.Q.S.* wines).

WINES OF THE LOIRE

WHITE WINES

The Loire is the longest river in France. Rising in what is picturesquely called the Massif Central—the great, wild mountains of central France—it flows through a placid countryside in a sweeping six-hundred-mile curve to the Atlantic, its watershed draining some five hundred thousand acres of vines. Even this is probably a low estimate—since in addition to all the regulated vineyards, nearly every peasant has a patch of vines in his own backyard to make wine for his own use. The Loire excels in its white wines, the driest of which are among the driest of all France, the sweetest being as sweet and "luscious" as any Sauternes or Barsac. In between the two extremes there are literally dozens of others, each with its own indisputable *terroir* or special individuality, derived from its own particular piece of soil.

Not too far from the headwaters, in the vicinity of the little market town of Pouilly-sur-Loire, are grown two white wines which, in the last decade or so, have undergone a spectacular rise in popularity among the wine drinkers of the world. The first of these is Pouilly-Fumé (not to be confused with the white Pouilly-Fuissé of Southern Burgundy), a dry, lightly perfumed white wine possessing what many connoisseurs describe as a "gunflint" flavor. Blanc-Fumé, an alternate name on labels for Pouilly-Fumé, means "white smoke," and the term derives from the particular way the *pourriture noble* in this section of France gives off a blue, misty dust that drifts across the vineyards at harvest time. Although the grape used here is the Petit Sauvignon, a cousin of one of the three principal white-wine grapes of Bordeaux, the *pourriture noble* in Pouilly-Fumé is not an integral part of the wine making. The climate of the upper Loire is not suited for late harvesting, and the wines are anything but sweet.[23]

---

[23] It is important to distinguish between two local appellations, the *Appellation Contrôlée* of *Blanc-Fumé-de-Pouilly* or *Pouilly-Fumé*, and that of *Pouilly-Sur-*

The second white wine from the upper Loire which has gained much favor in past years is that of Sancerre, a commune slightly below and across the river from Pouilly. Like those of the neighboring *Appellations Contrôlées* of Reuilly and Quincy, most Sancerres are bone dry—some of them almost to the point of outright acidity. The French themselves are unusually fond of these ultra-dry wines, drinking them with shellfish and oysters. In view of the always short supply (and rising cost) of the classic Chablis, many wine drinkers are turning to these dry whites of the upper Loire.

Yet another popular wine from the vicinity is St.-Porçain, predominantly made as white, though it may also be found as a *rosé*. St.-Porçain is the local wine, or *vin du pays*, of that famous French spa of Vichy visited periodically by many a French gourmand in order to put his liver right. Years before the magic powers of Vichy water were discovered, however, St.-Porçain was a famous wine. It was a St.-Porçain *oeil-de-perdix* (the ancient name for a *rosé*; literally, the color of a partridge's eye) which the French king Louis IX served to his guests to celebrate the coming of age of his son. St.-Porçain is dry and refreshing—some people describe it as smelling like freshly peeled apples. One might only add that after a liberal dose of Vichy water, almost any wine would taste like nectar and smell like ambrosia.

Just below the point where the ambling Loire straightens out and at long last plots its course for the ocean, it passes through what every tourist knows of as the Château Country—the celebrated playground of the French kings and their courts during the fifteenth and sixteenth centuries. Here, amid the elaborate country seats where the courtiers and their ladies danced away their boredom, sported their falcons and hunted the boar and the stag, one comes upon extensive white-wine vineyards, the wines of which are only just commencing to find their way in any abundance to the outside world. A short distance from the city of Tours, the geographical center of the Château Country, are the vineyards of Vouvray and Montlouis. Neither sweet nor dry, but instead a rather happy combination of the two, made principally from the

---

Loire. Wines of the latter are not made from the Sauvignon exclusively, but instead from the lowly Chasselas, a grape also used in Alsace, Algeria and California for generally inferior products.

local white Chenin blanc grape (also the source of one of the better California white wines, bearing that name), these wines differ from most other French whites in that they require considerable aging. For this purpose they are stored for several years in deep caves thought to date from prehistoric days, which have been carved into the steep chalk cliffs overhanging the Loire Valley. The rarest (and best) Vouvrays are *pétillant*—slightly fizzy. A Vouvray *pétillant* hardly tastes like wine at all: perhaps the best way to describe one is to liken it to an excellent, gently sparkling cider.

Unfortunately Vouvray *pétillants* do not travel well, and they require a high sugar content in order to pass through the second fermentation in the bottle. Thus they are usually only made in the best vintage years; in other years the wines are either produced as still wines or else turned into sparkling Vouvray (*mousseux*). In France, the best Vouvray *mousseux* is considered the finest sparkling white wine of the country, next to Champagne. We must confess that a still Vouvray or Montlouis always leaves us a little cold: they seem to require just that added touch imparted by a fizzle or a sparkle.

The most famous, as well as the most versatile vinicultural section of the Loire, is Anjou—that part lying closest to the mouth of the river. Anjou embraces a myriad of varied wines and *Appellations Contrôlées*, the best known being Saumur, Coteaux de la Loire, Coteaux du Layon, Coteaux de l'Aubance, Savennières, Quarts-de-Chaume, Rosé-d'Anjou and Anjou-Rosé-de-Cabernet. Fifty years ago the traditional vintages of Anjou were sweet—made, like Sauternes, with the aid of the *pourriture noble*—but nowadays wine drinkers rarely ask for sweet wines, and most of the vintners, like many of Sauternes and Barsac, are changing to drier versions, something which is simply accomplished by harvesting the grapes before the *pourriture noble* has set in.

From Saumur, the easternmost section of Anjou, comes a sparkling white wine (Saumur *mousseux*) which is often sweeter than sparkling Vouvray, and by no means of the same quality. The best dry wines, without exception, are from the area of the commune of Savennières, near Anjou's traditional capital of Angers. Its two outstanding vineyards, in fact, La Coulée de Serrant and La Roche aux Moines, approach such high quality in good years that they are allowed to hyphenate their own names to the *Appellation Contrôlée* of Savennières, giving them what would be a Grand Cru status (provided such were authorized for the Loire). Other superior dry wines are from the Château de la Fresnaye (Coteaux de Layon) and the Château de Parnay (Saumur).

For those who continue to like dessert wines—and we are among them—the traditional Anjous *liquoreux* will be found to possess perhaps even more character than Sauternes and Barsac. Amber in color, with a gentle perfume and a faint flavor of some exotic wild honey, they are among the finest white wines of France. Rabelais, a great connoisseur of wines of the Loire, once said that their aroma spreads itself "like a peacock's tail." Today they are rare; one of the few vineyards still producing them is known as the Quarts-de-Chaume which, as will be observed in Table H, is also entitled to an *Appellation Contrôlée* of its own. Now divided into four sections, this celebrated vineyard was once owned by an eminent physician so unusually bountiful and democratic that he kept only the wine of one-fourth the vineyard for himself and allowed his laborers to reap the profit of the rest. The doctor's own quarter is now known as the Ancien Domaine du Dr. Bernard, but the wines from it are not as good as those from yet another, the Château de Bellerive.

Finally, near the mouth of the river, are the scattered white-wine vineyards of Muscadet.[24] Much like Pouilly-Fumé and Sancerre, the Muscadets are light-textured and dry, with a unique lemony tang, and are most suitable with seafoods. Made predominantly from the Muscadet grape which, under the name of Melon, was brought from Burgundy many years ago, the Muscadets have recently undergone a considerable rise in popularity. Originally this transplanted Burgundian grape was tried out in Brittany, one of the few parts of France in which the *Vitis vinifera* has never seemed to flourish—or, as one writer succinctly put it, "the wines of Brittany are so bad that even the fishermen won't drink them." People in the wine trade can be as sharp tongued as any, and

---

[24] Not to be confused with dessert wines called Muscat in France, Muscatel in California, Moscatel in Portugal, etc.

the unfortunate vintners of Muscadets are locally subjected to cruel ribbing for their "Breton wines"—even though their vineyards lie predominantly in Anjou.

REDS AND *Rosés*

Although the red wines of the Loire live more in the past than in the present, there remains a handful of excellent ones that deserve brief mention, especially as some of them are beginning to reach foreign markets. At Orléans, in the central Loire (the site of Joan of Arc's victory over the British), there is made a pale red wine called Beaugency, as well as another comparable red known as St.-Jean-de-Braye. Centuries ago the red wines of Orléans had the reputation of being the strongest of France, and were great favorites with French connoisseurs, as well as with many traveling Englishmen. It was apparently the wine of Beaugency of which an English courtier noted in his journal during the visit of Charles I: "The wine of this place is so strong that the king's cupbearers are sworn never to give him any of it." Both Beaugency and St.-Jean-de-Braye require much age in the bottle before becoming really potable.

Rabelais's own vineyard, La Dévinière, was at Chinon—but there is sparse evidence that this talented stumblebum of French literature, whose chosen motto was the single word "Drink," confined himself to the wines of his own making. Along with the red wine of Chinon, two of his other favorites came from the nearby vineyards of St.-Nicolas-de-Bourgueil and Bourgueil. Wines with these two *Appellations Contrôlées* are still made today, and are probably the best red wines of the Loire. Although the predominating grape is the Breton, merely another name for the Cabernet franc of Bordeaux, these Loire reds are considerably coarser and harder than clarets, and also require long aging. In fact, the wines of Chinon and its vicinity need at least seven years in the bottle; some experts specify twice that. And, in common with Beaujolais, they are better when drunk cold.

The lower Loire Valley, especially the region of Anjou, produces excellent *rosé* wines, though for some palates they tend to be a little too sweet and cloying, not wearing as well the *rosés* of Tavel, Lirac and parts of Provence. Nor are they as fruity and delicate as many of increasingly popular *rosés* from Portugal. The best are marketed under one of the two special *Appellations Contrôlées* of Rosé-d'Anjou and Anjou-Rosé-de-Cabernet. Like all *rosés*, they should be consumed when young, for they improve very little in the bottle.

The best recent vintage years for the wines of the Loire are 1949, 1952, 1953, 1955, 1958 (except for wines from the Pouilly and Sancerre areas); 1959, 1961, 1962, 1964 and 1966. Table H gives the principal communes accorded authorized *Appelations Contrôlées*, as well as a list of the best-known vineyards.

SUMMARY

Of the dry, "flinty" white wines of the upper Loire, the most popular are Pouilly-Fumé and Sancerre (the former is not to be confused with Pouilly-Fuissé from Southern Burgundy). They are excellent with seafoods, good substitutes for the more expensive classic Chablis.

Vouvray, France's best sparkling wine (*mousseux*), is sweeter than most Champagne, but may often be used as a substitute.

The white wines of Anjou (lower Loire) are both dry and sweet. The best dry ones come from the commune of Savennières near Angers, the finest sweet dessert wines from the Quarts-de-Chaume vineyards. Anjou *rosés* are pleasant and satisfying, somewhat sweeter than most other French *rosés*.

Muscadet is a white wine with a lemony tang, inexpensive and popular.

Loire reds (Chinon, St.-Nicolas-de-Borgueil, etc.) are rare but extremely good when sufficiently aged (7 to 10 years).

WHITES

Appellation Contrôlée	*Vineyard*
Pouilly-Fumé (or Blanc-Fumé-de-Pouilly)*	Château du Nozet Coteaux des Loges La Loge aux Moines Coteau des Girarmes
Sancerre	Château de Sancerre Clos de la Poussie Chavignol Perrières
Quincy	Rimonet
Reuilly	Clos des Messieurs
Montlouis	Hameau de la Milletière
Vouvray	Clos le Mont Château Moncontour Clos de la Taiserie
Saumur	Château de Parnay (Clos Cristal)
Quarts-de-Chaume	Château de Bellerive Château de Surronde
Coteaux-du-Layon	Château de la Fresnaye
Coteaux de l'Aubance	Roche de Mûrs
Savennières	La Coulée de Serrant La Roche aux Moines Clos du Papillon Château de Savennières Château d'Épiré
Bonnézeaux	Château de Fesle
Muscadet	La Chapelle Châteauguy

---

* Not to be confused with the *Appellation Contrôlée* of Pouilly-sur-Loire, which wines are made from the Chasselas grape, and are the *ordinaires* of the region.

REDS

Appellation Contrôlée	*Vineyard*
†Vin de l'Orléanais	Beaugency (locality) St.-Jean-de-Braye (locality)
Chinon	Rochette-St.-Jean Le Closeaux
Bourgueil	Clos de la Salpêtrerie Clos des Perrières
St.-Nicolas-de-Bourgueil	Clos du Fondis
Saumur (Saumur-Champigny)	Château de Parnay Clos des Hospices

† *V.D.Q.S.* appellation.

OTHER FRENCH WINES

ALSACE

Alsace, the source of what are certainly the most fragrant and flowery white wines in all France, is a tiny district—a verdant little garden spot—tucked away behind the Vosges Mountains in the northeastern corner of the country. Along with its twin province of Lorraine (as the world so well remembers), it was captive German territory for almost fifty years preceding its liberation in 1918—a period which brought the wine industry of Alsace to the brink of disaster. A century ago Alsatian wines were of high quality. But the way to break a Frenchman's spirit is to ruin his wine, and this is exactly what the Germans attempted. Under the German occupation, quality was forgotten, and Alsatian viniculture was harnessed to the production of cheap wines for the German market.

In the years since 1918, the Alsatians—cruelly interrupted by the battles of World War II that raged in their vineyards and leveled many of their picturesque villages—have been valiantly putting the pieces back together. Their first act was once again to plant the traditional wine grapes, known in Alsace as "noble grapes," and in view of the dispersion of the old vineyard holdings which had taken place during the occupation, they wisely discarded the tradition that the name of a wine must be married to a particular piece of soil. Thus most Alsatian wines, comparable to the "varietal" wines of California, go by the name of the grapes from which they derive. Although the best of these are grapes ordinarily associated with Germany, it should be remembered that on Alsatian soil, they simply do not produce white wines which are really comparable to those of the Rhine or the Moselle—and one should not look for such. Alsatian wines are individualistic; if one allows them to stand on their own feet, many of them are very excellent indeed.

At the present time there is only the simplest, basic *Appellation Contrôlée* for the wines of Alsace, and this has only recently come into effect. Previous to 1962 the words were not required on a label, and the only control laws were locally-imposed ones which, in the course of its growing pains, the Alsatian wine industry had laid down for itself. Vineyard names, when found on labels, are still relatively unimportant. The term *Vin d'Alsace* indicates wine from the best or so-called "noble grapes," produced only in certain authorized areas; the highest qualitative appellations are the terms *Grand Vin d'Alsace*, *Grand Cru d'Alsace* or the word *Réserve*, all indicating wines of a higher alcoholic content, as well as ones the producer is proudest of.

There are no Alsatian reds worth mentioning; nor do the *rosés*, usually made from the Pinot noir and called in Alsace *vin gris*, constitute a very distinguished company. One will not need to experiment too long, either, before discerning that there is a vast difference in quality between the wines of one producer and those of another. Among the best *négociants* shipping to foreign markets are the firms of Hugel, Willm, that of Dopff and Irion, the Château de Mittelwihr and the Domaines Viticoles Schlumberger.

The following are the principal Alsatian wine types, in general order of excellence, all made from "noble grapes":

Riesling.   The Riesling grape is the source of all the great German "Rhine wines." In Alsace it produces a medium-dry white wine with a nice bouquet—thought by many to be the finest product of the district.

Traminer and Gewürztraminer.   Wines made from these grapes, especially the latter, compete in point of sheer strength of fragrance and perfume with almost any other white wine in the world. They also sometimes possess a barely perceptible seasonal effervescence, comparable to the *pétillant* white wines of Vouvray. The German word *gewürz* means spicy, and the Gewürztraminer is simply a "more-so-yet" variety of the commoner but already spice-like Traminer. In the best years a few producers sometimes make them with the *pourriture noble*. A more exotic redolent white wine than one of these rare Gewürztraminer *Auslesen* (from sweet, late-picked grapes) can hardly be found.[25]

Sylvaner.   A more ordinary grape than any of the above, the Sylvaner produces many of the lesser German wines, including the popular Liebfraumilch. In contrast, an Alsatian Sylvaner is apt to be acid and hard.

Muscat.   In Alsace this grape brings forth a dry white wine with a strong, enticing aroma that is never quite justified by the taste which follows. Nor is the typical "muscat" flavor in evidence.

Pinot Gris or Tokay.   Purportedly the grape of the celebrated Hungarian dessert wine, the "liqueur of wines." Actually, the relationship is doubtful, and is certainly not corroborated by Alsatian Tokay. This latter is simply dry, "flinty" and refreshing.

The *ordinaires* or most common wines of Alsace are called Zwickers, and are usually made from the Chasselas grape, a grape we have already referred to in connection with the inferior wine from the region (and with the *Appellation Contrôlée*) of Pouilly-sur-Loire. Better than these *ordinaires* are wines called Edelzwickers which, by local law, must be a blend of two or more of the above "noble grapes." Edelzwickers are not infrequently found outside of France, and are to be recommended when found with the label of a good producer.

Even the best and most carefully made Alsatian wines do not

---

[25] *Auslesen* labels usually bear the terms *Réserve* or *Cru Exceptionnelle*.

improve in the bottle, and the majority of them should be drunk young. Like the wines of Germany, they come in thin, tall bottles, here called *flûtes d'Alsace*. These wines, unusually light in color, are consumed in their native land from prettily decorated goblets, designed to enhance their gaiety. The best recent years in Alsace are 1958, 1959, 1961, 1962, 1964 and 1966.

Table I lists the famous communes of Alsace, along with the wines for which they are most noted.

WINES OF OTHER DISTRICTS

Other French wines from far-flung districts sometimes seen on foreign markets are those of the Jura, Monbazillac and Jurançon. The Jura is a small mountainous area, just east of the Côte d'Or. Chiefly noted for its amber-colored white wines, dry and rather heavy, and for its *rosés*, which latter are quite similar to (and compare favorably with) those of Anjou, the Jura also produces two vinous curiosities. One of these, formerly made in other parts of France (notably at Hermitage on the Rhône and in Alsace), is called *vin de paille* (straw wine). In effect, straw wine is raisin wine. The grapes are put out to dry in the sun on straw mats (hence the name) until they have reached a completely withered condition and attained an exceptionally high sugar content. The fermentation may require as much as a year; the wine, needless to say, is sweet and thick, and correspondingly strong.

The second curiosity of the Jura is made in the commune of Château-Châlon, and called *vin jaune* (yellow wine). This Sherry-like, dark-colored liquid derives from being allowed to remain, after its initial fermentation, in barrels open to the air for a period of six years or more. Bit by bit a crusty yeast forms on the surface of the wine, producing a progressive oxygenation which results in a yellow color and a somewhat bitter taste—though to many connoisseurs, not an unpleasant one. *Vin jaune* is really a very mild, unfortified Sherry—and in view of the history of the Jura, not too illogically so. For a brief period of time, as a result of one of those territorial jugglings that were always taking place through the intermarriages of Europe's nobility—the Jura was under Spanish control. No doubt this is the root of the close relationship between the wine of Château-Châlon and Sherry.

Château-Châlon has its own *Appellation Contrôlée*, and its yellow wines, bottled in individualistic square bottles, *clavelins*, are by no means as rare outside of France as one might suppose. The other two best-known wines from the Jura (white and *rosé*) go by the appellations of Arbois and Étoile. Vintage years for the district are roughly the same as for the Côte d'Or (see p. 54).

Monbazillac, the sweet white wine made in the Dordogne Valley upstream from St.-Émilion and Pomerol, is sometimes disparagingly referred to in France as "poor man's Sauternes." In our opinion, this accusation is not entirely fair. Made with the *pourriture noble*, and with the same grapes as those of Sauternes (though in different proportions), the wines of the *Appellation Contrôlée* of Monbazillac are softer and more mellow than the *liquoreux* of Bordeaux and lack the characteristic "rusty" taste of many Sauternes and Barsacs. Thus an appreciation of them need not be so often a matter of an acquired taste. They are endowed with sweetness and sunlight—and are considerably less costly than most other dessert wines. Children, among others, dote on them. Vintage years for Monbazillac correspond to those of Bordeaux (see p. 32).

The heady, orange-colored wines of Jurançon spring from an isolated district in the foothills of the Pyrénées, near the fashionable, fox-hunting town of Pau. Whether it was actually Jurançon (instead of the strong brandy from nearby Armagnac) which was so hastily brushed across the lips of the minutes-old Prince of Navarre—later to become Henry IV of France—is still a matter of considerable dispute among the respective publicizers of the two. In any event, Jurançon was to become one of the king's favorite wines, and its fame was spread far and wide by this native of the Béarn, himself born at Pau. Jurançon is made predominantly from two native grapes of the Pyrénées, the Marsencs (Gros and Petit). It has much fragrance and a peculiar musky tang, rather similar to what is often referred to as the "foxy" taste of New York State and other eastern American wines. Persons who are accustomed to these latter will find Jurançon an interesting comparison at least; to others it may almost be unrecognizable as a wine of France.

Jurançon possesses a reputation for an exceptionally long life in the bottle, and it, too, may be *pétillant*. In good years the *pourriture noble* is encouraged, giving the wine an extra sweetness. Almost all French wines have their folklore, and just as Château-neuf-du-Pape (thanks to its romping old marquis) is widely thought to be an aphrodisiac, Jurançon is considered a cure for marital discord and an accepted means of bringing estranged lovers together again. This, in itself, bodes well for its continued life on earth. Vintage years for Jurançon in general correspond with those of Bordeaux (see p. 32).

SUMMARY

Alsatian wines, nearly all white, are noted for their fragrances, and except for those labeled *Réserve* or *Cru Exceptionnelle*, they are all moderately dry. Like California "varietals," they are usually named after the grape from which they are made, and vineyard names are usually not too important. Alsace did not have *Appellations Contrôlée* regulations until 1962; previous to that year the term did not appear on labels. Often of excellent quality, they do not rank with the best German wines, even though most are made with the same grapes. Alsatian wines should be drunk young; the best recent years are 1958, 1959, 1961, 1962, 1964 and 1966.

The vineyards of the Jura Mountains produce good whites and even better *rosés*, the principal appellations being Arbois and Étoile. Jurançon, made near the Pyrénées, is orange-colored and heady; white Monbazillac, the most famous dessert wine of the Dordogne Valley, resembles Sauternes, though milder in taste. The best years for the Jura are roughly the same as for the Côte d'Or; those for Jurançon and Monbazillac parallel Bordeaux.

PRINCIPAL ALSATIAN WINES

Commune	*Wine for Which Commune Is Most Noted*
Barr	Sylvaner
Bambach	Riesling
Ribeauville	Tokay Riesling
Bergheim	Gewürztraminer
Hunawihr	Riesling Traminer Tokay
Riquewihr	Riesling Muscat Gewürztraminer
Mittelwihr	Gewürztraminer
Equisheim	Riesling
Soultzmatt	Sylvaner Riesling
Guebwiller	Gewürztraminer Traminer

WINES OF THE JURA, THE DORDOGNE AND THE PYRÉNÉES

JURA

Appellation Contrôlée	*Vineyard (or wine)*
Château-Châlon	Château-Châlon (yellow)
Étoile	(*rosé*, white)
Arbois	(*rosé*, white)

MONBAZILLAC (DORDOGNE)

Monbazillac   Château de Monbazillac (white)
Bergerac   Château de Monplaisir (red,
                              white)

PYRÉNÉES

Jurançon   Pourtau (white)
                            Perpigna (white)

THREE

Wines of Germany

NORTH COUNTRY VINEYARDS

The 50th parallel, which in Europe is considered the northernmost limit for the wine grape, slips between Land's End and the Scilly Isles, skirts the top of France, bisects the little Duchy of Luxembourg and passes close to the center of the greatest wine district of Germany. In fact, the northern part of this district is the sole exception to this vinicultural rule: for only the insignificant red-wine vineyards of the Ahr and those of the little river called the Moselle (Mosel), twisting and turning every which-way between its precipitous banks, are north of the parallel.

In comparison with France, Germany produces a mere trickle of wine—less than one-tenth as much. All the fine wines of Germany are white, and the finest of these are indelibly associated with the Riesling grape, which has been used in Germany for five hundred years. The Riesling is, *sine qua non*, the "noble" grape of the North Country. Although it is by no means unique to Germany, nowhere else does it truly excel. In California, Italy and Yugoslavia, for example, it produces comparatively watery and only mildly fragrant wines—though rather firmer and better ones, as we shall see, in Switzerland, Portugal, Chile and Hungary. In Bordeaux, especially in parts of Graves, it is often used for blending (though

94

not officially!); in Alsace it vies for high favor with the two Traminers. Yet nowhere in the world but in the Moselle and the Rhine
regions will one find a white wine as subtle, fragrant or as delicate.
A fine German wine made from the Riesling is a true aristocrat.

The Riesling is a lover of sun—and of poor, stony soil. If proof
were ever needed of the maxim that adversity is the ally of the
wine grape, here it is! There is a German saying that "where a
plow can go, no vine should grow," and certainly there are few
places in the world where wine is made under more tortuous and
impractical conditions. Almost without exception, the very greatest
wines of Germany come from vineyards that have been terraced
along the steep cliffs overlooking the Rhine and the Moselle, amid
outcroppings of rock where nothing else could possibly grow. The
stone-laden terraces themselves are oftentimes reached not by paths
or roads, but by flights of steps. When such earth as nature has
begrudged them is washed away, it must be carried back up the
cliffs in baskets or pails!

Nor is it just the terrain that taxes the German wine grower. For,
although in favorable years the aristocratic Riesling rewards him
for his pains several times over—and in the best years enables
him to make his justifiably celebrated sweet, fragrant wines—it
fails him badly in other years. In fact, the climate in this part of
Germany is so capricious that one is in luck to have as many as
three truly satisfactory years in a single decade. In other years, in
order to bring about a sufficient fermentation, the grapes in the
vat must be heavily sugared, which never enhances the quality of
wine—and even then, the product may be so poor that it must be
sold for the manufacture of *Sekt* (German Champagne), in the
process of which it is sweetened once again! Or perhaps the crop
—in a mediocre year—will go into Liebfraumilch or Moselblümchen, Germany's two most widely exported wines—the origin and
nature of which may be of some concern to the reader, who might
best receive clarification at the start.

One often hears the criticism that the classification and labeling
of German wines are overmeticulous, yet compared to the systems
of grading and labeling carried on in most other countries of the
world, this can be a blessing. Once one gets the hang of it, it is
possible to know from the language on most German bottles

exactly where the wine came from—and what it is. In some instances the origin of a German wine may be pinpointed right down to the identity of the very cask in which it was aged. Furthermore, this German system of labeling is nation-wide—something which does not hold true for any other important wine-producing country.

The two principal exceptions to the logic of German labels are Liebfraumilch and Moselblümchen. The former, perhaps the most popular of all German wines outside of Germany, is a generic name for what is often simply a haphazard blend of wines from the southern Rhineland; Moselblümchen is its equivalent from the region of the Moselle. Although neither of them are much drunk in Germany, this is not to say that when bottled and shipped by good producers (the firms of Sichel, Deinhard, Langenbach, Valkenberg and Anheuser are among the best) they cannot be drinkable wines, of good value. But it must be added that the aura of wines named Liebfraumilch (Milk of the Holy Virgin) and Moselblümchen (Little Flower of the Moselle)—terminology that artfully catches the imagination of the unknowing consumer—has frequently tempted German shippers and foreign importers to add between five and ten dollars to the fair value of a case. The real point is, of course, that one should not expect either wine to be any more distinguished in its way than a Bordeaux *Supérieur* or a communal blend from the Côte d'Or, or something simply labeled Châteauneuf-du-Pape without a vineyard name. Liebfraumilch and Moselblümchen are, in effect, the two principal "regional" wines of Germany.

With these two latter regional terms cleared away, one may then believe the statement that most German vintners sincerely do their utmost to assess and identify their wines for the consumer's benefit, and do a very thorough job of it. A proper German label invariably bears the name of the village or town from which the wine comes —in adjectival form. This latter form may at first be confusing, but if one keeps in mind the fact that the addition of the letters "er" to a proper name renders it an adjective, one will have little trouble. Hence the name Rüdesheim(er) means that the wine is "from" or "of" Rüdesheim. Similarly Hochheimer from Hochheim, Wormser from Worms. This is, after all, no more difficult to

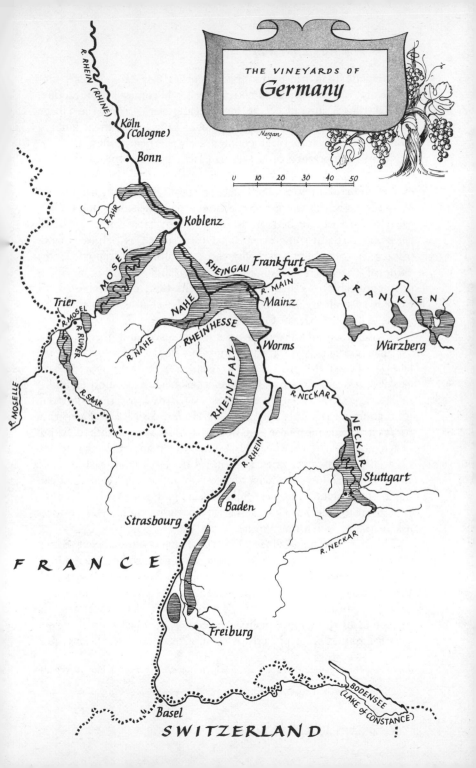

THE VINEYARDS OF
Germany

Morgan

0   10   20   30   40   50

R. RHEIN (RHINE)

Köln
(Cologne)

Bonn

R. AHR

Koblenz

MOSEL

RHEINGAU   Frankfurt

F R A N K E N

NAHE   R. MAIN

Mainz

Trier   Würzberg

R. MOSEL

R. RUWER   RHEINHESSE

R. NAHE   Worms

R. SAAR   RHEINPFALZ   R. NECKAR

R. MOSELLE   NECKAR

R. RHEIN   Stuttgart

Baden

Strasbourg

R. NECKAR

F R A N C E

Freiburg

BODENSEE
(LAKE of CONSTANCE)

Basel

SWITZERLAND

comprehend than the terms "New Yorker" or "Londoner". Occasionally one of these adjectival forms becomes a contraction, such as Binger instead of the logical Bingener—"from the village of Bingen." But such cases are unusual.[1] One learns them quickly enough, even from a brief contact with German wines.

Next in importance on a German label is the name of the particular vineyard. If one knows the language, many of these names evoke colorful pictures. Schlossberg means the vineyard on the hill with the castle; Sonnenberg, a vineyard on the sunny hill; Glöck, the vineyard of the bell or the clock; Schwarze Katz, the black cat's vineyard. In some exceptional cases (such as Schloss Johannisberg or Steinberg, two vineyards of universal renown), the name of the town is omitted from the label—but this, again, is only applicable to a sparse handful of the best, comparable to the French system of allowing a separate *Appellation Contrôlée* for Montrachet or Château Grillet.

Having established the town, the vineyard and the year, the German vintner (who always prints his name and address on the label) proceeds to inform the consumer of exactly what degree of sweetness the wine has, whether it has been estate-bottled and—in the case of the very finest wines—what cask it has come from. The commonest terms for casks are *Fuder*, *Stück* and *Fass*—thus *Fuder 129* will mean the one-hundred-and-twenty-ninth cask put down that particular year. Inasmuch as many German wines, especially the sweeter ones, vary in subtle ways from cask to cask, this courtesy allows the wine drinker the opportunity of duplicating a bottle which he may think especially fine—or of avoiding a repetition of one he doesn't like. What more could the consumer ask of the conscientious vintner?

The best German wines—like the French—are always estate-bottled. The most frequently seen term for estate-bottled is *Original-Abfüllung*[2] (original-bottled), although *Keller-Abfüllung* (cellar-bottled) and *Schlossabzug* (bottled at the castle or manor) are often substituted. The vintner's terminology for informing the consumer of the wine's quality—or rather, at what degree of ripeness the grapes were picked—is again a relatively simple one, pro-

---

[1] One will also notice that the year in which the wine is made is usually given in this same adjectival form, such as *1959er*.
[2] Often abbreviated to *Orig.-Abfg*.

vided one does not shy at those long, composite words so typical of the language. As one would assume for a country with so short a growing season, the most prized wines of Germany are the sweetest, made in the all too infrequent years in which the *pourriture noble* (the German term is *edelfäule*) has had time to settle. Thus a *Spätlese* (late picked) wine will be richer and sweeter than an ordinary wine; an *Auslese* (picked off) means an even sweeter one, from grapes that have been selected bunch by bunch. A *Beerenauslese* (picked off berries) or a *Trockenbeerenauslese* (raisined picked off berries) will be very sweet indeed, the grapes having been plucked one by one as they turned, or sometimes become so ripe and lush that they have fallen to the ground[3]. Logically these sweet wines—variously described by the words *feine* (fine), *feinste* (finest) and *hochfeinste* (very finest) or *edelste* (noblest)—are the most expensive of all German wines. In their native land, they are often taken between meals, very much as we drink coffee and tea.

Naturwein or *Ungezuckerter*[4] on a label will mean the wine has not been sugared. As we have implied, such is always a mark of quality. *Cabinet* or *Kabinett*, a term that originally specified wine which was put aside for the owner's exclusive use or for entertaining royalty, is nowadays more freely used—very much in the sense that the word *Réserve* in Alsace implies a wine that is its producer's particular pride and joy. Many German producers also go so far in their honesty as to print the name of the grape on the label. In place of the Riesling which, like all the superior wine grapes of the world, has a notably small yield, many of the lesser German vineyards use the more productive Sylvaner, or a hybrid known as the Müllar-Thurgau, a cross between the two. In certain parts of Germany, good wines are also made with the two white Traminers —grapes we have already met in nearby Alsace.

Inasmuch as most German vineyards *(Lagen)* are divided and subdivided among many owners, comparable to the situation on the Côte d'Or, the name of a reliable bottler or shipper on a label

---

[3] In certain unusual years frost—ordinarily the enemy of the wine grape elsewhere—enhances the quality of these very sweet wines. The product is called *Eiswein* (ice wine), the result of an even higher concentration of sugar than belatedly-picked grapes would ordinarily produce. 1961 and 1962 were both good years for *Eiswein*.

[4] Synonymous terms are: *Natur, Naturrein* and *Echt*. Wines of the highest quality—*Cabinet*, the various *Auslesen*, etc.,—are never sugared.

is always of importance, as the wine drinker will soon enough discover for himself by experience. However, on many German bottles one will find a basic guide to quality: a seal with a form-alized black eagle surrounded by the initials *V.D.N.V.* (representing a wine merchants' association known as the *Verband Deutscher Naturwein-Versteigerer*—German Natural Wine Sellers' Association). Bottles bearing this symbol, although not always qualitatively the very best, invariably contain good wine. Another auspicious signpost of quality may be found in wines from vineyards owned by the German state—of which there are a great many. Labels of state-produced wines bear the term *Staatsweinguter*—indicating products of traditional Teutonic thoroughness.

As with so many French wines, it is of primary importance to remember that a bottle without a year can only mean a poor year, or a blend of two years or more, and the wine should definitely be suspect—just as a bottle that does not carry a vineyard name will almost certainly be a blend. As we have said, abject slavery to a vintage chart is arch foolishness—yet it is perhaps less so in the case of German wines than of those of other countries. Good wines are made in poor years, but they are few and far between. The best recent vintage years (now applicable only to the sweeter varieties) have been 1952, 1953, 1955 and 1958. 1959 was excellent; the wines of 1960 were notably poor, whereas those of 1961, 1962, 1964 and 1966 were of good quality. Finally, it is well to remember that dry German wines are neither bottled nor shipped until they are ready to drink, and that with the exception of the various sweet *Auslesen, Spätlesen, Beerenauslesen*, etc., none of them profit by remaining long in the bottle.

THE SOUTHERN REGIONS
OF THE RHINE

Just beyond the point where the Rhine is finally swallowed up by Germany, north of the Alsatian city of Strasbourg, one comes to the first (and largest-producing) of the half-dozen famous German wine regions. This is the Rheinpfalz, or Palatinate—so named by the Romans, the first known cultivators of the wine grape in Germany, for one of Rome's seven hills. Unlike most of the up-and-down vineyard land in Germany, the Palatinate—a high plateau on the west bank of the Rhine which the Germans call the "Pfalz"—is a garden spot, a continuation of the terrain and way-of-life of neighboring Alsace. It is filled with orchards and truck gardens and vines, grotesque, timbered houses in villages with twisting, narrow streets. The sun shines longer and brighter in the Palatinate than in other parts of the Rhineland, and the predominant grape here, the Sylvaner, flourishes as nowhere else.

The best vineyards of the Palatinate, however, restrict themselves to the Riesling, and the finest wines all come from a small concentration of upland villages known locally as the Weinstrasse (wine street). Quarries abound in this part of the Palatinate, and the ground of many of the vineyards is covered with their rubble, holding the sun's heat throughout the cool nights. The wines, which have for years been uncommonly popular in England, are milder and less acid than those from any other part of the Rhineland, and mature faster. *Auslesen* and other sweet wines from the Palatinate are apt to be honey-sweet.

Although the Palatinate is Germany's largest wine-producing region, embracing some forty thousand acres in vines, the vineyards of the Weinstrasse total only about two thousand. The balance of the region is low-lying and nearer the river, and devoted almost solely to Sylvaner and lesser grapes for the production of *Könsumwein*—the *ordinaire* that the Rhinelanders drink themselves from pitchers and carafes. *Könsumweins* are relatively low in alcohol, harsh and undistinguished—with a *terroir* which is anything but pleasant. They are never exported. Wines of the Weinstrasse most often seen abroad are those of Ruppertsberg, Deidesheim, Forst and Wachenheim, though there are other villages, such as Bad Dürkheim, Ungstein and Königsbach that are nearly as famous.

Conterminous to the Palatinate, also on the west bank of the river, is a region producing markedly better wines, known as the Rheinhesse (Hessia or "Hesse"). The vineyards of the Rheinhesse, their vines neatly tailored on high wires, hug the riverbank all the way from Worms to Mainz. Again, in contrast to the northern regions of the Rhineland, the land rolls gently up from the river, and there is little need for terracing. The wines, the best known of which are perhaps the Niersteiners, are moderately dry, soft, fruity and pliant, with bountiful bouquets, and are readily acceptable to uninitiated palates. Most of them are raised on the red sandstone soil so typical of the region, as reflected by the names of many of the vineyards: Rotenberg (red hill), Scharlachberg (scarlet hill), Goldberg (golden hill).

In addition to being the home of such familiar wine names as Niersteiner, Oppenheimer and Bodenheimer, the region is also the fount of large quantities of the omnipresent Liebfraumilch. In fact, the finest *Lage* of Worms, a twenty-five-acre tract that surrounds the Liebfrauenkirche (Church of Our Lady), is probably the source of the term. In great years wines from the Liebfrauenkirche,[5] unquestionably one of the best vineyards of the Rheinhesse, can be as filled with multiple exotic tastes and subtleties as any. Any one who has tasted it at its best will perhaps not wonder why the name might have been plundered and dragged into the mud! Of the thirty thousand-odd acres of vineyards in the Rheinhesse, it has been estimated that all but about 2 per cent of their production emerges, one way or another, as Liebfraumilch—made in large part, of course, from the Sylvaner.

Although the vineyards of the Rheinhesse end abruptly where the river turns sharply westward at Mainz, technically the region includes the town of Bingen at the junction of the Rhine and the Nahe. Bingen is the source of some superb Rhine wines, well described by one connoisseur as "robust and racy." The town also once manufactured most of the corkscrews of Germany, known colloquially as "Bingen pencils." The apocryphal story behind this bit of wit has to do with a presiding bishop of Bingen who, having called a meeting of his priests and finding himself without a pencil with which to make the necessary notes asked if anybody perchance had brought one. The clerics obediently probed the depths of their habits—but not one could produce anything but a corkscrew. Names on labels of Bingen wines are often hyphenated with those of two nearby towns: Büdesheim (Büdesheimer) and Kempten

---

[5] Wine from this vineyard is called Liebfrauenstift or Liebfrauenstiftwein.

(Kempter); the adjectival form of Bingen on labels, as we have mentioned before, is Binger.

In order not to travel too far ahead of ourselves in this vinous journey down the Rhine, we must digress for a moment and cross the river to inspect two minor, though still significant, wine regions. These comprise the vineyards along the steeply sloped valley of the Neckar—the home of "student wines" to those who know the university city of Heidelberg—and those of Franconia, on the River Main. The wines of the Neckar are made under climatic conditions so severe that each winter the vines must be taken off their wires, laid on the ground and covered with straw to protect them against the frosts. Neckar wines only shine in the very best years—but when at their zenith they are entirely comparable, in delicacy and fragrance, to Moselles. The finest of them are made from the two Traminer grapes. The Neckar is also the traditional home of a German *rosé*, less popular now than formerly, called Schillerwein. The word (which is not related to the poet, Schiller) means "a glistening play of colors"—certainly a pretty word picture for a *rosé* and hardly less promotionally imaginative than the terms Liebfraumilch and Moselblümchen.

Franconia's wines (Steinwein or Frankenwein) hold a unique reputation, based in part on the squat flagons in which they have been traditionally bottled for generations. Unchanged in style or shape since the eighteenth century, this particular bottle is known as *Bocksbeutel* (or *Boxbeutel*), an entirely realistic word having to do with one-half of a part of a goat's anatomy. The name Steinwein is often construed to mean that these bottles were once made of stone; but the truth is that it derives from Würzburg's oldest vineyard, Stein, which lies close to the middle of this charming, ancient German city. Steinweins (like Liebfraumilch and Moselblümchen, the term is regional) are generally from the Sylvaner grape, or the hybrid cross, the Müller-Thurgau, and are rather different from the general run of German wines. Very dry, with an unsuspected alcoholic strength, they live a long time and often remind one of the white wines of northern France, such as those of Chablis. Some of them are exported and will be found to be relatively inexpensive—in terms of most German wines, a major asset in itself.

THE RHEINGAU

It will come as a surprise to many that out of Germany's comparatively minuscule total of one hundred and sixty thousand acres planted to wine grapes (compared with France's more than three million acres), only about twenty thousand produce superior wines. Certainly the greatest concentration of these latter is to be found in Germany's smallest (six thousand acres) region, the Rheingau—an impressive series of steep bluffs and hills running for about fifteen miles along the north bank of the Rhine, from its confluence with the Main to where it is joined by the Nahe at Bingen. Throughout this stretch the river's course turns almost due westward. The terraced vineyards, filled with coarse pieces of quartz and fragments of slate, literally stew in the sun, protected from the north winds by the forested Taurus Mountains behind.

It is said that the Emperor Charlemagne (whom we remember as the owner of vineyards in the Côte d'Or), while occupying the great palace he had built in Ingelheim, across the Rhine from the Rheingau, one day noticed a spot on the opposite bluffs where the snow melted sooner than elsewhere, and commanded the planting of the vines that now constitute the famous vineyards of Schloss Johannisberg. Charlemagne may have been the first member of Europe's nobility to note the virtues of the Rheingau, but he was certainly not the last. Among others, in later years, was Queen Victoria, whose fondness for German wines took the form of hypochondria. Visiting the Rheingau in the middle of the last century, so contagious was her enthusiasm that she managed to have a vineyard, Victoriaberg (by no means the best), named after her. Among others, one of the Queen's coined phrases was "Frankenwein is *krankenwein*"—the latter meaning wine for the sick; and it was the dour Queen herself who was responsible for the platitude of the last century: "Good hoc keeps off the doc."

She was referring of course, to the wines of the village of Hochheim, the first that one meets in the Rheingau. To the wines of this particular village the British term "Hock," throughout the British Isles a generic name for all German wine, owes its derivation.

Hochheim, whose vineyards in good years are capable of truly superior vintages, borders the Main and lies on relatively low ground—but as the river rounds the bend and starts on its westward course the hills and bluffs appear, and we are in the land of the gods. Here are the greatest vineyards of the Rheingau, if not of all Germany: Schloss Johannisberg and the nearby Steinberg—with Schloss Vollrads at Hattenheim and the Macrobrunn at Erbach ranking as close seconds.

Steinberg, the Clos de Vougeot of German vineyards, surrounded by a mile and a half of walls built by Cistercian monks in the twelfth century, is now owned by the German state. Schloss Johannisberg was founded as a Benedictine monastery in the same century, and has been owned for one hundred and fifty years by one of the oldest of all noble Germanic families, the Metternichs.[6] The present *Schloss* (castle), an imposing building overlooking its sloping vineyards and the Rhine, was used by the Germans as an observation post during World War II, and was consequently heavily bombed by the R.A.F. Happily, it has now been restored. Here are wines that have earned the praises of wine drinkers for centuries. Full of power and character, the dry ones are slightly piquant, the sweeter ones unbelievably fragrant. At both the Schloss and Steinberg, one finds the very epitome of German care and attention to detail in the art of wine making. To guard against contamination and infection of the vines, visitors must change their shoes before entering the vineyards; and the cellars—the first in Germany to install glass-lined steel tanks to replace wooden casks—are perhaps even more sanitary and free from contamination than a modern hospital.

The wines of Schloss Johannisberg, made in various grades (six in most years, more yet in the best years) are labeled in their own

6 A family of vinophiles for generations. It was, in fact, Prince Metternich who —in the course of negotiations for the hand of Marie-Louise of Austria—first brought to the attention of the lowly-born Emperor Napoleon the existence of the rare Sherry-like *vin jaune* of the Jura, Château-Châlon.

way. The lowest grade bears a red seal *(Rötlach)*. Next in quality comes the green seal *(Grünlach)*, followed by a rose or pink seal *(Roslach)*—this latter being at least a semisweet *Auslese* wine. The so-called *Kabinett* wines, the most expensive, will bear orange, white, blue or gold seals, in that order of excellence. But let us not whet the reader's thirst too hastily: he must be warned that a gold seal *Trockenbeerenauslese* from a great year may cost him $30.00 a bottle. A fine Steinberger may cost even more. Thus it is significant to know that although the wines of these particular vineyards are the indisputable best, there are other vineyards in the villages of Johannisberg and Hattenheim,[7] nearly as excellent, which are listed in Table J.

Another outstanding Rheingau wine comes from the village of Rüdesheim, the westernmost of the region, where the multitudinous terraced vineyards are scattered over the face of the steepest of bluffs. It is important to remember that Rüdesheim vineyards appending the word *Berg*—indicating that they are situated on the most precipitous part of the bluff—have the reputation of being the finest. (Examples: Berg Rottland, Berg Lay, etc.). Other villages with deservedly international fame are Winkel (Schloss Vollrads, the largest privately owned vineyard intact on the Rhine), Hallgarten, Erbach (the principle vineyard is Marcobrunn) and Rauenthal.

Although the average alcoholic content of German wines is appreciably lower than that of French wines (most Rhine wines rarely attain more than 10 per cent, and few Moselles more than 9 per cent) the wines of the Rheingau are exceptions. They are not only comparatively strong in alcohol, but also less sweet or sugary in the respective categories for wine made from late-picked grapes —*Spätlese, Auslese, Beerenauslese* and *Trockenbeerenauslese*. Aptly described by experts as "brisk and silky," they are certainly the most expensive of all German wines, and if for this reason only, it should not be forgotten that there are extreme variances in quality among poor, good and excellent years—and that a famous Rheingau of an inferior year can be as unappealing and undrinkable as any, and not worth any price. These wines are natural

---

[7] Wines are labeled adjectively Johanisberger and Hattenheimer after the villages, with labels supplemented by vineyard names.

pitfalls for the "wine snob". The reader should also not allow himself to become unduly concerned, especially in connection with these wines of the Rheingau, over the relative sameness of them. This latter is a criticism which has more than once been aimed at German wines as a whole, with a certain validity. German wines are versatile, to be sure, but there are subtleties of differences that are not always easily spotted by uninitiated palates. Thus the experimenting wine drinker should not lose patience if he cannot at first tell the difference between a Moselle and a Rheingau, or a Rheinpfalz and a Rheinhesse, much less a Schloss Johannisberg and a fine Steinberg. Even professional tasters experience difficulty in putting their finger on their relative merits and demerits, or sometimes even in telling them apart.

THE MOSELLE

The regional name for wines of the Moselle is printed on labels as *Mosel–Saar–Ruwer*[8]. Rising in that part of northern France which is one of the most fought-over territories on the earth, the Moselle River is shortly afterward joined by two tiny streams, the Saar and the Ruhr (Ruher), before commencing its snakelike route to the Rhine. In fact, so circuitous is the course of this extraordinarily beautiful little river that over a distance of forty miles, as the crow flies, it triples its length and—in its predominantly northeasterly path—runs eight times due north, seven times due south and once nearly due west!

All the best Mosel Saar Ruwer vineyards face south, thus some of them are on the left bank, others on the right, and most of them so precipitously placed as to induce violent vertigo. In the upper reaches of the region the finest wines come from the Schwarzhofberg and Schartzberg vineyards of the Saar, and the villages of Maximim Grünhaus and Eitelsbach on the Ruher. Made exclusively

---

[8] These German regional terms are not to be construed in the same light as French regional labels. For the convenience and information of the consumer, they simply establish the general geographical area in which the vineyard lies.

from the Riesling, reaching their zenith of perfection only once or twice in a decade, they are the most gracious and fragrant, fruity and above all crisp, of all German wines. They are also the palest of all German wines; and Moselles from the Saar and Ruhr watersheds, especially, are apt to be slightly *pétillant* (or *spritzig*), a quality which rarely detracts from the charm of any light white wine.

The five principal villages on the Moselle proper (known as the Mittel-Mosel), are Piesport, Wehlen, Zeltigen, Graach and Bernkastel. Concentrated in a small area at a place where the little river suffers its most active peristalsis, these villages are responsible for the majority of Moselles encountered in foreign countries. Concerning the wines of Zeltigen—the largest producer of the five villages, as well as the source of a great quantity of nondescript Moselblümchen—the reader should be forewarned that a wine simply labeled *Zeltiger* without a vineyard name will not necessarily be a distinguished product. Of the five, the wines of Piesport and Wehlen are traditionally considered the finest—equaled perhaps only by those of a few outstanding vineyards of Graach, the best of which is appropriately called Himmelreich (Kingdom of Heaven). Also at Graach is the superb vineyard of Josephshof, owned for a century by the old wine-making family of Kesselstatts. Always marketed under the vineyard name without mention of the village of Graach, few German wines of a great year can be as luscious or pervasively fragrant as a Josephshöfer *Beerenauslese*.

Ranking close, certainly in terms of international reputation, to Schloss Johannisberg and Steinberg, is the Moselle with the colorful name of Bernkastler Doktor—from the principal vineyard of the Bernkastel. Perhaps because of its picturesque and easy-to-remember name—comparable to the Côte d'Or's Volnay and Pommard—Bernkastler Doktor became one of the first Moselles to attain popularity in England and America. Some experts find a distinctive "smoky" flavor in it. In our opinion, the wine does not necessarily merit the high prices that it so often brings. If one must sample "the Doktor," however, the best is produced by one of the three owners of the vineyard, the Thanisch family, and will be labeled *Bernkastler Doktor und Graben.*

SCATTERED VINEYARDS

Other good German white wines are produced in the region of Nahe, which adjoins the Moselle to the south (see Table J for the best-known villages and their vineyards), and in the area of Baden in the foothills of the Black Forest, across the swift-flowing Rhine from Alsace. The best of the Baden (Badishe) wines, made near the city of Freiburg, derive from Sylvaner, Chasselas (here the Gutedal) or Pinot gris (here the Ruländer) grapes. Curiously enough, although neither the Chasselas nor the Pinot gris ever seem to constitute the sources of distinguished wines elsewhere, they bloom in this particular part of Germany. The best vineyards of Baden surround the villages of Ihringen, (Winklerberg), Achkarren (Schlossberg, Traubengarten), Durbach (Schlossberg), Endingen (Steingrube) and Oberrotweil (Henkenberg)—names of prophesiable value to drinkers of German wines in future years. Wines from the neighboring region of Württemberg are of less worth, as are those light, country wines known as *Seeweins*, grown along the placid shores of the Lake of Constance, the principal source of the Rhine. Delicious in their own habitat, they are not of sufficient character to warrant export.

The red wines of Germany, made in larger quantities than one might think, are almost all exclusively lowland wines. They are virtually never exported. The best of them, made on the lower Rhine in the Ahr Valley, near Bonn, usually derive from the German version of the Burgundian Pinot noir, here called the Spätburgunder (late Burgundy). Soft and too sweet for a red wine, they also lack character and require no further mention, except as a reminder to visitors of Germany that they often constitute a momentary (and most welcome) respite from what may be a plethora of whites.

With the exception of Steinweins and Frankenweins, most German wines come in tall, slim bottles known as *Flasche*. For purposes of quick identification, it is well to know that the wines of the Moselle and Rheinpfalz are shipped in green bottles, other German wines in brown bottles. The great years for German wines in the past decade have been 1959, 1961. and 1962, with those of 1955, 1957, 1958, 1964 and 1966 classified as good.

SUMMARY

All the best German wines are white, with the sweeter ones classified (and priced) according to their degree of sweetness: *Spätlese* (from late picked grapes); *Auslese* (usually picked even later); *Beerenauslese* (a definitely sweet wine); *Trockenbeerenauslese* (the sweetest). A *Cabinet* or *Kabinett* wine means one of which the producer is especially proud.

Liebfraumilch, Moselblümchen and Frankenweins are "regionals," or generics; the first two are usually overpriced for what they are.

Two basic guides to quality in German wines, to be found on labels, are the insignia of a black eagle surrounded by the letters *V.D.N.V.*, and the term *Staatsweinguter*, this latter indicating that the vineyard is state-controlled.

The finest German wines come from the regions of the Rheingau (on the Rhine) and the Moselle (Mosel). The former have more body and character; the latter are the more delicate and aromatic. Other lesser regions are the Rheinpfalz, the Rheinhesse, the Neckar and Franconia (Frankenwein or Steinwein, shipped in flagon-like bottles).

Most dry German wines are not released until ready to drink, thus need no further aging. The sweeter ones improve in the bottle. Recent *great* years are 1953, 1959, 1961 and 1962; *good* years are 1955, 1957, 1958 and 1964. Beware of wines from other years, especially those from 1960. Some 1965's—prophesied as a disastrous year—turned out to be excellent, though those of 1966 are more reliable.

RHEINPFALZ (PALATINATE)

Village	*Lagen (vineyards)*
Ruppertsberg	Hofstück, Nussbien Hoheburg Kreuz
Deidesheim	Dopp Hohenmorgen Kieselberg Grain
Wachenheim	Goldbächel Gerümpel Luginsland Böhlig
Forst	Kirchenstück Jesuitengarten Ungeheuer Freundstück

RHEINHESSE (HESSIA)

Worms	Liebfrauenstift Kirchenstück Klostergarten
Oppenheim	Sackträger Herrenberg Zuckerberg Goldberg
Nierstein	Glöck Brudersberg Taubennest Zehnmorgan

Nackenheim	Rothenberg
	Fenchelberg
	Engelsberg
Bodenheim	Westrum
	Kahlenberg
	Ebersberg
	Leidhecke
Bingen	Eiselberg
	Schlossberg
	Schwätzerchen
	Scharlachberg

NECKAR (WÜRTTEMBERG)

Brüssele	Spitze
	Schloss Shaubeck

FRANKEN (FRANCONIA)

Würzburg	Stein (Steinmantel, Jesuitenstein)
	Innere Leiste
	Felsenleiste
Escherndorf	Lump
	Kirchberg
	Eulengrube
Randersacker	Pfülben
	Hohberg
	Teufelskeller
	Spielburg

RHEINGAU

Hochheim	Domdechaney
	Hinter der Kirche
	Daubhaus

Village	Lagen (vineyards)
Eltville	Klümbchen
	Sonnenberg
	Taubenberg
	Kalbspflicht
Rauenthal	Baiken
	Gehrn
	Wieshell
	Rothenberg
Kiedrich	Gräfenberg
	Sandgrube
	Wasserrose
	Turmberg
Erbach	*Marcobrunn
	Brühl
	Siegelsberg
	Rheinhell
Hattenheim	*Steinberg
	Hassel
	Nussbrunnen
	Mannberg
	Wissellbrunn
Hallgarten	Schönhell
	Jungfer
	Mehrhölzchen
	Deutelsberg
Winkel	*Schloss Vollrads
	Hasensprung
	Dachsberg
	Jesuitengarten
Johannisberg	*Schloss Johannisberg
	Klaus
	Hölle
	Mittelhölle
	Kahlenberg

Geisenheim	Rothenberg
	Hoher Decker
	Mäuerchen
	Kosakenberg
Rüdesheim	Berg Bronnen
	Berg Bergweg
	Berg Rottland
	Berg Lay
	Berg Schlossberg

MOSEL—SAAR—RUWER (MOSELLE)

Wiltingen	*Scharzhofberg (Scharzberg)
	Braune Kupp
	Gottesfuss
	Dohr
Ockfen	Bockstein
	Herrenberg
	Geisberg
Maximim Grünhaus	Herrenberg
	Bruderberg
Eitelsbach	Karthäuser Hofberg
	Eitelsbacherberg
	Sonnenberg
	Marienholz
Trittenheim	Laurentiusberg
	Apotheke
	Altärchen
Neumagen	Rosengärtchen
	Laudamusberg
	Engelgrube
Piesport	Goldtröpfchen
	Falkenberg
	Lay
	Taubengarten
Bernkastel	Doktor und Graben (Thanisch)
	Doktor und Bratenhöfchen
	Badstude
	Lay

Village	Lagen (vineyards)
Wehlen	Sonnenuhr
	Lay
	Rosenberg
Graach	*Josephshof
	Himmelreich
	Domprobst
	Abtsberg
Uerzig	Würtzgarten
	Kranklay
	Lay
	Urglück
Zeltingen	Himmelreich
	Schlossberg
	Sonnenuhr
Erden	Treppchen
	Herrenberg
	Busslay
	Prälat
Zell	†Schwarze Katz

NAHE

Schloss Böckelheim	*Schloss Böckelheim
	Kupfergrube
	Königsberg
	Felsenberg
Kreuznach	Kautzenberg
	Brückes
	Kronenberg
	Hinklestein
Niederhäusen	Hermannsberg
	Hermannshöhle
	Rosenberg
	Rossel

---

* Designates that vineyard labels its wine only with vineyard name, without mention of the appropriate village.

† Nowadays usually a generic name, comparable to Moselblümchen.

FOUR

Italian Wines

WINES OF THE ALPS AND THE PLAINS

Although only a handful of Italian wines may ever be compared in quality with the best of France and Germany, this little nation, half the size of France, produces more wine than any country on earth. Italy holds three other vinous world's records, too. The first is for the exportation of table wine, a large part of which comes to the United States. The second is for the production of Vermouth, in which field she far outstrips her closest rival, France. The third is national per capita consumption: the average Italian drinks even more wine than the average Frenchman, at an annual rate approaching forty gallons.

Italy makes nine times as much red wine as white, and except for three or four of them, the Italians generally keep their still white wines at home. As is so amply illustrated by German wines, white-wine grapes flourish best closest to the northern limit of the wine belt. In fact, one might think of Italy as the converse of Germany, whose red wines, it will be recalled, are hardly worthy of mention.

One often hopes that it will not be too long in the future of the civilized world before someone comes up with a universal system for the naming and classifying of wines. Meanwhile, the wine drinker can only resort to familiarizing himself with the principles, such as they may be, behind each individual country's systems—and let experience (and many a mistake) teach him the finer points. The basic problem with Italian wines is simply the fact that their names, as found on labels, are divided between grape names and place names; the confusing aspect being that certain varieties of grapes are grown in many different parts of the country, while others are confined to small regions or even individual vineyards. Thus a wine called Barbera (from the grape of the same name) may be produced on the plains of Piedmont or in Tuscany, or among the Veronese hills, rendering it in effect a regional wine; whereas Soave, for example, is only made at Soave, a little hill town between Verona and Venice.

Perhaps the best rule of thumb is to remember that the five principal Italian wines named after grapes (all red) are Barbera, Nebbiolo, Dolcetto, Freisa and Grignolino—and assume that any other name on a label is a place or vineyard name. Since the superior wines of the world always derive from the most suitable soils, it goes without saying that those Italian wines which are named geographically are the best. There is one infamous exception: Chianti. Chianti is a specific place name—a small delimited region. But several million gallons of it produced each year just don't come from there!

Wine is in the blood of Italians. Just as many an Italian in the United States buys California or New York grapes and makes his own wine in his cellar, the wine grape is also grown in every backyard from the boot top to the toe of the Italian peninsula, and on the islands of Sardinia and Sicily. Yet there are, in effect, only seven major vineyard areas responsible for superior Italian table wines—all of them surprisingly small. From north to south, these are the mountainous Tyrol in the north, once part of Austria; the plains of Lombardy and Piedmont, the latter largely famous as the source of Asti, the best-known Italian sparkling wine (*spumante*); Verona in the province of Venetia (Venice); Chianti, south of Florence; the region of Orvieto in Umbria; and finally the slopes of volcanic Mount Vesuvius below Naples.

As would be expected, the vineyards of the Tyrolean Alps, sky-high in the valleys and steep approaches of the Brenner Pass to Austria, are predominantly filled with Austrian and German wine grapes, and their best wines are the aromatic whites that derive

THE VINEYARDS OF
Italy, Sicily and Corsica

0   50   100   150
MILES

SWITZERLAND

•Innsbruck

Brenner Pass

AUSTRIA

FRANCE

Turin
Asti
Milan
LAKE GARDA
Verona
R. PO
Venice
R. PIAVE
Trieste

YUGOSLAVIA

Genoa

Nice

Florence
R. ARNO
Siena

Orvieto
R. TIBER
Rome

ADRIATIC SEA

I T A L Y

CORSICA (french)

SARDINIA (ital.)

Naples
Capri

TYRRHENIAN

SEA

Palermo
Messina

Marsala
SICILY
Catania

TUNISIA

from the Traminer, the Sylvaner and the Riesling. Wine from the Riesling (which comes in tall, green Rhine-wine type bottles) is usually known as Terlano; that from the Traminer is appropriately called *Traminer aromatico.* Also grown in the Tyrol are several excellent reds, Guncina, Santa Giustina and another with the somewhat incongruous name—for an Italian wine, at any rate —of Kuchelberger (no doubt a relic of the Austrian days). These Tyrolean Alps are also the source of a lively *rosé* called Lagrein Rosato, deliciously fruity and fragrant, probably the best Italian *rosé.* Although none are truly outstanding, the white and *rosé* wines of the Tyrol are fresh, fragrant and pleasant. Long popular with the Swiss and the Austrians, the day may not be far off when they will be exported elsewhere. Three red wines of the Tyrol are also to be recommended: Lago di Caldaro, Santa Maddelena and Valttellina.

The vineyards of Piedmont, that part of Italy closest to France, are split in two by the River Po, Italy's longest river. Near the headwaters, in the rolling country south of industrial Turin— whose grime and soot is exonerated once one knows it as the Mecca for such gastronomic treasures as the celebrated lavender truffle and those thin, crispy Italian breadsticks called *grissini*—is a tremendous stretch of vineyards, said to produce three times more wine than all the vineyards of New York State and California put together. Most of this is of inferior quality: white, sweetish Moscatello, used either as a basis for herb-laden Vermouth, or for the manufacture of Italy's best known "Champagne," Asti Spumante, a sparkling white wine with an unmistakable Muscatel flavor. But Piedmont is also noted for some excellent regionals (those named for the grape). Perhaps the best white is the green-gold Cortese, made from the grape of the same name, a dry *(secco)* pale wine that is best when sold under the label of Gavi. The reds include Freisa, fragrant and fruity, and Barbera (a wine grape, as we have mentioned, found in other parts of Italy, as well as California). The Piedmont version of Barbera is sturdy and coarse, and like many another Italian common red wine it is apt to be *frizzante (pétillant).* The Italians themselves think of this as adding to the charm of a red wine. When made for export, however, they are still wines.

In that part of the region north of the Po, Piedmont is responsible for four or five superior wines, all red—perhaps the only Italian wines to which the adjective "great" may be justly applied at all. These are, respectively, Gattinera, Bardolino (the Beaujolais of Italy), Carema, Barbaresco and Barolo—all named for the villages in which they are grown. Made from the indigenous Nebbiolo grape, here are wines that are full-bodied and slow to mature, reminiscent in aroma and taste of good Burgundies. Barolo is often called the "Prince of Piedmont." Sometimes startlingly alcoholic, it is universally acknowledged as the best of the lot. If one is fortunate enough to come across an old bottle (or has the patience to wait for a young one to mature), one will not be disappointed. Another celebrated Piedmont red, possibly more of a curiosity to the average wine drinker than anything else, is the local sweet Dolcetto, one of the few unfortified red dessert wines in the world. Wine snobs—and many another!—will find it both incongruent and distasteful.

Piedmont is also the source of Nebbiolo Spumante, a ruby colored, sweetish *(abboccato)* equivalent of Sparkling Burgundy, at its best when made by a process similar to the *méthode champenoise* of the Champagne district in France, which will be described in Chapter VIII. But most wine drinkers will agree, we think, that the most commendable sparkling wines of Piedmont are the white Astis.

In the United States and England an increasingly popular Italian dry white wine is Soave, which owes its name to an intriguing little walled town just east of the city of Verona, on the road to Venice. Soave might well be called the Italian Chablis. Exceptionally light in color, it is dry and mild (*soave* means suave or mild). As with Chablis, the vines are grown on chalky soil, giving the wine a comparable "flinty" quality. Soave is shipped in tall, slender bottles similar to those of Alsace and Germany, and it is an excellent companion to almost any dish demanding a light white wine, especially fish. One may be certain that it will offend few palates.

Three excellent reds of Venetia are the twins Valpolicella and Valpantena, fragrant and soft and subtle, and Bardolino, a coarser and sturdier wine than the others, rather similar to the ordinary, ubiquitous Chianti. Valpolicella was a great favorite of Julius Caesar; today a bottle of Valpolicella *Superiore*, well-aged, is considered to be one of Italy's "greats." But Bardolino has a more modern glamour in that it is raised in what are probably the most spectacular vineyards in the world, overlooking the fabulously beautiful Lake Garda. High above this jewel of all Italian inland seas, its crystal-blue waters mirroring the peaks of the surrounding mountains, the tiny village of Bardolino is one from which many a traveler has found it all but impossible to part. Nearby is the village of Chiaretto, the source of an excellent *rosé* of the same name. *Rosé* wines of the surrounding region are usually sold under the name of Chiarello. They are all good—but poor travelers.

Two rare white wines are natives of Venetia. One is Verdiso, dry and delicate; the other, better known, is the sweeter, redolent Prosecco, usually found as a sparkling wine, though better when made as a still one. The Prosecco grape, known as the Glera, was well known in the days of the Romans, when it was religiously thought to possess the power to prolong life.

WINES FROM THE HILL TOWNS

Ordinary red Chianti, the most exported table wine on earth, has probably had a larger part in alienating novice wine drinkers than all the other inferior wines from all countries of the world taken together. Shipped the world over in those squat, round bottles known as *fiaschi*, picturesquely wrapped in straw jackets and enticingly decorated with red, white and green strands reflecting the Italian tri-color, 90 per cent of it is haphazardly made, improperly aged and inadequately corked. The end result, more often than not, is a sour, bitter liquid with an overpowering, unpleasant "burnt" taste. With well-made Chianti—a comparatively scarce wine—this same "burnt" flavor is one of its most attractive elements.

In one sense red Chianti may be likened to Liebfraumilch and Moselblümchen—it may be almost anything. Made in the province of Tuscany around Florence, it is among the cheapest of all red wines, and its production is enormous—one single plant (producing Chianti *ordinaire*) in the village of Poggibonsi alone has a daily capacity of five thousand cases. Much of it is simply a base of any common Tuscan wine, doctored and flavored with heavily boiled-down grape juice concentrate—contributing the desirable "burnt" flavor.

But there is such a thing as fine Chianti, coming from the traditional or "classic" zone that embraces parts (and only parts) of ten villages strung along the Via Chiantigiana, the ancient (and now comparatively untraveled) winding hill road running south from Florence to Siena and thence to Rome. Not so long ago the entire Chianti region was as much of a caldron of graft and fraudulence as the Côte d'Or in the 1920's and 1930's; but in recent years, under the able guidance of the Barone Ricasoli—whose Brolio Chianti is among the very best on the market—the growers of these ten little villages have successfully organized themselves. This is a group called the *Consorzio per la Difesa del Vino Tipico del Chianti* (The Society for the Protection of Genuine Chianti Wines), whose mark or symbol (*Marco Gallo*) on bottles is a black cockerel. Bottles bearing the *Marco Gallo*—especially from such houses as Ricasoli, Serristore-Machiavelli, Ruffino and Marchese Antinori—are what the consumer should look for. The very finest, often labeled *Chianti Classico* to indicate superior wine from these best vineyards, are usually not shipped in the straw-jacketed *fiaschi*, but in ordinary bottles resembling those of Bordeaux. Other marks of distinction are the word *Riserva (Réserve)* and the term *Imbottigliato alla tenuta* or *al Castello*, meaning estate- or castle-bottled, expensive wines that demand an age of from ten to twenty years.

Certain other Chiantis, not made in the "classic" zone of the Via Chiantigiana, are authorized to use the mark or symbol of a cherub on labels. The latter is by no means the qualitative equal of that of the black cockerel, but the reader may at least know that a *fiascha* decorated by a cherub is better than one unadorned. Italy, incidentally, has no true equivalent of the French *Appellations Contrôlées* laws, except for a red seal that appears on all exported bottles, bearing the words *Italia Marchio Nazionale* (National Trademark). This is simply an official guarantee that the wine comes from where the label indicates.[1] Wines not conforming to this simple geographic regulation must be marked with the word *tipo* (type).

A well-made, aged Chianti, much like the traditional Châteauneuf-du-Pape, has body and substance—for *Riserva* or *Classico* Chiantis are among the rare Italian wines made from a blend of several grapes. In the case of the reds, three native ones are used: the San Gioveto, the Canaiolo nero and the Trebbiano—to which are added the juices of either the Cabernet or the Malbec, both of which, as the reader will remember, are ingredients of red Bordeaux. White Chianti—a dry and rather dull wine—may contain a certain amount of the Burgundian Chardonnay, or sometimes of the Roussanne, one of the two sources of white Hermitage. The best white Chianti comes from the village of Pomino; but it is no exception to the general rule that the finest dry white wines are made in northern climes.

Another white of central Italy, from the vineyards of Montefiasconi on Lake Bolseno, goes by the intriguing name of Est! Est!! Est!!! The words, which bear the ring of some advertising stunt more than the ancient name of a wine, are actually the Latin for "It is! It is!! It is!!!" The rather incredible story behind them involves a bibulous German bishop, whose practice when traveling was to send his valet ahead to assess the wines at the various inns en route. With taverns offering outstanding wines the valet had instructions to chalk on the inn's outside wall the word *Est*—thus conveying to the master who followed that the wine *Est bonum* (is good). In this instance the servant exceeded himself in recording his enthusiasm over the Moscatello wine of the Umbrian village of Montefiascone. The bishop spent the night there, naturally—but the tale ends gloomily. He drank himself to death. Anyone who doubts the legend may visit the bishop's nearby tomb.

Est! Est!! Est!!! is made in two versions, one a dry wine, the other a dessert wine. This latter is one of the few Italian white dessert wines that is produced as such. Except for the potent white Cinque-Terre[2] from Liguria near Genoa, perhaps its only serious rival comes from the region of Orvieto (also in Central Italy), the source of two other white wines, one also dry, the other sweet.

---

[1] An alternate (also red) seal denoting authenticity (but not necessarily quality) is that of the commercially slanted *Istituto Nazionale per l'Esportazione* (*I.N.E.*) —the National Institute for Exportation of Wines.

[2] Also to be found as a red and as a rare *rosé*, the latter being especially delicious.

Like ordinary Chianti, Orvieto is sold in old-fashioned flasklike bottles, known as *pulcianelli*. Dry Orvieto,[3] exported in considerable quantity, has a peculiar, leathery taste all its own, not unlike a typical white Graves. We hazard the guess that the reader will prefer the sweet version, which he should find excellent with fruits and desserts. Other whites from this region are Frascati from Rome, Verdicchio (or Castelli) di Jesi and Velletri. All of them are strong in alcohol, markedly golden in color, and dry. Verdicchio (Castelli) di Jesi, made close to the Adriatic coast near the port of Ancona and shipped in green amphora-shaped bottles, has a delightfully spicy, individualistic quality, comparable to an Alsatian Traminer. Nowadays a considerable quantity of it is exported.

Except for Marsala and Moscato, the fortified wines of Sicily (the counterparts of Sherry and Port), the only remaining Italian wines of importance are Lacryma Christi (Tears of Christ) and Capri. Lacryma Christi is raised on the slopes of Mount Vesuvius. It is principally a dry white wine with a treacherously high alcoholic content; but it may also be found as a slightly sweet and entirely excellent sparkling wine, one of Italy's best sparkling "generics"—although it is rarely made on or near the slopes of Vesuvius. There is also a sparse amount of red and *rosé* Lacryma Christi, but neither is as good as the white. The white wines from the island of Capri are dry and refreshing, though hardly notable. Most of them have never seen the Isle of the Blue Grotto—but are made on the mainland around the Bay of Naples.

One need pay little attention to vintage years in Italy, even those from the northernmost region, the cool Italian Tyrol of the Alpine valleys. Years rarely appear on labels—but should a year be mentioned for an Italian red (especially on a bottle from one of the northern and central regions)—the reader may be reasonably sure that it is one which the producer hopes he will have the patience to age. In all likelihood the temporary abstention will be amply rewarding.

---

[3] Like the Portuguese wines of Vinho Verde (see Chapter V), most Orvieto grapes are grown under what are usually considered impossible vinicultural conditions—what the Italians call *coltura promiscua*. The vines are not grown in conventional vineyards, but as part of small-farm crops, being allowed to climb trees or trellesis, or seek out their livelihood among garden crops of potatoes and cabbages.

SUMMARY

Although Italy produces a handful of good white wines, nine-tenths of her output are in reds, in which she excels. Confusingly, some Italian wines are named after grapes and may come from almost any part of the country (and thus vary greatly in quality); others are named for places and vineyards, these latter being the best. A good rule of thumb: remember that the following five Italian wines (all red) are named after grapes—Barbera, Nebbiolo, Dolcetto, Friesa and Grignolino—and assume that all others are place or vineyard names.

The exception is Chianti—the name of a small area which is bootlegged by producers from a vast one. Legitimate Chiantis, usually labeled *Classico,* bear a seal with a black cockerel. The best are shipped in standard (Bordeaux-type) bottles—not the familiar flagon covered with basketwork. A superior Chianti *Classico* needs age: ten years is a good minimum.

Barbaresco, Barolo, Valpolicella and Valpantena are four other excellent Italian reds, unfortunately not yet exported in much quantity. Two good exported dry whites are Soave and Verdicchio (Castelli) di Jesi; the best *rosés* are Lagrein Rosato from the Tyrolean Alps, and Chiaretto (Chiarello) from the Lake of Garda.

Vintage years for Italian wines are not important; except that a year on a bottle of a superior red variety (from North or Central Italy) usually means the producer hopes the wine drinker will have the patience to allow it sufficient age. Usually these years will be 1955, 1956, 1957, 1958, 1961, 1962 and 1964.

~§ TABLE K   *Principal Italian Wines*

Wine	Region
REDS	
Caldero	Italian Tyrol
Santa Maddalena[1]	Italian Tyrol
*†Dolcetto	Piedmont (principally)
Gattinara	Northern Piedmont
Barbaresco	Piedmont
*Barbera	Piedmont (principally)
Barolo	Piedmont
*Freisa	Piedmont (principally)
*Grignolino	Piedmont (principally)
Cinque-Terre	Genoa
Bardolino	Venetia (Verona)
Carema	Piedmont
Valpantena	Venetia (Verona)
Valpolicella	Venetia (Verona)
Valtellina	Italian Alps
Chianti	Tuscany
Salaparuta	Sicily
WHITES	
Terlano	Italian Tyrol
*Traminer (*Aromatico*)	Italian Tyrol
Cortese	Piedmont
†Cinque-Terre	Genoa
Verdiso	Venetia
Soave	Venetia (Verona)
†Prosecco	Venetia
Chianti	Tuscany (Florence)
‡Est! Est!! Est!!!	Umbria
‡Orvieto	Umbria
*Verdicchio di Jesi (or Castelli di Jesi)	Adriatic
Frascati	Rome

[1] Known in Switzerland and Austria, where it is inexpensive and popular, as St. Magdalener.

Wine	*Region*
Lacryma Christi	Campania (Naples)
Capri	Campania (Naples)
Salaparuta	Sicily

ROSÉS

Lagrein Rosato	Italian Tyrol
Chiaretto (Chiarello)	Lombardy
Cinque-Terre	Genoa

SPARKLINGS

Asti Spumante (white)	Piedmont
Lacryma Christi (white) (generic)	Naples (and other regions)
*Nebbiolo (red)	Piedmont

---

* Grape name.
† Sweet.
‡ Made both as a dry and a sweet.

FIVE

The Wines of
Portugal and Spain

CONSUMOS, PASTOS AND RESERVAS

The wines of the Iberian Peninsula—those of Spain and her plucky little neighbor, Portugal—once served to slacken the thirst of Rome. Cicero alludes to the lush vineyards of Lusitania (the Roman name for Portugal); and it is a matter of record that wines were being shipped from the Roman port of Tarragona, on Spain's Mediterranean coast, long before the legendary conversion of the Iberians by St. Paul. In fact, the Iberian vineyards of that day appear to have been even more widespread and bountiful than those of southern France.

Yet perhaps the most intriguing thing about wine making in Portugal and Spain in our time is that modernity has barely caught up at all. In Portugal the grapes travel from vine to vat—over roads paved exactly as the Romans paved them centuries ago—in primitive basketwork ox carts with solid wooden wheels and creaking axles, of a design unchanged since Roman times. In both countries the grapes are more often than not tread with human feet; every part and appendage of the grape that nature intended for wine—

animal, vegetable and mineral—may be found in the fermenting vats. Only at a few progressive vineyards does one come across that newfangled contraption used today throughout most of the wine-making world—the *éggrapoir*. Such short-cut methods of stripping the grapes from their stems and stalks, to produce a lighter and faster maturing wine, is looked on with suspicion. The end result, as is to be expected, is wine which, when young, is coarse and usually distasteful—overburdened with tannin and acids —yet when adequately aged often proves to be of unusual quality. And because of the current rate of exchange with the two countries, it will also be of exceptional value.

The wine drinker is to be cautioned, even so, that he will not find Iberian wines similar to French or German wines—however much writers on the subject have sought to compare and liken them. There is no Spanish Château Lafite-Rothschild, nor a Portuguese Schloss Johannisberg. Iberian soils and climates differ vastly from those of France and Germany; most Iberian wine grapes are indigenous, unrelated to those found elsewhere. The wines simply have a different taste; one needs to get used to them. Yet once their harshness and robust youth have been placated by time, one will hardly fail to spot a unique richness and depth of flavor which can only be the result of sound (and commendably old-fashioned!) vinicultural practices. The best Iberian wines are still made as wines were made in France a hundred years ago.

Both Portugal and Spain rely heavily on wine as an integral part of their national diets—and, for the most part, very bad wine it is. The *ordinaires*—those known as *vinhos de consumo* in Portugal and *vinos de pasto* in Spain—are unbelievably raw concoctions. They are always consumed very young—and with the exception of the so-called *Vinhos Verdes* (young wines) of Portugal—happily never come our way. Red *consumos* and *pastos* pucker the mouth and cloy the throat; the whites may smell disarmingly enchanting —like fresh apples or peaches, perhaps—but when swallowed give rise to incipient ulcers. Unless one has never known anything better, they simply cannot be said to be potable.

In both countries the finer wines almost invariably go by the classification of *Reserva*—a term used to indicate the proudest product of a producer from a vintage year he considers superior.

THE VINEYARDS OF
Portugal
and Spain

0   50   100   150
MILES

Bay of Biscay

FRANCE

GALICIA

Haro

RIOJA

R. MIÑO

VINHO
VERDE

DOURO
(PORT)

R. DUERO

Valladolid

Barcelona

Oporto

R. DOURO

Tarragona

DÃO

S   P   A   I   N

COLARES

R. TAJO (TAGUS)

Madrid
Toledo

VALDEPEÑAS

BUCELAS
Lisbon

R. EBRO

SETÚBAL

PORTUGAL

R. GUADIANA

ALGARVE

R. GUADALQUIVIR

SHERRY

MÁLAGA

Jerez
Cádiz

Málaga

ATLANTIC

MEDITERRANEAN   SEA

OCEAN

MOROCCO

ATLANTIC

SPAIN

OCEAN

Lisbon

PORTUGAL

Madrid

Madeira
Is.(Port)

600 MILES

MOROCCO

Before it is released for sale a white Portuguese or Spanish *Reserva* will usually be at least five years old; a red, ten. This will have involved two or three years in the barrel, followed by approximately the same period in the bottle for the whites—and a minimum of five years in the barrel for the reds. In the Rioja region of northern Spain, the universally acknowledged source of the finest wines of that country, some of the top producers age their red wines "in the wood" for ten years, followed by fifteen or more in the bottle! For good Iberian wines this is none too much—and by local standards, of course, *Reservas* are expensive wines. Yet when one learns that a glass of *consumo* or *pasto* at a Portuguese or Spanish bar costs only $.02 in terms of American currency, it follows that even the price of a *Reserva* abroad cannot be high. In view of the spiraling prices of wines from other European countries, one may safely prophesy that we shall see more Iberian wines.

Reservas are vintage wines—but with a difference. Whereas the advent of a bountiful year, such as 1959 in France or Germany, sent every vintner scurrying—virtually before his grapes were crushed—to market his wine in a bottle bearing the magic year, a *Reserva* of Portugal or Spain is never designated as such until it has been at least two years in the barrel. At that time its intrinsic quality is assessed and, if it passes the test, it is chosen for a *Reserva* status and a long life. Otherwise it is bottled forthwith and released. The word for vintage on Portuguese labels is *Colheita;* on Spanish ones, *Cosecha.* The important point for the wine drinker to bear in mind is that the presence of either of these two words with a year does not necessarily indicate that a wine has been given sufficient age in the producer's cellar to become truly fine. We shall cover this aspect more fully when dealing with the wines of the two countries separately.

PORTUGUESE WINES

Portugal, in many ways, may be numbered among the more modern countries of Europe. A land of happy and incredibly hospitable people, it is endowed (thanks to the Romans) with well-engineered roads, blessed with a low rate of unemployment, an enviably diversified agriculture, the best sardines and the finest cork—and what is perhaps the most enlightened dictatorship the world has ever known. (The Portuguese themselves prefer the term "enlightened leadership"). Its wine industry, however, is only beginning to come into its own. As recently as thirty years ago, with the exception of the fortified dessert wines of Port and Madeira, only three Portuguese wines were known at all to the outside world —the balance being of a mediocre grade for internal consumption. These were the sweetish white Moscatel of Setúbal; a dry white wine known as Bucelas; and the strong and oftentimes unappealingly harsh red Colares. During the past three decades, however, the Portuguese government has made every effort to develop its wine industry, with emphasis on exports. Although much remains to be done before any vast number of Portuguese table wines become readily acceptable to most foreign palates, under the supervision of the *Junta Nacional do Vinho* (National Wine Board) great progress has been made in selecting the most suitable grapes and in educating the vintners.

The *Junta Nacional*, additionally, runs state-owned cooperative cellars to serve the small vintners, and even conducts schools for wine waiters—a vital innovation in a country where perhaps only at the ultra-cosmopolitan Ritz Hotel in Lisbon may one, even nowadays, find wineglasses of suitable size and proportion, or waiters who do not persist in filling them to the very brim. In almost any Iberian restaurant a red wine on its way to your table may have been shaken like a Daiquiri; it may well arrive in one's glass well chilled—whereas its white sister, as often as not, will be the temperature of warm broth.

A white wine in Portuguese is a *vinho branco;* a red is a *vinho tinto* (incidentally, the same word, *tinto,* is used for red in Spain). A *rosé* is *rosé* or a *maduro;* and all table wines go by the term *vinhos de mesa. Doce* is the usual term for sweet wine; *adamado* (literally: "for dames") the colloquial one. In addition to the two regions producing Port and Madeira, the *Junta Nacional* officially recognizes six other regions for the production of *vinhos de mesa,* for each of which it has established rules and vinicultural specifications comparable to the *Appellations Contrôlées* of France. Wines from each of these six regions are authorized to bear the insignia of their respective *Uniao Vinicola Regional* (Vinicultural Union) —abbreviated on labels as *U.V.R.* Whereas the presence of an official sticker is a guaranty of genuineness, it should not be automatically construed, as will be seen in Table L, that there are not other good Portuguese wines from as-yet-unregulated sections of the country. The wines of Portugal are among the oldest in Europe—but the industry, and its regulation, is still in its adolescence.

Proceeding from north to south, the officially recognized regions and their wines are as follows:

Vinho Verde (or Minho).   The northwestern section of Portugal, extending from the Douro River (the home of Port) northward to the Spanish border. In addition to being one of the more beautiful and verdant parts of Portugal, the Vinho Verde region has certain unique, not to say picturesque, vinicultural practices, comparable only to the Orvieto section of Italy. The vines are trained high on trees along the fence rows (a practice which gives rise to many accidents during harvesting!), or strung on trellises surrounding each field, which latter is always planted to other crops, such as corn and potatoes. The Vinho Verde is a country of small landowners, and each square of land is so planned that if one crop fails or falters, the profits from another will bring the family through the winter. And since the vines grow along with crops of fruits, grains and vegetables, they receive a copious fertilization— the exact opposite of the usual treatment of the wine grape in other parts of the world.

Vinho Verde (the wine), which may be red, white or *rosé*, is not, as one might expect, "green" wine—but young wine. Intended to be drunk young, for home consumption it is customarily bottled very early in the spring following its birth, when it is undergoing a second, or so-called malolactic, fermentation. This renders it mildly sparkling (*pétillant*) and is responsible for a great part of its charm. Unfortunately, when exported to the United States—because of the extremely high tax levied on anything of a sparkling nature—it must be a still wine.

White Vinho Verde, slightly acid and relatively low in alcohol, is especially pleasant as an accompaniment to those many fish and seafood dishes for which the Portuguese are so renowned. The *rosé*, usually less acid, is perhaps even more delicious. Red Vinho Verde, a very popular *vinho de consumo* among the Portuguese, is something else again. Smelling enticingly like a concentrate of fresh raspberries, its particular degree of rawness strips the very lining from the mouth and throat. (Uninitiated professional wine tasters are even warned against spilling a drop of it on a white shirt, lest it leave an indelible stain!) The Vinho Verdes are all made from indigenous grapes, the predominant red one being the Vinão (with varying dosages of many another unfamiliar: the Borraçal, the Espadeiro, the Azal Tinto, the Cainhos and the Brancelho). White Vinho Verde comes principally from the Azal Branco and the Dourado.

Dão.   The fertile, rolling countryside along the River Dão in central Portugal, surrounding the quaint town of Viseu—the source of both red and white wines that are becoming increasingly well known to the outside world—is the largest and most important area of Portugal producing *vinhos de mesa*. Well-aged reds from the Dão—labels should at least bear the word *Velho* (old), *Garrafiera* (selected) or better yet, *Reserva*—are all wines of much character, with strong bouquets reminiscent of red Burgundies. The similarity is not coincidental. Although in years gone by Dão wines were made from half a dozen or more indigenous grapes, Dão vintners have recently been concentrating on a grape known as the Pinta Pinheira, recently identified as the Pinot aigret, once used for the celebrated (though now virtually nonexistent) still red wines of Champagne and extreme northern Burgundy. Although promising efforts are being made by many of the Dão producers to make their younger wines more palatable and attractive, Dão reds at the moment usually require an aging of ten years. The *Reservas* are often found at twice this age.

The white wines of the Dão—once again those of the *Reserva* category are preferable—are perhaps the most universally appealing whites of Portugal. Made principally from the Arinto grape (a version of the Riesling), sometimes with the addition of a little juice of the Sémillon (of Bordeaux), they possess body and smoothness, and are comparable both in taste and character to a white Hermitage or any other sound white wine of the central Rhône.

Bucelas. White Bucelas, once known in England as "Lisbon Hock," and before that, in Shakespeare's day, as Charneco (Charneca is a village in the authorized Bucelas region), is one of the three traditional *vinhos de mesa* of Portugal to have been exported in any quantity. Also made from the Arinto or Riesling, in the hands of good producers it is a clean, very dry wine, reminiscent of a superior Graves. At those periods in history when French wines were either barred from England or subject to a prohibitive tariff, Bucelas from Portugal always took a sharp rise in popularity. It eventually fell from grace, however, when Portuguese vintners gave in to the temptation (so prevalent throughout Iberia in the last century) of fortifying it with brandy, comparable to Port and Madeira. Nowadays, under the guidance of an enlightened officialdom, Bucelas is again coming into its own, and its vineyards, spread across a lovely up-and-down countryside fifty miles north of Lisbon, are on the increase.

Colares. Red Colares is another of the classic wines of Portugal. Traditionally known as "Ocean Wine" because of the proximity of its vineyards to the sea, it is produced from the Ramisco grape—a distinct native to Portugal—under conditions that are certainly among the most extraordinary in the world. North of Lisbon's fashionable seaside resort of Estoril (Coast of the Sun), the road zigzags along a jagged, mountainous coastline, covered with heather and dotted with round stone windmills. High on a bleak promontory in the distance is the lighthouse of Cabo de Roca— the westernmost point of Europe. Suddenly the road descends steeply to a level countryside where magnificent beaches line the coast, and where for several miles inland a receding ocean has left a land of pure sand. Once upon a time the vineyards of Colares occupied the beaches themselves—but today these have been taken over by cheap villas and cabanas, and the vines have been driven inland.

The only crops at Colares are pines and vines. As one trudges laboriously through the groves of turpentine pines, one never expects to come across a clearing filled with grapevines nor—unless one stumbles on a vineyard which is being newly planted—would

one ever guess that the roots of these particular vines often penetrate thirty feet of sand to obtain moisture from a basic clay subsoil. In fact, planting the vines at Colares is no simple affair: to dig
a narrow trench in thirty feet of sand requires shoring up the sides,
and as the excavation proceeds, the diggers cover their heads
with ludicrous wicker baskets that may allow them to breathe for
a time in the event of a cave-in. When the roots are finally em-
bedded in the moist clay, the trenches are filled up gradually, year
by year, as the shoots of the vines lengthen. Frequently the original ground level is not obtained for four or five years.

The sandy vineyards (*areias*) of Colares are additionally unique
in that they have never been beset by the *phylloxera*, which at one
time devastated nearly all the vineyards of Europe. The sands of
Colares are too fine and deep for the tiny aphids to burrow through
and reach the roots. In consequence, Colares is one of the few wines
extant which is still made from grapes not grafted to American
wild-grape root stock. Strong in taste and exceptionally high in
alcohol, it is often called the "claret of Portugal." Of all Portuguese red wines, it probably requires more age in the barrel and
bottle than any other; but when adequately matured it does possess a softness and a flowerlike bouquet comparable to that of a
good St.-Émilion. White Colares, made from the Arinto grape,
lacks the distinction of the red. And like so many white wines of
southern countries, it is disappointingly devoid of bouquet.

Carcavelos and Moscatel de Setúbal.   Known in Portugal as
vinhos generosos, meaning table wines fortified with alcohol (even
though they are not subjected to the same aging and special blending processes of Port or Madeira). Carcavelos, called "Lisbon
Wine" because it comes from a small (and fast-disappearing) group
of vineyards in the western suburbs of Lisbon, is a sweetish red
with an alcoholic content approaching 20 per cent. Almond-
flavored and definitely demanding an acquired taste, it is drunk as
an *apéritif* and is exported chiefly to Scandinavia. Despite the
fact that the *Junta Nacional* has designated the Carcavelos region
as an authorized *Uniao Vinicola*, the government does not presently
appear to be encouraging its production.

Moscatel de Setúbal is produced both as a red and a white wine
—the latter being, loosely speaking, the Sauternes of Portugal. Made,

as its name implies, from various varieties of the same Muscat grape responsible for many another fortified wine (including France's Roussillon and Muscat de Frontignan), the best of it is labeled under the names of Palmela and Azietão—two villages in which it is most successfully produced. The vineyards lie on the peninsula south of Lisbon, in a warm pocket behind the Arrabida Mountains just west of the fishing town of Setúbal. Moscatels are heavily fortified, and have a characteristic grapy, Muscat flavor by no means appealing to everyone. Because of the lagging world demand for sweet dessert wines, valiant efforts are being made by the producers to develop an attractive dry wine that will be below 15 per cent in alcohol. To date the results have not been outstanding; much of it is currently exported to Germany for the manufacture of Sekt.

The Setúbal region is also the best-known source of another prevalent Portuguese red, Periquita, made from the grape of the same name. Like the Ramisco, the Periquita flourishes in sandy soil, and until comparatively recently the Periquita vineyards of Setúbal were free of the *phylloxera*. Periquita has an enticing aroma—but the reader is cautioned to beware of tasting it until it has attained a hoary old age.

By now many a veteran wine drinker will no doubt have wondered why we have not yet mentioned Portuguese *rosés*. We have saved them for the end, for Portuguese *rosés* are in a class by themselves: they need neither to be *Reservas* nor *Garrafeiras*—and many of them are among the best and most palatable *rosés* in existance. *Rosés* are made all over Portugal with equal success. Certainly one of the pleasantest goes by the brand name of Mateus, which comes in an attractive brown *bocksbeutel* and is made near the town of Vila Real on the northern outskirts of the Douro (Port) region. A blend of strictly local grapes—the Alvarelhão, the Bastardo, the Touriga and the Souzão—Mateus is found abroad both as a still and as a carbonated wine. In our opinion, the former is far preferable. Its strongest competitor, sold in Portugal as Faisca and abroad as Lancers, comes from the Setúbal region, and tends to be a harsher wine—attributable, no doubt, to the presence of the virulent Periquita in the mixture. Two other *rosés*, almost equally recommendable, are Lagosta (lobster) from the Vinho Verde region and Moura Basto. Portuguese *rosés* are always ready to drink when bottled, and their labels rarely carry a vintage year.

Unlike the wines of France or Germany, the best of Portugal are almost never associated with a vineyard *(quinta)*, but instead carry a regional or brand name. For this reason we have included in our listings of Portuguese wines (Table L) the names of some of the more reliable winehouses *(adegas)*, the quality of whose wines may in general be counted on.

REDS (*Tintos*)

Bussaco (Buçaco)

A so-called "claret" from central Portugal. Two of the best come from the Quinta de San Miguel and the Caves do Mosteiro.

*Carcavelos

A sweet, fortified red wine, best as an *apéritif*. Not properly a table wine.

Cartaxo

One of the few good reds from the vast wine-producing region of Ribatejo, in the Tagus Valley north of Lisbon. Also one of the few Portuguese reds not requiring much age. The best is produced by the Adega Cunhas.

*Colares

Portugal's traditionally finest red. To be potable it should be at least ten years old, and preferably twice that. Three of the best producers are the Visconde de Salreu, Jorge da Silva and the firm of Tavares and Rodrigues. (A white Colares, of inferior quality, is also made.)

*Dão

Dão reds, when sufficiently aged (preferably of *Reserva* status) are among Portugal's best. Two outstanding names are Grão Vasco and San Pedro. The finest vineyards of the Dão region are those of the village of Tondella, near Viseu.

Douro

One outstanding red from the Douro (Port) region is called Imperial Evel—a lively and slightly tart wine, resembling a California Zinfandel.

Grantom (and Lagoa)

Few good wines are made in Algarve, the southernmost province of Portugal, but the reds of Grantom and Lagoa—appealing light, red wines—are an exception.

Mealhada

A fragrant red from a district north of Lisbon, requiring much age. Among its best producers is the firm of Carvalho, Ribeiro and Ferreira.

Pinhel

A light and pleasant red, likened by some to a claret, made in central Portugal to the south of the Douro region. The Pinhel region is slated to become officially recognized by the *Junta Nacional* and its wines will soon bear the official *U.V.R.* sticker.

Serradayres

Traditional brand name for an excellent red table wine, with a nice tart "bite," the best of which is made in the province of Estremadura in central Portugal, near the Spanish border.

WHITES (*Brancos*)

*Bucelas

White Bucelas, made from the Arinto or Riesling grape, is a dry wine reminiscent of a white Graves. The best producer is J. Camillo Alves, whose reds are also excellent.

Bussaco (Buçaco)

White Bussacos tend to resemble the whites of the central Loire. They are clean and slightly sweet, with delicious, mild aromas. Those from the Caves do Mosteiro are to be highly recommended.

Douro

Some excellent white wines are made in the Douro (Port) region,

Douro (*Cont.*)

although only Port itself is entitled to the official *U.V.R.* sticker. One called Granjo, slightly sweet but with excellent body, resembles French Monbazillac. Other recommendable whites are Planalto, Campo Grande and Grão Vasco Blanco. Yet another excellent Douro white is called Ermida.

Lagoa

A dry white with a lovely yellow tinge, from Algarve on the southern coast, where very little good wine is produced. Low in alcohol.

*Moscatel de Setúbal

The best is bottled as Palmela and Azeitão. A sweet wine fortified with grape alcohol to attain a content of 18 per cent. Often called the Sauternes of Portugal. The principal producer is José Maria da Fonseca, which firm also produces a dry Moscatel ("Branco Seco").

Óbidos

A walled town north of Lisbon, every tourist's first stop on a journey north from the capital. The whites of Obidos are peculiarly light and refreshing, with a nice aroma. One of the best comes from the Quinta Gaieras.

Santarém

A town north of Lisbon on the Tagus River. The white wines of Santarém are fruity and dry, with a pleasing aftertaste. The best (and rarest) comes from the Quinta Abidis.

*Vinho Verde

"Young wine" from northern Portugal. Acid and light, it can be

---

* Indicates an officially recognized region, table wines from which are entitled to bear the authorized *U.V.R.* sticker. In the Douro region—the source of several excellent wines—only Port is allowed this official insignia.

Vinho Verde (*Cont.*)

most refreshing—although hardly
what one New York merchant
recently advertised as the "Montrachet of Portugal." Two excellent brands: Casel Garcia and
Moura Basto. Perhaps the most
highly prized and rarest of all
from the Vinho Verde region is
Moncão—light and mellow, with a
delicate bouquet of wild flowers,
called Alvarinho.

ROSÉS

Among the best Portuguese *rosés* now exported are Mateus (Douro),
Lancers (Setúbal), Lagosta (Vinho Verde), Borges Maduro, and Moura
Basto. The first two are produced also as sparklings, the product of
Lancers being called Fiasca.

The following is a partial list of reliable Portuguese winehouses.

Recommended Winehouses

Carvalho, Ribeiro and Ferreira
Caves Aliança
José Maria da Fonseca
Real Compania Vinicola do Norte de Portugal
Sociedade Agricola de Quinta da Aveleda
Sociedade Agricola E Comercial dos Vinhos Messias
Sociedade Agricola Moura Basto
Sociedade Comercial dos Vinhos de Mesa de Portugal (Sogrape)
Sociedade dos Vinhos Borges and Irmão
Tavares and Rodrigues
Vinícola do Vale do Dão

SPAIN: "COUNTRY" WINES AND "CITY" WINES

There is probably no better bargain in the world than a fine
old vintage of Spain—and oftentimes nothing harder to find, even
in Spain itself. The truly good wines of Spain are produced in

lamentably small quantities, and almost entirely for domestic consumption. Furthermore, Spanish wine making in general can only be described by the word "casual"—a fault which has been the basis for the often-heard criticism of them: their variability. Not only between year and year, but even between one bottle and another of the *same* year from the *same* vineyard and with identical labels Spanish wines may vary enormously. Regrettably, Spanish government agencies responsible for guiding the industry reflect this very same casualness. Nominal regulations and standards exist for the vineyards of most of Spain's forty-nine provinces—and many Spanish wines are entitled to an official label of quality, *Denominacion de Origen*—yet an official sticker on a bottle of Spanish wine remains all but meaningless. In fact, it may frankly be said that the only reliable mark of quality on any bottle of Spanish wine is that of the unofficial organization of vintners of the Rioja region (*Garantia de Origen*), the indisputable source of Spain's best wines.

Leaving the wines of the Rioja aside for the moment, most other Spanish table wines may be divided into two classes: the regional or "country" wines (*vinos del pais* or *vinos de la tierra*) and those known as "city" or "town" wines, ones from a particular set of vineyards associated with a specific town. Far and away the most popular and widespread of the regionals, often called the Beaujolais of Spain, is the wine of Valdepeñas (valley of stones). Valdepeñas may be either red or white, though the red is far better, and more frequently exported. It is produced in tremendous quantity on the arid high tablelands of New Castile, south of Toledo in the central part of the country. High in tannin, often more than a little vinegary, it is almost always drunk in its native land when less than a year old. Because of its power (not necessarily alcoholic), the Spaniards call it *peléon*—a word which means fighter. The fact that a *chato* or small glass of it costs the equivalent of a penny in a Madrid bar has no bearing on the fierceness of the fighter: even in small quantity *peléon* can be a most invigorating drink.

The second most popular regional wine of Spain is Ribero, (or Ribeiro), from the lovely province of Galicia, north of the Portuguese border. Galician vineyards are in effect merely a continuation of the vinicultural pattern of Portugal's Vinho Verde region to the south. Galicia is also a country of small landowners, where each individual plot of corn or oats has its quota of grapevines climbing the trees or strung on neat trellises along the walls or hedgerows, and its tomblike little corncrib raised high on granite posts and surmounted with a cross. Like the wines of the Vinho Verde, Ribero is usually *pétillant* and rather acid—nonetheless, much coveted by the Spaniards. The best of it is white. Curiously, the most popular drink among the Galicians themselves is the excellent sparkling cider that abounds in this particular corner of Spain.

Among other regional wines are those called Prioratos, or Tarragona wines, from the Mediterranean city of the same name— rough wines that were once fortified with brandy and, as such, known to our forefathers as "Tarragona Port." Now many Tarragona wines go to France to be made into *apéritifs*, as does much of the white (and very pleasant) wine of Alicante, that Mediterranean city of Spain where "the sky is always the bluest." Tarragona wines (the best of which is called Barbier), can be red, white or *rosé*. But they are none of them as acceptable to foreign palates as Perelada, yet another regional (also red, white and *rosé*) made north of Barcelona along the foreboding but extraordinarily beautiful Costa Brava (hard coast).

Of the so-called "city" wines, the best known is Alella, a rather heavy and sweet white, also made near Barcelona. Alella comes in slim, tall bottles, comparable to those of Germany; the best known is the white Mafiel, though there is also a red Alella of lesser quality. Far superior to Alella, however, is the rare and exceptionally delicate white Rueda, from Vallalodid, northwest of Madrid. Considered by many to be the finest white wine of Spain, and certainly in a class with the whites of the Rioja, Rueda is hard to find away from its home ground, and it is rumored that much of it is surreptitiously used for blending with inferior whites. Yet another fragrant white wine comes from Yepes, a small town east of Toledo in central Spain.

Only two reds among these "city" wines are really worthy of mention. Although one often hears that no wine but Sherry is made in the region of Jerez de la Frontera, the fact is that this area is the source of two of the pleasantest red wines of Spain. One of them, known as Carlo, is a fragrant wine from Sanlúcar de Barrameda, a seaside town on the southern coast just above the gleaming, whitewashed port of Cádiz; and from the village of Rota, a few miles down the coast, comes a light red wine, much savored by Spaniards, known as Tintillo. Unfortunately, neither is exported, but this is a situation which may well change.

WINES OF THE RIOJA

The best proof of the comparative excellence of Riojan wines is that on the wine lists of nearly every good hotel and restaurant in Spain they appear almost to the exclusion of all others—the exceptions being an occasional "city" wine, such as an Alella or a Rueda, or perhaps the regional Valdepeñas.

The Rioja is the Côte d'Or of Spain—and of about the same size and proportions. Its center is the little wine town of Haro, which lies on the Ebro River in the northeastern part of the country, just south of the foothills of the Pyrénées. The climate of the Rioja is more rigorous, and the summers shorter, than on the southern tablelands where the mass of Spanish wine is produced, and the resultant wines more resemble those of northern countries, such as Germany and France. In fact, the Ebro at Haro could be taken for a mountain river of France itself. Lush fields and groves of poplars line its gravelly banks, and the swift-flowing, opaquely green mountain water abounds with fish. To the north is the high protective plateau of the Sierra de Urbasa, over the top of which a fifty-mile-long, low-lying cloud is apt to appear and slide dramatically down into the valley—like a great white blanket not tucked in—where it dissipates as it meets the tepid air below.

Unlike most other vineyard areas of the world, the Riojan countryside, dotted with little landlocked lakes and walled hill towns that bespeak the days of a more prosperous Spain—a Spain with colonies and a world trade—is one of diversified agriculture. The vines are interspersed with crops of wheat, olives and fruits; the soil is unusually fertile for vineyard land—bright red clay, filled with small stones. One phenomenon of the region is that until the beginning of our century it was free of the *phylloxera*—and thus for more than thirty years an important source of wine for other European nations at a time when their own vineyards were only giving forth a comparative trickle. This undoubtedly is the origin of the labeling practice of so many Riojan wines with quasi-French names—"Spanish Claret," "Spanish Chablis," "Spanish Burgundy" and so on—terms which are now being gradually discarded, except for the cheaper export wines, by Riojan producers.

Needless to say, no white Rioja ever really tasted like a Chablis or a Rhine wine, and a well-aged Rioja red—a *Reserva*—can only be remotely compared to a good Burgundy or a Bordeaux.[1] The old wives' tale so often heard, that the Rioja was colonized by Bordeaux vintners in the 1880's who introduced French grapes and taught the Riojans how to make wine in the French manner, is hotly denied by the Riojans themselves, who are justly proud of their own wine-making traditions. The truth of the matter appears to be that a Riojan delegation, visiting France some thirty years before the *phylloxera* was ever heard of, did bring back a certain number of French vines to be tried out on the banks of the Ebro. Of these, only two seem to have survived, and then only in a minor capacity—Bordeaux's red Cabernet-Sauvignon, and the Grenache, itself by no means strictly French. As with Portuguese wines, the grapes used in Spain are indigenous varieties whose connection with the accepted ones of France, Germany and Italy have never been thoroughly traced. Riojan wines are made chiefly from the native Tempranillo (the *tinto* for the reds, the *blanco* for the whites), along with several other natives called Graciano, Mazuelo and Viura.

However little the French had a hand in it, the fact remains that the best wines of the Rioja are still fermented and aged very much as those of Bordeaux and Burgundy were a hundred years ago—without any short-cut methods. This accounts for their extreme rawness when young—as well as the fact that a properly

---

[1] Some Riojan producers do still make a distinction between what they conceive of as a Bordeaux type (claret or *Cepa Burdeos*) and a Burgundy type (*Cepa Borgoña*). Neither actually involves the use of French grapes—the only difference being that the Burgundy type is made as a lighter and less dry wine.

aged *Reserva*, once its copious dosages of tannins and acids have been sufficiently "married," may be a very good wine indeed. The best Riojan whites have a softness and body one rarely finds elsewhere; the reds possess an almost overpowering bouquet, a richness of color and a *finesse* that renders them among the finest. The Rioja region is traditionally divided into four quarters, the best of which is known as the Rioja Alta (upper), adjoining Haro. Alta Rioja wines are lighter in alcohol than others of the region, and are acknowledged to possess the greatest "breeding"; those of the Rioja Baja (lower), the quarter surrounding the industrial town of Alfaro to the southeast, are of only slightly less repute. The other two quarters (the Rioja Media, near Logroño, and Alavasa, on the north bank of the river) are in general the sources of what the Spaniards deem "wines for ready drinking."[2] These are raw wines, referred to by the producers as "commercials," released when young and palatable only to the Spaniards themselves. More often than not they are the Riojas that reach foreign shores, by no means enhancing the reputation of Spanish wines as a whole, or of Riojan wines in particular.

A vintage year in Spain is known as a *cosecha*—and Spanish labels often bear the adjectival variation *cosechado*, meaning "of the vintage" of such-and-such a year. On the label of a good producer the term *Escogida* (specially chosen) may have significance; but the reader should be warned that the two most common terms used for "old"—*Pasado* and *Viejo*—mean about as little on a label as a Spanish government sticker on the bottle. The best producers give the *cosecha*, or else the terms 5° Ano, 6° Ano, etc., to indicate how long the wine was kept in barrel and bottle before release. As with Portuguese wines, good or bad vintage years do not exist in the sense that they do for France and Germany. A year for a *Reserva* is purely a matter of a decision on the part of a particular vintner that a wine is deserving of further age—and this decision is not made until the wine has been in the barrel for several years. For example, 1932 may be a *Reserva* year for one producer,

[2] Two notable exceptions are the *Bodega* (winehouse) of the Marqués de Murrieta, near Logroño in the Rioja Media; and in Alevesa, that of the Marqués de Riscal.

whereas 1934 might be for his neighbor. The wine drinker may be certain, however, that in the case of the best Riojan producers, the word *Reserva* with a year on the label is a guaranty of quality.

Riojan wines are not labeled with vineyard or geographical names, but instead have a trade or house name bestowed upon them by their producers, whose establishments throughout Spain are called *bodegas*—the equivalent of *caves* in France and *adegas* in Portugal. Table M lists a number of the best Riojan producers.

SUMMARY

Portuguese and Spanish wines are made from native grapes (and thus taste differently from other European wines), as well as by old-fashioned methods that require more aging than most other wines. A well-made, five-year-old white is usually just ready to drink—a red needs much more time yet.

The best are "vintage wines" called (in both countries) *Reservas*. Other terms meaning "very old" or "selected," generally indicative of quality are: *Garrafeira* (Port.) and *Escogida* (Sp.). Common terms meaning "old" (*Velho*, Port.; *Pasado, Viejo*, Sp.) cannot be relied on.

The Portuguese excel in *rosé* wines and in their white Vinhos Verdes. The best traditional Portuguese wines are white Bucelas and red Colares, rarely exported. Dão reds are excellent when ten years old or more—especially if the word *Reserva* is present on the label.

Spain's most popular red—its Beaujolais—is vinegary, young Valdepeñas. But the indisputably best wines of Spain come from the small northern Rioja region. Inexpensive Riojas (usually intended for export) are labeled with quasi-French names: "Spanish Claret," "Spanish Chablis," etc. They are almost always wines of poor quality. For the best Riojas, all bearing the trade names of the traditionally finest winehouses or *bodegas*, see Table M.

Vintage years for both countries are inconsequential. A vintage year of a *Reserva* is meaningful: but principally as an indication of the wine's true age.

"COUNTRY" (REGIONAL) AND "CITY" (LOCAL) WINES

REDS (*Tintos*)

Wine	Locality
Alella	Mediterranean
Carlo	Cádiz
Perelada	Mediterranean
Priorato (Tarragona)	Mediterranean
Ribero (or Ribeiro)	Galicia
Rota Tintillo	Cádiz
Valdepeñas (El Morenito)	Central Spain

WHITES (*Blancos*)

Alella (Marfil)	Mediterranean
Alicante	Mediterranean
Perelada (*rosé* also recommended)	Mediterranean
Ribero (or Ribeiro)	Galicia
Rueda	Northern Spain
Yepes	Central Spain
Valdepeñas (El Morenito)	Central Spain

TRADITIONAL WINEHOUSES (*BODEGAS*) AND WINES OF THE RIOJA*

REDS (*Tintos*)

Compañia Vinícola del Norte de España	Cune Imperial Reserve Viña Real *Reserva Oro*
Franco Españolas	"Royal Claret"
La Rioja Alta	Viña Ardanza Reservas "904" and "890"
López de Heredia	Viña Tondonia *Reserva* Viña Bosconia *Reserva*
Marqués de Murrieta	Castillo Ygay Ygay

---

* Trade or house names are given in the right column.

Marqués de Riscal	(Formerly one of the finest producers of the Rioja, wines of the *bodegas* of the Marqués de Riscal have not been up to standard in recent years. The *Reservas* and the older wines are still to be recommended, however.)
Palacios, Ignacio	*Reserva* Especial
Paternina, Frederico	All *Reservas*
Vega Sicilia	Anada Valbuena (Not strictly Riojan wines, the reds of the *bodegas* of Vega Sicilia are among the best in Spain. The vineyards have been recently taken over as a government experimental station, but excellent old wines from this house are still in circulation.)

WHITES (*Blancos*)

Compañia Vincola del Norte de España	*Cune* Monopole *Reserva*
La Rioja Alta	*Reserva* Blanco Extra
López de Heredia	Viña Tondonia Viña Zaconia
Marqués de Murrieta	Castillo Ygay

ROSÉS (*Rosados*)

Rosé wines from López de Heredia and the Marqués de Murrieta are especially recommended. Riojan *rosés*, locally called *Ojo de Gallo* (cock's eye), are strong in taste and color and may be likened to those of the lower Rhône in France. Bottles rarely carry a vintage year (*cosecha*). Excellent sparkling Riojan whites are made by the *Bodegas* Bilbenas.

SIX

Wines of Other European Countries

SWITZERLAND

In proportion to her size, the little country of Switzerland consumes a great deal of wine, most of which is imported. She is Spain's best customer, as well as Italy's, and each year the produce of many of France's top vineyards are cornered by the Swiss. Beaujolais is a great favorite—and strange as it may seem, a bottle of Romanée-Conti or Chambertin is a far more common sight in the window of a Swiss wineshop than in a French one.

Very few Swiss wines reach other countries. The great majority of them are white, the best made from either the Riesling (in Switzerland imitatively called the Johannisberg) or the Fendant, another name for the Chasselas. If the lowly Chasselas, which we have already met in Alsace and at Pouilly-sur-Loire, can be said to excel anywhere, it does on the high, terraced vineyards of Switzerland, the loftiest in the world.

Switzerland's best vineyards are to be found in the Canton of Valais, near the mouth of the Simplon Tunnel, on the headwaters of the Rhône above the Lake of Geneva. Here the most popular

white is called Fendant de Sion, the latter being the name of the
capital of the canton. It is a pale, quite dry wine, without much
bouquet, an excellent accompaniment to Swiss national dishes—
among others, cheese fondue. Also produced in the Valais is a passable red wine, Dôle, made from a blend of the Burgundian Pinot
noir and the Gamay of Beaujolais. Dôle de Valais is a nicely scented
wine which—as would be expected—tastes like a cross between a
mediocre Beaujolais and something fairly undistinguished from the
Côte d'Or. A pure Pinot Noir, so labeled is better.

Other Valais wines, all of them white, go by grape names. Of
these the best are the Johannisberg, usually blended with Riesling,
the Sylvaner (the second grape of the Rhine), the Muscat and the
Malvasia. As we have said, the Riesling in Switzerland is called the
Johannisberg, the name deriving [as with California's Johannis-
berg(er) Riesling] from the celebrated Schloss Johannisberg on the
Rhine. The Valais also makes another imitative white known as
Ermitage, so-called because it comes from the Marsanne grape,
which is partially responsible for white Hermitage of the Rhône.

The other two principal wine-producing areas of Switzerland
are along the northern shores of the Lake of Geneva—and on lovely
Lake Neuchâtel. Many Swiss white wines have a certain *pétillant*
quality, and are locally called "star wines"—a bit of realistic terminology for rising bubbles. The whites of Neuchâtel, which are
unusually light and pleasant, are perhaps the best vinous examples
of "star wines." As is the case with the Vinhos Verdes of Portugal,
under United States tariff regulations they may not be imported
to this country without being subjected to what is for them,—
considering their intrinsic worth as wine—a prohibitively high tariff
on sparkling wines.

The region of Neuchâtel is also responsible for reds, the best
of which is a light-colored wine called Cortaillod—often labeled
oeil-de-perdrix (partridge's eye) or *grain d'orge* (barley grain).
Not strictly a *rosé*, but simply a weakly tinted product of the Pinot
noir, it is comparable (in shade, at least) to those let-down reds
once shipped to England from Bordeaux that went by the name
of *clairet*.

Of those wines from the shores of the Lake of Geneva, the most noted of which come from east of the city of Lausanne, the ones to watch for are St. Saphorin, Épesses, Dézaley and Yvorne or Aigle. The last three are exported in small quantity and are reasonably priced. Freshness and vigor constitute the charm of all Swiss wines and—as may be said of the wines of almost any land— they are at their best when served with native dishes. They should be consumed when young, and vintage years are of little conse- quence. Swiss 1965's, for example, were excellent. Swiss wines offer few inexpensive "finds": it pays to buy the more costly ones. Among the best producers are: Château d'Auvernier and Chatenay (Neuchâtel), Gillard and Clos des Chevaliers (Valais), Badoux, Fonjallaz, Comtesse and Testuz (Vaud—Lake of Geneva).

HUNGARY AND YUGOSLAVIA

Among the few wines to emerge from behind the Iron Curtain are those of Hungary—a country which, prior to the *phylloxera* period, ranked fourth among the wine-producing nations of Eu- rope. Though few may have tasted it, nearly everyone has heard of Tokay (Tokaji), the legendary sweet wine of Hungary, which at its best is more like a liqueur than a wine. But the honey-sweet Tokay is by no means the only Hungarian wine of excellence. The Hungarians have known how to make good wine for a thousand years, and their government—whatever else one may think of it— seems not to have impeded them.

The finest wines of Hungary come from the tiny wine district of Somló in western Hungary and from Lake Balaton, a large lake southwest of Budapest which the landlocked Hungarians call "Our Hungarian Sea." The wines of the Balaton region are all white, and the best are either from the Riesling grape or the Hun- garian Furmint, this latter also being the grape responsible for Tokay. Olasz Rizling, the most famous (note the Hungarian spell- ing of Riesling), is a full-bodied white wine with a lovely flowery fragrance. Badacsonyi Kéknyelű, the most expensive (and tongue- twisting), is a delicate dessert wine with a marked aroma, tradi- tionally drunk in its own land from bowls large enough to accommodate the nose.[1] Another popular Balaton wine is Furmint of Balaton, a pleasant and light white which—according to one distinguished Hungarian expert anyway—is supposed to have had its origin in the hills of northern Italy.

The tiny Somló region, locally known as Somló Hill, is an extinct volcano that rises like an island in a sea of wheat plains in the western part of the province of Vesztera in central Hungary. Somló Hill might be called the Clos de Vougeot of Hungary. Its wines were known for their excellence long before Tokay was ever heard of, and owe their long and distinguished existence to Stephen I, the first king of Hungary, who sagely perpetuated the vineyards in the thirteenth century by founding a nunnery on the site. As with the Clos de Vougeot, passing troops are habitually halted and brought to attention to salute Somló Hill.

The white wines of Somló are pungent and an unusually brilliant green.[2] Their traditional medicinal and curative qualities are almost too numerous to mention. Reputedly they aid the digestion, clear the kidneys, combat anemia—as well as being an "appetizer which causes neither headache nor dyspepsia." A traditional custom of the Hapsburg family was to take a glass of Somló before their nuptials to insure the procreation of male offspring.

Tokay, Hungary's most renowned wine, is made near the northeastern village of the same name, on the River Tisa. There are two forms of Tokay, sweet and dry. The latter is usually called Szamarodni, and is the more prevalently exported. It can be a good wine, but never a distinguished one. Sweet Tokay—Eszencia or Tokay Aszú—is basically made from selected (aszú) grapes that have all but dried on the vine. The unpressed juice or seepage from these, very sweet and syrupy, is then added to the "must" or wine of ordinary ripe grapes in varying proportions, depending upon how sweet the producer wishes the wine to be. The terminology for this proportion is known as *puttonys*[3] (actually the name for the collecting-baskets used locally in the vineyards). The greater the number of *puttonys* indicated on the label, the sweeter the wine.

Tokay Aszú is dark golden in color, and highly perfumed. The

---

[1] When exported, Kéknyelü is not a dessert wine, but a dry and refreshing one.

[2] The Californians, whose wine industry owes so much to the Hungarian Count Haraszthy, make a wine called "Green Hungarian"—thought by many experts to be related.

[3] An often seen alternate spelling is *puttonos*.

legendary wonders of this rarest of all wines became so exaggerated throughout the civilized world that at one time it was actually believed to contain gold. The legend was further expanded when an Italian humanist, after visiting Hungary, asserted that the hills of Tokay contained veins of gold ore, and that golden shoots were to be found on some of the vine stocks. This report in turn prompted the immediate visit to Hungary of the most brilliant Swiss alchemist of his time, a man named Parcellus. Parcellus conducted prolonged experiments with wine, grapes and soils—only to come up with the rather lame diagnosis that the soil of Tokay was unusually blessed with minerals, and that Hungarian sunshine, "like a thread of gold, passes through stock and roots into the rock." Hungarian Tokay, incidentally, should not be confused with either the Tokay of Alsace, a dry wine which bears little resemblance even to Szamarodni, or to that of California.

Although the majority of Hungary's good wines are white, two excellent reds, Egri Bikavér (Bull's Blood) and Nemeskadar, nowadays both found on foreign wine shelves, are distinctive wines and good bargains. The former, certainly one of the world's most imaginatively named wines, is made from a combination of Pinot noir and red Bordeaux grapes. It has a peculiar clovelike fragrance, and when given sufficient age, it may be a wine of considerable character.

The wines of Yugoslavia have been known to Europe since the Middle Ages, carried thence by traders journeying from the Middle East. In recent years they have been seen increasingly on foreign markets. They are not of the same quality as those of Hungary, nor have they been improved by the imposition of Marshal Tito's wine cooperatives. They are, however, relatively inexpensive. The best of them—and even these tend to be watery and without much character—come from Slovenia, that part of Yugoslavia adjacent to Italy and Austria.

Most Yugoslavian white wines are named after their grapes, such as Traminer, Sylvaner, Riesling and a local grape known as the Sipon (Chipon). This latter produces a dry and fairly palatable white that the wine drinker, in this day of high prices, may find useful for daily drinking.

Yugoslavian reds are in general inferior to the whites, and the labels usually bear French grape names, such as Merlot, Cabernet and Pinot. The country also produces a sweetish red called Prošek, and a popular, pleasing *rosé*, Ruzica.

AUSTRIA

The Austrians are a traditionally gay and light-hearted people, with a sparkling humor and the watchword of *gemütlichkeit* (cheerfulness). Vienna in its heyday was the capital of "Wine, Women and Song"—and as many a tourist knows, the atmosphere of an Austrian *Weinstube* (wine café) is anything but heavy-footed. Wine aptly fits the national mood.

Austria is seeking to export her wine, and we may see many of them in the months and years to come. Austrian wines may be likened to German wines—except that they do not reach such towering heights. Although the common ones, or *ordinaires*, of the country are generally made from the Chasselas, the finest spring from the best German grapes: the Riesling, the Sylvaner, the two Traminers, as well as the Veltliner. Some of the finest Austrian vineyards are to be found in the suburbs of Vienna, of which Grinzing (the wine is called Grinzinger) is probably the most famous. Fifty miles or so up the picturesque Danube is the wine region of Wachau, which produces well-known whites called Dürn-steiner, Loubner and another somewhat less-distinguished wine named after the region itself, Wachauer.

It is from south of Vienna, however, in what is known as the "wine quarter" of Burgenland, where Austria's best-known and most frequently exported wine is produced. This is called Gumpold-skirchener—a spicy and charmingly scented white, whose red counterpart is rather disappointing in its coarseness. Certainly a better and milder red, also from the Burgenland, is Voslauer.

Austrian labels bear not only the town name, but that of the grape as well—and, comparable to German wines, a good year brings forth a *Spätlese* or an *Auslese*, or even a *Trockenbeerenaus-lese*. It is well to bear in mind that these latter will not be as sweet or luscious as their German namesakes, but one may be assured they will be much easier on the pocketbook. Vintage years for Austria are generally the same as for Germany (see p. 110).

GREECE

The wines of Greece were once considered the best of the world. Times have changed—or, properly speaking, tastes changed as the northern wine-growing sections of Europe were developed. Nonetheless, Greece exports a good deal of wine today, inferior wines which go principally to France for blends to make *ordinaires* and to Germany for the equivalent: *Könsumwein.*

Greek wines divide into three general classes: sweet, dessert wines containing a fairly high percentage of alcohol, of which the one called Mavrodaphne is the most commonly seen abroad; ordinary table wines, red and white and *rosé*, perhaps the best being a delicate white called Pallini; and "doctored wines", those which derive from the early periods of Grecian wine making, when neither bottles nor corks existed, and wine was stored in decorative crocks called *amphorae* (singular: *amphora*), these latter sealed with skins to keep out the air. Even though wine in that ancient day was drunk young and almost always watered, the *amphora* system was usually anything but successful in terms of preserving or aging the wine. Thus the wine—to combat the vinegar-making bacteria and many another airborne enemy—was doctored with spices such as cloves, peppercorns, various aromatics and (chiefly) sandarac, a resin used elsewhere today principally in the manufacture of varnishes. Yet it should not necessarily come as a surprise for the reader to learn that in modern Greece resinated wine is still preferred. Wine is so often a matter of habit and usage. Just as many a farm child brought up on whole milk rebels at the taste of pasteurized milk; or as the native of northern Portugal, accustomed all his life to the cloying red Vinho Verde, spurns anything else—so the Greek prefers his Retzina that tastes like pine needles! Some authorities say that after several bottles of it, one overlooks the pine needles and begins to taste wine! As a matter of vital statistics, however, none of these authorities ever seems to mention whether the several bottles should be consumed all in the same sitting or in easy dosages.

As is always taking place in France, Italy and many another European country, wine-loving travellers in Greece have unearthed many a strictly local ("unknown") wine to their liking. Although none of these latter bear mention by name in these pages, perhaps we shall see more of them soon in our own country.

SUMMARY

Few Swiss wines are exported, but among the best to be found abroad will be whites called Fendant de Sion, Neuchâtel, Aigle and Dézaley, all appropriate to cheese dishes and Swiss food in general.

The finest Hungarian wine is the very sweet Tokay (Eszencia), but it is a rarity. A dry version (Szamarodni) is exported. Two excellent Hungarian reds are Egri Bikavér (Bull's Blood) and Nemeskadar.

Yugoslavian wines, usually named after French or German grapes (the chief exception is Sipon, a dry white), are not always very well made—but their low price renders them worth a try.

The best Austrian wines are white, all made from German grapes, such as the Riesling, the Sylvaner and the two Traminers. They are similar to German wines, and less expensive—but one should not look for any "greats." One of the most popular is Gumpolds-kirchener.

In Greece, wine of the Retzina type—originally instilled with resin as a preservative—is still considered a delicacy. Two other more potable wines (to the European-trained palate) are sweet Maphrodaphnes (often seen in the U.S.) and the delicate white Pallini and Santa Helena.

SWITZERLAND

WHITE	RED
Fendant	Dôle (de Valais)
Johannisberg	Cortaillod (*rosé*)
Neuchâtel	Pinot noir
St. Saphorin	
Villette	
Yvorne	
Aigle	
Dézaley	
Épesses	

HUNGARY

WHITE	RED
Tokay (Tokaji) Aszú (Eszencia) (sweet);	Egri Bikavér
Tokay (Tokaji) Furmint (dry)	Nemeskadar
Olasz Rizling (dry)	
Badaczonyi Kéknyelű (sweet)	
Somlói Furmint (dry)	
Szamarodni (dry and sweet)	

YUGOSLAVIA

WHITE	RED
Sipon (Chipon) (de Maribor)	Prošek (sweet)
Traminer	Ruzica (*rosé*)
Sylvaner (Château de Maribor)	Cabernet (Château de Dobrovo)
Riesling	Merlot (de Breda)
Sauvignon	Pinot

AUSTRIA

WHITE	RED
Grinzinger	Voslauer
Dürnsteiner	Gumpoldskirchener
Gumpoldskirchener	
Loubner	
Wachauer	
Riesling	
Gewürztraminer	
Traminer	

GREECE

WHITE	RED
Retzina (Retsina) (resinated)	Maphrodaphne (sweet)
Maphrodaphne (sweet)	Pendeli
Pallini (dry; and semisweet)	
Hymettus (dry)	
Muscat of Samos (sweet)	
Santa Helena (dry)	

ISRAEL

WHITE	RED
Israeli Hock (dry)	Château Richon
Château de la Montagne (semi-sweet)	(semisweet)

SEVEN

Wines of the
New World

CALIFORNIA

Few Americans—even Californians—know that the State of California produces seven times more table wine than is imported into the United States from all other countries of the world. This is in addition to nearly a hundred million gallons of California Port, Sherry and other "fortified" wines. California itself, furthermore, not only drinks almost half of what it produces, but also consumes nearly a quarter of all United States imports. This is simply part of the truism that the people of wine-growing areas of the world like and drink wine. According to the Wine Institute in San Francisco, the average American drinks thirty-two gallons of milk a year (roughly three gallons less milk than a Frenchman or an Italian drinks wine), one and three-tenths gallons of spirits, and a little more than a gallon of wine. California has the highest wine consumption per capita of any state in the nation—a little over two gallons. Iowa, incidentally, has the lowest. But what will really start the heads rolling within the inner sanctum of the W.C.T.U. is the statistic that the state which most closely coincides with the national average is that little rock-ribbed republic of conservatism and temperance: Vermont.

Although all the principal grapes used in California—unlike those of New York State and other parts of the country—are of European origin, California wines cannot truthfully be said to taste much like European wines. There are certain obvious resemblances, and one or two California producers have succeeded—with infinite pains and at considerable expense—in making something that is more than just reminiscent of its European counterpart. But beyond the point of a few notable exceptions, we can only be fooling ourselves if we attempt to draw similarities. More important yet, we would be doing a considerable disservice to all concerned. California Cabernet Sauvignon, made from the principal red Bordeaux grape, does—in the hands of the best producers —taste and smell considerably like a Médoc or a red Graves; but a Cabernet Sauvignon also tastes and smells like itself. In a California Pinot Noir (from the Burgundy grape) one often finds the intriguing bouquet of a red from the Côte d'Or—a Musigny, perhaps—yet for any devotee of the wines of the Golden Slope, the anticipated ensuing tastes are just not there. And anyone who goes along with the sanguine promoters of that California white wine known as Chardonnay, made from the grape of Chablis and the Côte d'Or, and claims an absolute identity with the great white Burgundies, should have both his head and his palate examined.

In fact it is an almost tragic truth that the more Californians persist in trying to make a white Burgundy, the more they seem to bring out the worst characteristics of the Chardonnay[1]—and the farther they stray from their goal. Sensible Alsatians have long since abandoned the idea of promoting their wines as "Vins du Rhin" and attempting to produce something to rival a Schloss Johannisberg—and Californians could well take a lesson. A California Chardonnay, when allowed to stand by itself, is a light dry wine, somewhat deficient in fragrance, but quite acceptable to the veteran European wine drinker (provided he doesn't think of it as a white Burgundy), and quite delicious to many an American who has been drinking it all his life. In anyone's preferences for

---

[1] In actuality, there are far fewer bona fide Chardonnay vines in California than the numerous bottles so labeled indicate.

wines, be he an Italian peasant, a Burgundian, or a resident of the Finger Lakes, there is far more to habit and usage than meets the eye.

In comparison to the confusing systems of names and classifications of most European wines, the terms on California labels may be unfolded with a disarming simplicity. California table wines divide into two groups. The first, called "generics," are nearly always blends, and are sold under European names such as "California Burgundy," "Chablis," "Claret," "Rhine Wine," and "Sauterne" (the latter spelled in California without an "s" on the end). Just because these are blended wines it does not follow that, when made by a conscientious producer, they will not be of good value. The reds as a whole are better than the whites. Many of them are sold in bottles or jugs larger than a fifth or a quart, and they are inexpensive: for example, in San Francisco one can buy a gallon of a good generic "Chablis" or "Claret" for $3.50. The important thing to bear in mind is that the wine will not even taste like a third cousin thrice-removed of its European namesake.

The second, and higher category of California wines are known to the trade as "varietals." These are the wines in which the producers take the most pride. They are almost invariably sold by the bottle—and they all go by the name of the principal grape from which they are made. Although by law a varietal need only contain 51 per cent of the juice of the variety whose name appears on its label, in the case of the best producers it will usually be a pure product of that grape. Even so, it matters little. For shocking as this seemingly arbitrary *Appellation Contrôlée* might appear to a Frenchman, it has its distinct advantages in an industry which is, after all, hardly more than a hundred years old. Many a producer of California varietals is by no means dedicated to the god of mass production, and granted that the law allows some producers to pass off poor and/or blended wines under a label indicative of high quality, it is a blessing to others who wish to experiment and improve their vintages.

The following is a list of the most common California varietals:

Red Wines

Cabernet Sauvignon.   A red wine made from the principal grape of Bordeaux. Unquestionably the most successful (according

THE VINEYARDS OF
California

Morgan

SACRAMENTO VALLEY

Sonoma

Napa

Sacramento

San
Francisco

Livermore

Santa Clara

SAN JOAQUIN VALLEY

Santa Cruz

Hollister

Fresno

PACIFIC OCEAN

San
Bernadino

Cucamonga

Los
Angeles

0   25   50   75   100
MILES

to European standards) of all California reds. Usually an unblended product.

Pinot Noir.   The grape of the Côte d'Or. It is by no means as successful in California as the Cabernet Sauvignon, and particularly those whose taste buds are accustomed to red Burgundies may find it a bit insipid, with an unfamiliar sweet aftertaste.

Gamay.   (Sometimes seen on varietal labels as "Gamay-Beaujolais.") This is the grape that makes the jubilant red Beaujolais of Southern Burgundy, the wine which the citizens of Lyons—and any other Frenchmen who can get hold of it—let pass down their throats with such alacrity. In California the Gamay results in a softly refreshing wine, faintly resembling—but in no way rivaling—its French counterpart in vitality and fruitiness. The Gamay and the Zinfandel (see below) are usually the basis for most generic, blended California "Burgundy."

Zinfandel.   Supposedly of Hungarian origin (though not found in Hungary), this red grape may have been introduced into California in the last century by a fortune seeker of the Hungarian nobility, Count Haraszthy—nowadays known in the industry as the "Father of California wines." Many people consider Zinfandel to be the Beaujolais of California. It is light and tasty, if sometimes a little too acid, and notably better when produced in the so-called North Coast Counties around San Francisco Bay. Zinfandel improves appreciably with age.

Barbera.   The red grape used with such success in the Piedmont region of Northern Italy. The wine is rather rough and coarse, like so many Italian reds. Good varietal Barberas are produced in the North Coast Counties—notably Mendocino and Sonoma—as well as in the Central Valley and Cucamonga districts in the southern part of the state.

Petite Sirah.   Possibly the red Syrah of the Côte Rôtie and Hermitage on the Rhône. Now it is rarely, if ever, seen as a California varietal, but more often used for blending. In its pure state, however, and with sufficient age, the wine strongly resembles its purported French cousins.

White Wines

Chardonnay.   The grape responsible for all the best white wines from Champagne to Mâcon, which Californians persist in likening to a white Burgundy. A well-made, bona fide Chardonnay can be dry and refreshing; a poorly made one will have a metallic first taste and a medicinal aftertaste. Californians use this comparatively rare grape to great advantage in the production of California "Champagnes."

Pinot Blanc. A grape also used to good advantage in California for "Champagne." Considerable confusion—not to say contention—rages in California as to what this particular grape really is. In Burgundy the term Pinot blanc is colloquially interchangeable with Pinot Chardonnay, or Chardonnay; but actually the relationship is distant. In California the Pinot blanc is, in turn, frequently confused with another white grape, the Chenin blanc of the Loire. A California Pinot Blanc varietal wine will, in any event, generally be inferior either to a legitimate Chardonnay or a Chenin Blanc.

Chenin Blanc. Responsible for Vouvray of the Loire, as well as the wines of Anjou. The California version is often gratifyingly reminiscent of a Vouvray, and slightly on the sweet side. One of the best California whites.

Traminer. The Gewürztraminer and the Traminer, as the reader will remember, are the sources of those beautifully spicy and highly perfumed white wines of Alsace, Austria and the Italian Alps. The California product now being developed is quite comparable to the European types—and very much like the Chenin Blanc above, stands up well of itself.

Sylvaner. In California the "second" grape of Germany makes a wine that is dry and pleasant, though somewhat watery.

Johannisberg(er) or *White Riesling.* The Californians have appropriated the name Johannisberg(er) (from Schloss Johannisberg) to indicate the true Riesling. Though comparison should never be made with its European equivalents, in the hands of good producers it has a nice, mild bouquet, and is neither sweet nor dry. Bottles labeled Gray Riesling or Emerald Riesling are not made from the same grape.

Folle Blanche. In France, wine of the Folle blanche grape is atrocious—yet when distilled, it is responsible for French Cognac, universally accepted as the finest brandy on earth. (See Chapter X.) Used in California largely to blend with the Pinot noir and the Chardonnay for "Champagnes" and other sparkling wines, it is offered as a varietal by a few producers. Generally tart and rather high in acidity—but many people like their wine this way!

Sauvignon Blanc.   Made from one of three white grapes used for dry Graves and sweet dessert wines of Sauternes and Barsac. Most Californian vintners ferment the Sauvignon blanc into a tart white wine of considerable character. California sweet Sauterne is not a varietal (see below).

Semillon.   The name of another of the three white-wine grapes of Bordeaux. In its pure state, it is responsible for one of the most successful dry white varietals of California. A well-made Dry Semillon (emphasis on the Dry) may be almost indistinguishable from a French Graves—sometimes even a little better—and without any trace of the metallic overtones common to so many California whites. Because the *pourriture noble,* or "noble rot" we have already met in Bordeaux, the Rhine and elsewhere, does not flourish in California, it is a rare thing to find a California dessert or *liquoreux* wine in the classic European tradition. One exception is a wine produced after years of extensive research at the Cresta Blanca Vineyards in the Livermore Valley. Here the "noble rot" is cultured and sprayed on the grapes in specially air-conditioned and humidified rooms. Known as a Premier Semillon, made in very limited quantity, it is only available at the Pump Room in Chicago, the Colony in New York, Antoine's in New Orleans and a few other top-bracket, expensive eating establishments. Although experts agree that it may not be substantially distinguished from the genuine French product, its current price of $4.00 or more a bottle even exceeds that of the very finest French Sauterne. Methods for making it more cheaply and in greater quantity are still to be worked out.

Grenache (rosé).   The grape responsible for most of the good *rosé* wines of Europe—especially those of Tavel and Provence. When produced in one of the northern regions of California, it holds its head up well against many an imported one. Even more distinguished Californian *rosés* are made from the Gamay and the Cabernet; others from the Grignolino and the Zinfandel. Without fail, the best of them all come from the North Coast Countries in the vicinity of San Francisco.

Champagne. California "Champagnes," which we will deal
with more fully in Chapter VIII, are not strictly varietals, though
a few producers do sometimes make them from the Chardonnay,
in which case they will usually be so labeled.

As we have so often witnessed in the case of the wine-growing
countries of the world, once again it is to the Church—in this
instance the Spanish missions—that credit must go for the introduction of the wine grape to California, where the first plantings of
the *Vitis vinifera* appear to have taken place near San Diego about
1770. Later the Franciscans took the grape northward to the cooler
climates of the Sonoma and Napa valleys, north of San Francisco
Bay. These were grapes of Spanish origin—only one of which, the
so-called Mission, is used to any extent in the industry today. The
monastics did not sell their wines to the outside world, but kept
them for their own uses.

About the middle of the nineteenth century, California commenced to experience an invasion of vinous fortune seekers—
Frenchmen, Germans and the famed Count Haraszthy from Hungary. Most of these Europeans were already conversant in the
art of wine making, and they either imported or brought with them
many thousands of cuttings of European vines. The majority of
them, to their dying day, labored under the rather sad hallucina-
tion that European wines could be duplicated—or perhaps even
surpassed—on California soil. As we have seen so frequently, certain
grapes excel—to make fine wines—on certain soils; but wines are
never "duplicated."

By 1875 California was producing more than four million gallons of wine. Paralleling the experience of the Franciscans before
them, it was discovered that the best areas for wine making lay in
the North Coast Countries, in the vicinity of San Francisco Bay:
the Napa and Sonoma valleys, Alameda (no relation to Almadén
Vineyards), Santa Clara and Santa Cruz. In the other wine-growing
regions of the state—the vast Central Valley between the coastal
range and the Sierras, the Cucamonga district near Los Angeles
(now the sources of nearly 75 per cent of all California vinous
produce, and largely devoted to generics and fortified wines)—
the climate was too hot, and the grapes reached maturity with

more sugar and less acid than is requisite for good table wine of 14 per cent or less.[2] Today a few good varietals are raised in the Cucamonga district—notably from Barbera and Zinfandel grapes; but in general the inland regions of California are the lands of wine in the jug, of imitation Chiantis, or Ports and Sherries and Vermouths that are akin to their European counterparts in name only. There are some exceptions, however. Gallo Chablis and Tawny Port, as well as Guild Burgundy, all represent surprising quality for their low prices.

Many vineyards of the North Coast Counties, where the wine grape *Vitis vinifera* truly flourishes, are still owned by descendants of the founding families. Inglenook Vineyard, with its imposing ivy-covered winery reminiscent of the Old World, today is managed by the great-nephew of its founder. Similarly Beaulieu Vineyard, of comparable fame and charm, belongs to the descendants of its original French owner, Georges de Latour. Another name hallowed by Californians is that of Louis Martini, a comparative newcomer from Italy, who has succeeded in making some of the best varietals in the state, and whose cuttings are in great demand by other vineyard owners. The century-old firm of Charles Krug, a Prussian who pressed his first grapes in the Napa Valley with a cider press, has been taken over by yet another old wine-making family, the Mondavis. Southeast of San Francisco, in the Livermore Valley, a region most noted for its white wines, the sons of Karl Wente, another German, still operate the vineyards. And even the vast empire of Almadén, comprising more than two thousand acres divided between Los Gatos and San Benito, has been acquired by a group of men dedicated to the perpetuation of the high ideals of Charles Le Franc, owner of the original minuscle Almadén. It is impossible to name them all; but it is encouraging to know that their company is continuously being joined by small vineyard owners—retired businessmen, former ambassadors or just plain people who are intrigued with living on the soil and making good wine. All of these producers are ably aided by the Department of Viticulture and Enology of the University of California—for California, with considerably more than

---

[2] Among the best-known vineyards in these areas today are those of Gallo, Cribari and Sons, Roma, Guild and Petri.

four hundred thousand acres in grapes (nearly three times the acreage of Germany), and an annual production of one hundred sixty million gallons of wine, is by no means unaware of the importance of the industry.

Even though most North Coast vintners, especially those who produce varietals, are impelled to make better and better wine— and this bodes well for the consumer—there are certain trends in the industry that are not exactly encouraging, and of which the consumer should be aware for his own protection. One of these is embodied in our perennial American emphasis on "marketing." California produces more wine than our country drinks—and our exports are negligible. With the exception of a very few vineyards, there is always a certain surplus to every California wine crop, and most producers are forced by the competition to employ elaborate sales staffs. Inevitably, this has led nearly every one of them (even the best) into thinking that he must produce a full "line"; that in order to compete he must make a Cabernet Sauvignon, a Semillon, a Sauvignon Blanc, a Zinfandel, a Chardonnay—and many another. Some producers, for example, make as many as five or six Champagnes. One has to be dry, one sweet, one pink, another red (to compete with Sparkling Burgundy), the last perhaps a "Crackling Rosé" to rival the effervescent Portuguese products that are attempting to capture the market.

Obviously nothing could be more ridiculous—nor more dangerous to the California wine industry as a whole. If someone could persuade each California producer to make a *few* wines, namely the ones best suited to his soil, and forget about the "lines," he would do both the industry and the average wine drinker an inestimable favor. In the matter of utilizing appropriate soils for appropriate grapes, of respecting what the French call *terroir* (the special, intangible character that a particular piece of soil imparts to its wine), California vintners have much to learn. It is like the old Hollywood boast that a producer need not move out of the state to obtain any backdrop in the world—whether the scene be the Via Appia, the peaks of the Andes or the Bay of Bengal.

The Californians have much yet to discover about *terroir*, but there are some encouraging signs. In the Livermore Valley, for example, where the soil is best suited for white-wine grapes, some producers now devote their local acreage to the production of whites, and—in order to fill out the inescapable "line"—buy red grapes elsewhere. This procedure is obviously more sensible than producing red wine on soil that is more appropriate to white— though it has one technical disadvantage, in that it prevents the use on varietal labels of the highest allowable appellation: the words *Produced and Bottled By.*[3] Federal law forbids the use of this latter term for any wine made from less than 75 per cent of grapes harvested on the land of the vintner, or from another district or county; otherwise the label may only bear the words *Made and Bottled By.* This is a distinction not generally known by the public, and perhaps not one to be emphasized: the proof is, after all, in the drinking.

Another lesson in European tradition from which the Californians —along with the wine-drinking public—might well profit, involves the absurd bugaboo about sediment. California producers go to inordinate lengths to insure that there is neither sediment nor cloudiness, nor in fact anything but the vision of virginal purity in any of their wines. The tiniest speck floating in a limpid white, the slightest trace of a dreg in a red, destines any bottle on the production line to cruel oblivion. There is room here for the education of all concerned. No Frenchman or Italian would think twice about a few specks in a bottle of Pouilly-Fuissé or Soave— and as the reader should know by now, the presence of a teaspoon- full or so of dregs in any European red wine is not only entirely allowable, but an indication that the wine has been well made and properly aged. Most California wines, unfortunately, are not produced with aging in view; nor is there any doubt but what many of the elaborate filtering devices used in deference to this silly bugaboo are simply not good for the wine.

Finally, there is the matter of years for California—good and bad. One often hears that vintages in California are nonexistent— and this is, in general, true. The temperate and dependable climate, as compared with that of Chablis or the Moselle, say, renders vintage

---

[3] Another higher, rarely seen (and only *semi-official*) appellation embodies the words "estate-bottled"—meaning wine made in a winery adjacent to the vineyards where the grapes are grown.

years of far less significance than those of northern Europe. But nearly every California vintner will admit, in private, that such things as good and bad years do exist.

As with the *Reservas* of Spain and Portugal, one vintner may have had good luck in 1960 with his Cabernet Sauvignon, whereas across the road or in the next valley the vineyards may have been subjected to some quixotic rainfall or the visitation of some pest or blight, perhaps inhibiting spontaneous fermentation and involving costly and damaging delays. Certain Californians, no doubt because they are afraid that a (good) year on a label will prevent the marketing of wines of a less good one, bridle at so much as the mention of the word vintage. Others proclaim with fervor that California definitely has its vintage years, and that it is only fair to the consumer to mention them. Some producers, in the European tradition, print the vintage year on labels of wines they are exceptionally proud of.

The point is, of course, that a good California wine, especially a red, needs as much age in cask and bottle as any, and certainly it would seem that the public is entitled to know the age of the wine it buys, regardless of the wishes or marketing policies of the producer. In this respect, the wine drinker is fortunate in having a handy—though not infallible—little custom on his side, although not everyone is aware of it. Most manufacturers of American wine bottles blow a record of the year in which the bottle was made into the bottle's base. This generally appears in two-digit form ('58, '59, '60) to the right of an easily spotted hallmark. Thus if one knows, in addition, that in the hands of the best producers of varietals, red wines usually stay two years or more in the barrel before bottling, white wines one year and *rosés* somewhat less— one is provided with a fairly accurate index for gauging the age of the wine.

SUMMARY

California wines are labeled either as "generics"—usually blends carrying European names such as "Burgundy," "Chablis," etc. —or as "varietals," these being named for the grape from which they are predominantly made—"Pinot Noir," "Cabernet Sauvignon," etc. The latter, usually sold in bottles instead of jugs, are the best, especially if they come from the North Counties of Napa or Sonoma, the Livermore Valley or other regions surrounding San Francisco Bay. The best reds are Cabernet Sauvignon, Pinot Noir, Gamay and Zinfandel; the best whites are Chardonnay, Dry Semillon, Chenin Blanc, Johannisberg(er) (White) Riesling and Traminer. The two finest *rosés* are the Gamay and Grenache. The Livermore Valley excels in whites; the Napa and Sonoma regions are most famed for their reds and "Champagnes."

Vintage years in California are not important, although most of the good producers put them on labels so that consumer will know how old the wine is. Should the label not have the year, one may *usually* learn when the wine was bottled by looking for a two-digit date (*'58, '59, '60*) that manufacturers blow into the bottle's base. To estimate the actual age of the wine, allow two years before bottling for the reds, one for the whites and *rosés*.

Table O lists most of the finer North Coast vineyards, though certain varietals do excel with the skills and soils of their producers:

WHITE WINE	RED WINE
Chardonnay: Wente; Beaulieu	*Cabernet Sauvignon:* Beaulieu; Concannon
Chenin Blanc: Mondavi; Inglenook	*Pinot Noir:* Mondavi; Inglenook
Sylvaner: Beaulieu	*Zinfandel:* Wente; Souverain
Traminer: Inglenook	*Petite Sirah:* Concannon
Gewurztraminer: Almadén	*Gamay Beaujolais:* Mondavi; Beaulieu
Johannisberg Riesling: Souverain; Mondavi	
Dry Semillon: Wente	ROSÉ
Sweet Semillon (Sauterne): Wente	*Grenache:* Almadén
Sauvignon: Almadén	*Vin Rosé:* Wente; Mondavi

SONOMA COUNTY

Buena Vista Vineyards   F. Korbel and Brothers

NAPA COUNTY

Louis M. Martini   Heitz Wine Cellars
Charles Krug Winery   Beaulieu Vineyard
Inglenook Vineyard Company   Hanns Kornell Champagne Cellars
Stony Hill Vineyard (A small but   Souverain Cellars
   excellent vineyard producing   Robert Mondavi Winery
   white wines only.)

ALAMEDA COUNTY
(Livermore Valley)

Wente Brothers   Concannon Vineyards

SANTA CLARA–SANTA
CRUZ–SAN BENITO REGION

Almadén Vineyards   Mirassau Vineyards
Paul Masson Vineyards

NEW YORK STATE, OHIO
AND LAKE ONTARIO

As every American school child knows, the Nordic discoverers of North America called our country Vinland or "Wineland." Vines in tremendous abundance, from Massachusetts to Georgia, greeted the settlers wherever they landed, and it was thought that only a little attention and proper pruning would turn the whole continent—or what was then known of it—into a bountiful vineyard. But our sanguine forebears suffered disappointment after disappointment. The native grape turned out not to be the wine grape, *Vitis vinifera*, but instead, another variety, *Vitis labrusca*. And when this latter was cultivated, a mysterious sickness took hold of the vines that could neither be cured nor explained.

When all efforts to tame the wild grapes of Massachusetts, New York, Maryland, Virginia and elsewhere failed, attempts were made to plant European grapes. Lord Delaware imported French vines and vintners; the Huguenots made serious attempts at viniculture in the Carolinas; late in the eighteenth century cuttings from Portugal were brought to Georgia. In all cases the vines suffered from inexplicable plagues and withered away. From what we know now, this second failure was probably attributable to the dread *phylloxera*, to which all European *Vitis vinifera* vines fall prey. It was as tragic as a gold rush without gold.

Had it not been for a Swiss immigrant named Jean Dufour, who persisted with his European cuttings in Kentucky, the American wine industry might well have disappeared for good and all. Dufour's Kentucky plantings were not exactly spectacular—only one survived. This was a vine bearing a hitherto unknown black grape, reputedly imported as a seed from the Cape of Good Hope and thought to be of *vinifera* origin (though vinicultural authorities of today are skeptical on the subject, and tend to believe it was an accidental cross between a European and an indigenous vine). Called the Cape, or Alexander, in any event it made wine, and its success gave American vintners the courage to experiment further and develop others. The first of these of any lasting importance were two distinctly native grapes, both from coastal North Carolina: the Catawba, whose still and sparkling wines, produced by the Longworth family in Ohio, were acknowledgedly the best of eastern wines previous to Prohibition days, and the Scuppernong. Somewhat later their numbers were augmented by the Delaware, the Niagara, the "Missouri Riesling" and others—all of the *Vitis labrusca* variety.

Only about 10 per cent of all the wine made in the United States is produced outside of California, and the greatest part of this derives from the New York State vineyards of the Finger Lakes, Niagara and Chautauqua, from the shores and islands of Lake Erie in Ohio, and the Lake Ontario regions of the United States and Canada. It should be mentioned in passing that a few good wines are now being made in the Hudson Valley and at the Boordy Vineyards in Maryland. These latter, which show considerable promise, are outstanding examples of wines from imported French hybrid vines and, along with the recent successes of the Gold Seal Vineyards and the Konstantin Frank Cellars in the Finger Lakes represent the first successful attempts on the eastern seaboard to approximate European tastes and flavors. Both red and white wines are made—but production is limited.

Although the New York and Ohio wine industries are persistently experimenting with hybrid European vines, the reputation of these century-old vineyards rests on the production of wines from *Vitis labrusca* vines. As we have already mentioned, wines from native American grapes have a flavor all their own—universally described by the word "foxy"—denoting a raw, musky or grapelike flavor that is anything but pleasing to the wine drinker who has been brought up on European or California wines. *Labrusca* grapes are higher in acid than the *vinifera* variety; and inasmuch as it is the acid that largely carries the taste and the aroma we experience in wines, it is for this reason that the "Champagnes" and sparkling wines made from these grapes—by virtue of the added sugar necessary for "Champagne" making—are less "foxy" and more acceptable to European-trained palates. Two Finger Lake varieties of "Champagne" in particular, Great Western and those made by a Frenchman named Charles Fournier (Gold Seal Vineyards), have been popular with the public for many years—and are only rivaled by a few other domestic brands, such as the California "Champagne" made by Kornell Champagne Cellars, Korbel, and Almadén Vineyards. Like many European *mousseux* and Californian "Champagnes," these superior New York State "Champagnes" are made by the true French Champagne process, meaning that they undergo their second fermentation in the bottle. They are principally blends of Catawba, Delaware and Elvira grapes. In Ohio the unblended Catawba also makes a creditable sparkling wine.

As with California brands, New York still wines have their

generic names, such as New York State "Burgundy," New York State "Chablis," etc. These are probably the most misleading of all wine terms on earth: a New York State "Burgundy" carries an even lesser relationship to true Burgundy than a California blend of the same name—which latter is at least derived from European grapes, though they may not be the Pinot Noir or the Gamay. Similarly, the sole resemblance between a New York State "Chablis" and a French one is that of color. New York State varietals, however, follow the California pattern and are named after the grapes themselves. The most successful of these are Niagara (white), Delaware (both red and white), Isabella (red) and Catawba and Diana (both white). Probably the best New York State *labruscas* are made by the Widmer Wine Cellars at Naples, New York—though the two other firms already mentioned, Great Western Producers and Gold Seal Vineyards, along with the Taylor Wine Company (New York) and Meier Wine Cellars (Ohio), all have excellent reputations. As already mentioned, Gold Seal Vineyards have made great strides in the development of *vinifera* varieties, especially with Riesling and Chardonnay grapes; and the recent appearance of the wines of the Vinifera Wine Cellars of Dr. Konstantin Frank—a Russian onologist whose experimental vineyards at Hammondsport are an increasing source of amazement to his contemporaries—represents a conclusive breakthrough in the hitherto unknown art of producing European-type wines east of the Rockies.

SUMMARY

New York State and Ohio wines, which are almost never made from European wine grapes, taste differently from wines of Europe and California. The best come from the Finger Lakes and Niagara districts of New York, four outstanding firms being Gold Seal Vineyards (New York), Widmer Wine Cellars (New York), the Taylor Wine Company (New York) and the Meier Wine Cellars (Ohio). The two most noted "Champagnes" are made by Great Western Producers and Gold Seal Vineyards (both New York).

Like California wines, eastern wines are classified as generics (New York State "Burgundy," New York State "Chablis," etc.) and as varietals, these latter named after the principal grape. The most successful varietals are Niagara (white), Delaware (red and white), Isabella (red) and Catawba and Diana (both white). Gold Seal Vineyards produces excellent European-type Rieslings and Chardonnays, along with Konstantin Frank's Vinifera Wine Cellars—both at Hammondsport. Except for the latter, eastern wines do not have significant vintage years.

Some Recommended New York State Still Wines

Vinifera Wine Cellars (Konstantin Frank) (Hammondsport)
Johannisberger Riesling Spätlese (white)
Pinot Chardonnay (white)

Muscat Ottenel (white)
Gewürztraminer (white)

Gold Seal Vineyards (Hammondsport)
Johannisberger Riesling Spätlese (white)

Catawba (white)

Pleasant Valley Wine Co. (Great Western) (Hammondsport)
Delaware (white)

Vin Rouge (red)

Widmer's Wine Cellars (Naples)
Lake Niagara (white)

Isabella (red)

SOUTH AMERICA (CHILE)

South American countries produce roughly one-tenth of the world's wine, and along with not inconsiderable imports from Europe, drink almost all of it. In fact, the per capita consumption of wine in both Chile and the Argentine compares favorably with that of Spain, and only ranks below those of the world's three greatest wine-drinking nations: Portugal, Italy and France. In terms of world production of table wines, country by country, the Argentine is fourth. Among South American countries, Chile comes next, making more than one hundred million gallons of what is generally considered the best wine of the continent.

Although European grapes are employed, most wine from South American countries is coarse, comparable to European *ordinaires* and not worth exporting. Fifty years ago the wines of Peru gained a certain popularity in England; today nearly the only wines found on export markets are those of Chile, that narrow little strip of a nation on the Pacific side of the continent, two hundred and fifty miles across at its widest, and more than two thousand miles long.

The northern section of Chile is arid desert, the southern part a storm-lashed forest. The important vineyard areas are in the central part of the country, at Huasco and Cahapoal and somewhat further south near Talcahuano—all located between the 34th and 38th parallels, south latitude, the latter being the southernmost limit for the wine grape on the continent. The climate of the vineyard districts resembles northern California, the soil is volcanic and unusually fertile for the successful production of good wines. The vineyards are irrigated by streams draining the snow fields of the Andes— some of whose peaks reach heights of more than twenty thousand feet—and it has been said that the land has never been invaded by the *phylloxera* or any other serious plague of the wine grape. A majority of the vineyards are owned by small owners, and nearly all the wine is made in cooperatives.

Nearly every important European wine grape is grown in Chile, including the Pinot noir of Burgundy and the Cabernets of Bordeaux for the reds, the Chardonnay, the Sylvaner and the Riesling for the whites. Labels usually bear the grape names, as with United States and Alsatian varietals, along with such qualitative words as *Reservado, Especial* and *Gran Vino* (the highest appellation). The best producers also add vineyard or area names on labels—names which, by dint of some curious promotional sleight of hand, nearly always seem to coincide with the names of the producers themselves. The best of these are Carmen, Conchalí, Concho y Toro, Tocornal, Santa Rita, Linderose and Undurraga.

Chilean reds are light in color and tend to be rather muddy tasting, but the *rosés* are often excellent. The whites—especially the Rieslings—are very dry, with an appealing purity. In the United States these latter are usually inexpensive, and are particularly to be recommended. Chilean Rieslings and Rhine wines are usually sold in squat, dark green *bocksbeutels*, comparable to those used for German Steinweins and Frankenweins. Chilean "Champagnes," rarely exported, are nearly as good as second-string French ones. Except for bottles labeled "Rhine wine," the generic blends and imitations of European types (*Tipo*) are to be avoided. One bottle of blended wine that recently came to our attention bore words supplying an unexpectedly candid history: *Chilean White Wine Tipo Chablis. Elaborated and bottled by*. . . .

AUSTRALIA

Australia produces almost 30 million gallons of *vinifera* wines annually, of which about half are turned into distillates. Exported to Britain and other parts of the world for years, they are gaining in reputation. Nearly all the vineyards are in the southeastern section—New South Wales—stretching from Sydney to Adelaide. The best regions are the Hunter, Murrumbidgee and Barossa Valleys; the significant exporting firms are Glenloth, Lindeman, Orlando, Reynell (Château Reynella) and Seppelt. To European ears many Australian labels have a cacophonous ring: Chardonnay Sauternes, Hermitage Claret, etc. Yet to the tone-deaf wine lover, many of the wines (especially the varietals) are excellent: the reds possess exciting, exotic bouquets; the whites are clean and well made. Australian Sherry can be better than Californian.

SUMMARY

South American countries make (and drink) large quantities of wines, but the only country to export them in any quantity is Chile.

Chilean reds (named varietally after the grapes) include wines from the Pinot noir and the Cabernet; but Chile excels in its clean, dry whites and *rosés*. The best vineyards (or producers) are Undurraga, Carmen, Conchalí, Concho y Toro, Tocornal, Santa Rita and Linderose. Wines made from the Chardonnay, the Sylvaner and especially the Riesling are all excellent. Labels bear qualitative terms such as *Reservado, Especial* and *Gran Vino*—the latter being the highest.

Except for bottles specifically labeled "Rhine Wine," Chilean generic wines—whose labels often carry the word *Tipo* (type)—are to be avoided.

Australia produces European-type (*vinifera*) wines, many of which are excellent. The reds possess astounding bouquets, and the whites are clean and well made.

EIGHT

Champagnes
and Sparkling Wines

FRENCH CHAMPAGNE: THE "KING OF WINES"

Although its name is borrowed the world over, there is no true Champagne but French Champagne—the "King of Wines." This is made in a strictly demarcated area of northern France, in the vicinity of the city of Reims on the Marne River, by more than one hundred and fifty firms, each of which uses its own particular secret formula. The grapes used for Champagne are two we have already met in the Côte d'Or and elsewhere: the red Pinot noir and the white Chardonnay. But Champagne is never made from the grapes of one vineyard alone—and, in most instances, it is not even the product of a single year. Grapes from all over the district are purchased by the individual firms; the wines themselves are in turn blended according to the manufacturer's formula, and may derive from several years.

Vintage Champagnes (those bearing a year on the bottle) are only made in the best years; even so, they are blends of wines from that particular year. These only constitute a small part of the total production; but they are the acknowledged best and, needless to say, the most expensive. Champagnes—and for that matter, all imported sparkling wines—are a luxury. To begin with, they are taxed as though they were jewelry; the United States duty on sparkling wine (roughly $10.00 a case) is nearly ten times that placed on still wine. Again, because sparkling wines are universally considered to be a rich man's drink, or something to embellish a special occasion, restaurants and retail stores feel privileged to charge a mountainous mark-up.

Another factor that renders Champagne so expensive is the basic cost of manufacturing it. The process known in France as the *méthode champenoise* is long and complicated. Since the wine is made in large part from the red-skinned Pinot, a very careful pressing (involving considerable waste) is necessary to insure that no pink tinge appears in the juice.[1] After fermentation, the wine is kept in casks through the winter, to be bottled in the spring. At this time its sugar content is carefully measured, and when the wine is bottled it is infused with more sugar yet and a culture of yeast, in order to bring about a second fermentation. The bottle is then securely capped to prevent any gases from escaping, and now begins a long period of storage in the bottle (which with the best Champagnes may last two or more years), during which time the wine both matures and builds up its carbonation.

When the product is adequately aged, the bottles are placed in racks, their necks pointing downward, to begin the very specialized treatment which so contributes to the wine's ultimate cost. For several months each downward-pointing bottle is twisted by hand, part of a turn each day, allowing the sediment to settle on top of the cork. Now the wine is ready for its final processing. With the cork still downward, a skilled worker uncorks the bottle to allow only the sediment to escape, quickly turns it right side up, injects more sugar to sweeten the wine, a bit of brandy to arrest any further fermentation and recorks and wires the bottle. When done by an experienced worker, the whole process is accomplished in the space of a few seconds, and none of the valuable natural carbonation is lost.

---

[1] Pink *(Rosé)* Champagne, sometimes called *Oeil-de-perdrix,* once much more popular than it is nowadays, is made either by continuing with the pressing until a pink tinge is obtained or by a mixture of red and white wines.

In recent years another process, never used for superior French Champagnes, has been employed by the makers of sparkling wines and so-called "Champagnes" as a time- and labor-saving device. Called the bulk method, it became possible only with the invention of high-pressure glass-lined tanks. The bulk method involves a rapid second fermentation in the tank, from which the wine is siphoned off from the top, eliminating the protracted hand labor of rotating and disgorging. Many inexpensive sparkling wines, including most German *Sekt* and much California "Champagne," are made in this way. Obviously a cheaper procedure than the *méthode champenoise*, with wines carbonated by the bulk method there is almost always an unpleasant trace of residual yeast; nor does it necessarily require the palate of an expert to detect that the wine has usually not been properly aged. Only with the best and most conscientious bulk method producers are the two processes combined: the wine is actually aged in the bottle and then transferred to the tank for settling. Even so, the taint of dead yeast cells always remains to a certain extent.

No one quite knows how the evolution of making natural sparkling wines came about. As we have mentioned, many wines—the whites of Alsace, Vouvray and Château Grillet are examples—oftentimes undergo of their own accord a repetitive, seasonal secondary fermentation in the bottle, unintended by their makers. This is known to the experts as malolactic fermentation—but even the experts are at a loss to explain certain of its phenomena; and many an expert whose experience should have taught him otherwise refuses to face all the evidence! Usually occurring in the spring of the year—beginning about the time the sap is rising in vineyards and lasting only a few months—the wine takes on a gentle fizziness, producing a slight prickle on the tongue. Occasionally one may observe minuscule bubbles. Perplexingly enough, this can happen with wines stored in a perfectly air-conditioned cellar —under ideal conditions and unvarying temperatures—and the phenomenon repeats itself year in and year out, often until the wine is itself no longer good, or "spent."

Wines with this natural faint effervescence are called by the French *pétillants*, as opposed to *mousseux*, the latter term being used for Champagnes and sparkling wines in which bona fide bubbles have been induced by a purposeful second fermentation in the bottle, or by direct carbonation. It is apparent that the wines of the Champagne district—which until several hundred years ago were always marketed as still wines—must have also contained a potential for these *pétillant* characteristics. Dim as history is on the subject, we do know that they were first popular in England, and that in those days the French had neither strong bottles nor proper, airtight corks. The English, on the other hand, had both; and evidence points to the fact that it was Champagne shipped as still wine in casks to England, and bottled there, that was responsible for the innovation. Only some years later did the French themselves commence to imitate this "sparkly," as the English called it.[2]

Legendarily the invention of Champagne is attributed to a certain Dom Pérignon, a monk and the cellarer of a Benedictine Abbey near Hautvilliers in the Champagne district. But there is no real evidence that Dom Pérignon—whose chief contribution to Champagne was to perfect the art of blending—put sugar and yeast cultures into his bottles to supplement natural effervescence. This procedure, obviously conceived to insure a year-round effervescence, apparently came later. Nor did Champagne—today the most fashionable drink among the French themselves—come into its own in its native land until comparatively recently. Ignored for almost two centuries in France, elsewhere in Europe, especially across the Channel, its popularity grew by leaps and bounds. This latter is no doubt why a bottle labeled *English Cuvée* or *English Market* almost invariably represents the cream of the crop from any one of the many firms of the Champagne district.

The Champagne district operates under regulations laid down by the *Appellations Contrôlées* laws, but these words—so important a guaranty of quality with most French wines—do not appear on labels. Nor are there any classifications for Champagnes except those arbitrarily placed on the labels by the manufacturers themselves: the words *Premier Cru* or *Grand Cru* on a bottle, for example, mean nothing official. Champagnes are graded by the

---

[2] Thomas Jefferson, visiting Champagne about this time, reported that "While the sparklings are little drunk in France . . . they are endeavoring to make all they can. This is done by bottling in the Spring, from March till June. If it succeeds, they lose an abundance of bottles. This is another cause for increasing the price."

manufacturing firms according to their degree of dryness—the driest and best of which is generally known as a *Brut*.[3] Next comes *Extra Sec* (extra dry), followed by *Sec* (a French word essentially meaning dry, but in the case of Champagnes and other *mousseux* wines indicates something moderately sweet). Bottles labeled *Demi-Sec* and *Demi-Doux*, like those bearing the mysterious terms *Goût Américain* or *Drâpeau Américain*, are usually made for South American and Slavic countries, where the sweetest Champagnes are much appreciated. Other terms on Champagne labels—*Réserve*, *Privat*, *Spéciale* and *Première Cuvée*—are all relatively pointless, with the exception of the last, which is a guaranty that the wine has come from the first (always the best) pressing of the grapes. A Champagne labeled *Blanc de Blancs* means that only the white Chardonnay grape has been used, without an admixture of the Pinot noir. A *Blanc de Blancs* of a named vintage year will be ultra dry, and a superlative product.

Champagne is one wine that fits with almost any food, and may be served throughout a meal. Another use for it, about which we shall have more to say in Chapter XI, is in place of a cocktail, as an *apéritif* (before a meal) planned to show off the qualities of good wines. One is often asked what are the best Champagnes. Unfortunately the answer is not easy to come by—for Champagnes are blends that do not spring from any particular piece of soil, and their quality and particular character is dependent upon their producers. Furthermore, each one of us generally has his own favorite, the result of long experimentation. One may commence by saying, however, that a vintage Champagne, one with a year on the label, is invariably better than a nonvintage one— though not perhaps always really worth the appreciable difference in price. One of the most expensive (and considered by many the best) brands is produced by the firm of Moët et Chandon, and named after the traditional "Father of Champagne," the Benedictine Dom Pérignon. Dom Pérignon is always Vintage. Two other superb Champagnes, manufactured in several degrees of sweetness, are made by the two firms of Krug and Bollinger. For the balance we have appendid a list (Table P) of a dozen or so

---

[3] An exception is the well-known firm of Krug (not to be confused with California's Charles Krug Wineries), whose *Extra Sec* is traditionally drier than the *Brut*.

others, with any of which the wine drinker cannot go far wrong —though he may wish to experiment with several before he has found one truly to his liking.

As is the case of all wines, Champagne is better when it comes from a larger bottle than from a smaller. Champagne bottle sizes have a wide range: they include the split (quarter bottle), the half bottle and the bottle, the Magnum (double bottle), the Jeroboam (four bottles). Of these perhaps the Magnum is the most practicable, provided as much as two bottles is to be served. Actually, there are four yet larger traditional ones: the Methuselah, the Salmanasar, the Balthazar and the Nebuchadnezzar (the last containing the equivalent of twenty bottles). Although theoretically Champagne from one of these would be preferable, it requires little stretch of the imagination to realize that as they progress in size they become increasingly difficult to cool and to handle around the dinner table—and serve their best purposes in show windows.

Recent good years for Vintage Champagnes are 1952, 1953, 1955, 1959, 1961 and 1962.

⤙ TABLE P   *Recommended French Champagne Manufacturers*

Ayala	Moët et Chandon
Bollinger	(Dom Pérignon)
Delbeck	Mumm
Goulet	Perrier-Jouet
Charles Heidsieck	Piper-Heidsieck
Heidsieck Monopole	Pommery et Greno
Irroy	Pol Roger
Krug	Roederer
Lanson	Ruinart
	Veuve Clicquot

"CHAMPAGNES" AND SPARKLING WINES

Under French law no *mousseux* or sparkling wine, unless it be made in the Champagne district itself, may be called Champagne. Vouvray, for example, is Vouvray or "Vouvray *Mousseux*," not "Vouvray Champagne." Although the United States is not one, many nations—at the request of the French—refrain from calling their sparkling products Champagnes. The Germans call theirs *Sekt*; the Portuguese and Spanish use their own terms (and for export purposes often add the words "Sparkling Wine"); the Italians also have terms of their own, such as *Spumante or Frizzante*.[4]

Though there is no sparkling wine that duplicates the special quality given by the sun, the soil and the grapes of Champagne—there are many substitutes, and good ones. We have already mentioned Sparkling Vouvray and Saumur of the Loire Valley, semi-sweet wines that correspond to the Champagne grading of *Sec*. Made from the Chenin blanc grape, they have a slightly different flavor—but they are considerably less expensive than the "King of Wines" and are frequently a practical substitute. The only other important sparkling wine of France is Sparkling (Red) Burgundy, which of course has its California and New York State namesakes. Having begun these pages with the statement that there is some wine to suit nearly everyone's tastes, we should not be on very firm ground if we gave vent to our own personal prejudices in the case of Sparkling Burgundy. But what the reader should know, simply put, is that Sparkling Burgundy—not usually made by the *méthode champenoise*—was conceived for the sole purpose of disposing of poor, surplus wine. Sparkling Burgundy rarely comes from the little royal ribbon of vineyards on the Côte d'Or; it is

---

[4] Portuguese "Champagnes" are called *Espumantes;* Spanish, *Xampáns* or *Gran Cremants*. Chilean "Champagnes" are of excellent value but never exported; in the Argentine, the home of large quantities of low quality wine, the exception to the rule is a "Champagne" made by a division of the French firm of Moët et Chandon, from a combination of three European grapes: the Chardonnay (Burgundy), the Ugni blanc (Cognac) and the Sémillon (Bordeaux).

only infrequently made with the juice of the Pinot noir; it is always heavily sugared. No Burgundian would drink it himself; in fact, it is never seen on any wine list in the Côte d'Or, and rarely on any French one. The only thing to recommend it, as opposed to its Californian or New York State cousins, is that it is at least made of Old World grapes on Old World soils— and thus its taste carries a certain hint of Old World *terroir*.

Again, there are many good substitutes for true Champagne that are not even necessarily French *mousseux*. The experimenting wine drinker will probably find that one of the most satisfactory, in terms of taste and price, is the Italian Lacryma Christi, a wine made by the *méthode champenoise*, though not always from grapes grown on the slopes of volcanic Mount Vesuvius! The classic Italian "Champagne," generally sweeter than Lacryma Christi, is Asti Spumante. Either of these two wines—or their Portuguese and Spanish equivalents mentioned below—may be substituted at weddings or other festive occasions: their costs range from one-half to two-thirds the price of French Champagne and, especially after the first glass or so, few of the guests will know the difference.

German "Champagne," *Sekt,* is (logically) not made from superior wine, for it is usually the product of the poorest years, when good still wines cannot be made in an unsugared state. A great quantity of sugar must be added to *Sekt* to blanket its extreme acidity— and no amount of dosing or blending can ever serve to disguise an inferior product. By contrast, both Spain and Portugal make excellent sparkling wines. The best of the Portuguese, now beginning to be seen on world markets, are Raposeira and Messias, both *Brut* (very dry). Two other good exported ones are Borges and Royal *Brut*. The finest Spanish ones are the *Extra Bruts* of the firms of Castellblanch and Codorniú.

In all frankness, many domestic brands of "Champagne" are infrequently worth the price. Even the driest and rarest of California, fermented in the bottle without added sugar (which goes by the grading of *Nature*) is grossly overpriced when compared to a Portuguese or Italian import. Cheap California "Champagnes" made by the bulk method are of even less value. As already mentioned, among the better and more expensive California producers are Korbel, Kornell and Almadén. California "Champagne" terms are *Brut, Extra Dry, Dry* or *Sec* and *Sweet*, or *Doux*, in that order. Pink "Champagne" often goes by the name of *Oeil-de-perdrix* (partridge's eye), the ancient term for a French rosé.

Most New York "Champagne" is labeled *Brut*, or *Brut Special* (the driest of all), *Special Reserve* (somewhat less dry) and finally, *Extra Dry* (which paradoxically indicates an almost cloying sweetness). The Gold Seal Vineyards of the Finger Lakes produces a Charles Fournier *Brut* "Champagne," named after the firm's president, which—if one does not object to its slight foxiness—one will acknowledge to be of exceptional quality. Fournier *Natur*, another Gold Seal product, is not a *mousseux* but a *pétillant*, cheaper than the *Brut*, and appreciated by many. Great Western "Champagnes," of course, have been the "Standard of the East" for years.

SUMMARY

Most French Champagnes are blends, sometimes containing wines of two or more years, made by private formulas of the individual manufacturers. Vintage Champagnes—those with a year on the label—are the best, but also the most expensive and sometimes not worth the price. They are only made in the best years.

French Champagnes are graded in order of dryness: *Brut* (the driest); *Extra Sec* (extra dry); *Sec* (sweetish); *Demi Sec* and *Demi Doux* (very sweet). The only other terms on a label with any meaning are: *Blanc de Blancs* (indicating the wine is made exclusively from white grapes); *Première Cuvée* (meaning from the first and best pressing of the grapes); *English Cuvée*, or *English Market* (indicative of the producer's best quality).

Other "Sparkling Wines"—French, Italian, Portuguese and Spanish—may be good, inexpensive substitutes for French Champagne. Of these the best are Italian Lacryma Christi and Asti Spumante, Portuguese Raposiera *Brut*, Messias *Brut*, and Royal *Brut*, Spanish Castellblanch *Extra Brut* and Codorniú *Extra Brut*. German "Champagne" (*Sekt*) is usually a doctored wine of poor quality.

California and New York State "Champagnes" are usually overpriced and do not compete in quality with many imported "Sparkling Wines." Among the better producers are F. Korbel and Brothers, Hanns Kornell Cellars, Almadén Vineyards (all California); Great Western, Taylor and Gold Seal Vineyards (New York State).

NINE

Fortified Wines

Port, Sherry and Madeira, together with Sicilian Marsala, Californian Angelica and many another, are known as fortified wines—meaning that they are all basically table wine, either red or white, to which a certain amount of brandy or alcohol (and sometimes sugar) has been added. In Portugal and Spain they are called, respectively, *vinhos* or *vinos generosos* (noble wines); in Italy, *vinos di lusso* (*lusso* is also the Italian term for "luxurious"); in France, *vins de liqueur* (sweet or luscious).

The practice that began in earnest in the eighteenth century, of "spiking" or fortifying something that we must assume to have been a perfectly good table wine in its own right, appears in all instances to have had its roots in economic rather than gastronomic ground. One of these springs from the simple biological fact that wine with 18 per cent alcohol or more is all but immune to the hoards of harmful bacteria (its natural enemies) ever-present in the air. Fortified wines, for example, may evaporate—but they do not turn to vinegar. Thus brandy was added to wine as a preservative. Another reason is that wine low in alcohol does not travel well—or at least didn't in the days of long, hot voyages. By contrast, some fortified wines—Madeira, for one—are even improved by travel.

A perhaps more significant reason yet for fortification is the fact that in countries not in the wine belt, not producing wines themselves, there has always been more of a predilection for the alcohol in wine than for wine itself! This applies alike to the British Isles and Dominions, to Scandinavia and the Portuguese African colonies. Here is certainly the true explanation for the survival of Sherry and Port, and many another fortified wine (either extant or extinct). By comparison, the Spanish drink almost no Sherry; virtually the only Portuguese who drink Port or Madeira are ones in the Port or Madeira trade, or those who have learned to drink and appreciate them in foreign lands.

Many a fine table wine in history has had its reputation ruined —or at least temporarily eclipsed—by vintners who gave in to the temptation of making it (i.e., for export) a stronger wine than nature intended it to be. Among dozens of them we may count Portuguese Colares and Bucelas, the wines from Tarragona in Spain (Tarragona Port) and the once reputedly excellent Constantia from South Africa—with the result that the former, two of Portugal's traditional best, temporarily lost favor on the export market, and the latter two have sunk into a worse state of oblivion.

The fact remains, however, that wines of certain parts of the world—the forbidding Douro Valley in Portugal, the little triangular area surrounding Jerez de la Frontera in southern Spain, the volcanic island of Madeira off the African coast—are ones that time has shown to be better suited to fortification than not, and these have been the classic survivors. Though the vogue for fortified wines can hardly be said to be increasing, one hopes that the pendulum may once again swing the other way: for even though sweet dessert wines may be a thing of the past, there is still a place for dry fortified wines in the civilized world of table wines. Port, especially dry White Port, dry Sherry and crisp Madeira are all excellent as *apéritifs*, and far better for the human race than the habitual strong cocktail. And there is no doubt whatsoever but what—like Champagne—they are better suited to precede wine, a true appreciation of which is never enhanced by spiritous liquors.

PORT

Port—Red Port, that is—is a dessert wine; Sherry, the best of which is very dry, is an *apéritif*; in terms of uses Madeira falls between the two—it may be either.

Of all the fortified wines, Port is made and comes to maturity by the simplest processes, and therefore may be said to be the purest. A prophet without much honor in its own land, Port has for generations been known as the Englishman's drink. Its origin is typically commercial—as opposed to gastronomic. During the eighteenth century, as a result of a ban on French wines, Portuguese table wines had gained considerable popularity in the British Isles. History does not record the name or names of the Portuguese merchants who, shipping their wines from the little fishing town of Viana do Castello on the River Lima, chose in poor years to adulterate table wines destined for England with a little alcohol, adding the juice of elderberries "to improve the color." The use of elderberry juice met with understandable disfavor and was shortly abandoned; but the taste for stronger and stronger wine (not called "Port" until the industry was later centralized in the city of Oporto) caught on so indelibly that numbers of Englishmen were soon journeying to Portugal to take part in the production of this new British national drink. Some of these Englishmen stayed on to enter the trade: hence many of the names found on Port labels—Cockburn, Graham, Robertson, Sandeman, Dow and Yeatman, all shipping firms at Vila Nova de Gaia, the "Port" town opposite the city of Oporto at the mouth of the Douro River.

The birthplace of Port is the steep and narrow Douro Valley in central Portugal—a veritable furnace where high mountains shut off any possible moisture or coolness from the ocean, and where during the growing season the temperature in the depths of the valley may rise to 110 degrees in the shade. For five months of the year the Douro dries to a mere trickle; at the valley's bottom one sleeps at night on the bare earth to benefit by any coolness it might afford; high on the precipitous mountainsides, where the best vineyards lie, the workers sometimes lack sufficient water in which to cook their vegetables. Somehow the vines miraculously acquire enough moisture from the rocky granite and schistose soil of the terraces to produce a grape that comes to a quick maturity, with an exceptionally high sugar content. Unlike most other fortified wines, no sugar need ever be added to Port; in fact, it is forbidden by law.

Although Port is born a thousand feet above the Douro amid

these humanly untenable conditions, the wine only remains there during its infancy. Shortly after fermentation has taken place in the *quintas* (winehouses) situated on the valley floor far below the high vineyards, it is taken in small casks or "pipes" down the river to the "wine lodges" at Vila Nova de Gaia, to complete its adolescent stage of aging and blending. In days gone by the journey was made in the late fall or early winter, when the river comes in flood, by means of shallow-draft boats with flaring square sails and rudders uniquely designed to pass the dangerous rapids. Nowadays Port is carried off to its second home less romantically, by means of lorry and railroad.

Port is made almost entirely from grapes strictly indigenous to the Douro, sometimes from an admixture of several dozens of them. During the fermentation process, in the case of Red Port, the grape's natural sugar is allowed to convert to alcohol only until such time as the wine's sugar content is reduced to the particular degree desired by the producer—at which point all further fermentation is arrested by the addition of brandy or grape alcohol. The result is a wine with an alcoholic content ranging from 18 to 23 per cent, and 8 or 10 degrees sugar. White Port, actually preferred by the Portuguese themselves, is made of white grapes, and the best of it is drier as a result of having been allowed to ferment to nature's full limit (roughly 15 per cent alcohol) before the brandy is added. This is one reason why White Ports make such excellent *apéritifs.*

White Ports are never blended in the winehouses of Vila Nova de Gaia, but are always a product of their own "pipe." In this sense they are much like the type known as Vintage Port—the most highly prized abroad, especially in England. Vintage Port, though it may be a blend, is always one of a single year, a year that the shippers' organization at Vila Nova have decided on as outstanding. As opposed to other types—"Ports from the wood," which mature in the cask and are ready to drink when bottled— Vintage Port only remains in the casks for two years, and grows up in bottles. This is a slow process: many a Vintage Port does not come into its own until it has rested in the bottle for forty years or more.

Port is classified by its producers into six general categories:

Full, Red, Ruby, Light, Tawny and White—although labels now rarely carry more than a brand name or some company's special promotional invention accompanied by one of the three classifications of *Ruby*, *Tawny* or *White*. Of these the first, Ruby Port, is a deep, rich color—as its name implies—a blend of new and old wines that may be consumed relatively young, say at the age of ten. Tawny Port, more expensive, is lighter, with a brownish tinge, and has simply received more blending and more age than Ruby (although some inferior Tawnys, called "short cuts" in the trade, are made from a blend of red and white wines). Like Sherry, Port is usually at its best when slightly chilled, and since its aroma is definitely an integral part of its charm, it should never be served in a small glass—but instead, in one which is large enough to allow sufficient evaporation. Very old Ports, especially Vintage Ports, cast a heavy sediment, a "crust," and should in all cases be decanted.

SHERRY

The name Sherry is an Anglicization of Jerez de la Frontera, the Andalusian town that is the epicenter of Sherry making, in the province of Cádiz in the southeastern corner of Spain. Like Port, Sherry is more often spoken of as a British drink than a Spanish one.

Although Sherry is made principally from two sweet white-wine grapes, the Palomino and the Pedro Ximénez (thought by some to be a cousin of the Riesling), and is a *vino generoso*, even its sweetest version is definitely not a dessert wine. In fact, until the last century the English name for Sherry as we now know it was Sack or Sherris-Sack, terms deriving from *wyne sec* or *seck*, meaning dry. The history of Sherry as a fortified wine closely parallels that of Port. The wines of Cádiz were introduced into England as early as the twelfth century, probably by returning Crusaders, at the time when Jerez de la Frontera—as well as most of southern Spain and Portugal—was under Moorish domination. It was not until comparatively recently that it became a fortified wine. As with Port, it was the proclivity of the Dutch and the British for wine strong in alcohol that established the type.

Sherry is raised under almost ideal climatic conditions for growing wine grapes. On the Cádiz peninsula, rains abound in winter, and the spring and summer are extremely hot and dry. The calciferous soil on which the Sherry grapes thrive—almost as dazzlingly white as the whitewashed seaport city of Cádiz itself—is too poor for anything else. If one digs a well among the inland vineyards, one comes across roots of the vines that have probed thirty feet or more through lime and rock in their search for moisture. Yet the Cádiz peninsula is a beautiful part of the world: apart from the vineyards, and principally near the coast, olives and chestnuts and oaks, grains and citrus fruits and even cotton and sugar cane all flourish.

The making of Sherry differs from that of Port in two distinct ways. The first is the utilization of what is called the *flor* yeast, a bacteria presumably native to Jerez (although it is successfully cultured elsewhere) that gluts itself on both oxygen and alcohol and, as it grows, spreads a thick, protective crust or white film over the aging wine. *Flor* means flower in Spanish, but the resemblance is slight; in actuality the sight of the *flor* crust floating on top of the wine is all but repulsive. Its useful purposes with Sherry are to shut out harmful bacteria, and to give the wine the individualistic "nutty" flavor and aroma that differentiates it from other fortified wines.

The other unique factor in Sherry making is the blending process known as the *solera* system. Sherry is always a blend, and the *solera* system entails rows or tiers of casks, sometimes five or six lines of them arranged above each other, through which the wine passes slowly from the top tier to the bottom one in the course of its aging. Each year new wine is put into the top of the system from the "*solera* school"—and, in the best tradition of Sherry making, it may require nine years before it graduates, mixed little by little with more mature wines. Thus fine Sherries that bear dates on their labels should never be thought to derive entirely from that year. A year on a Sherry label means the year the oldest cask of the *solera* was put down—and it might be added that if any one

Sherry were left in its cask for fifty years or so, unblended with new wines, it would be totally undrinkable, even with the benefit of fortification. Unlike Port, which is fortified at the finish of its fermentation, Sherry acquires its brandy at the end of the *solera* process. At this time it is also colored with evaporated grape juice, and sweetened. More sugar goes into Sherry intended for export than for that made for home consumption, since most Spaniards prefer their Sherry absolutely bone dry.

The best Sherries, as we have said, are dry, and for this reason useful as *apéritifs*. They are generally classified as Fino, which is moderately dry and rarely acid. the *ordinaire* of the field; Manzanilla (also the Spanish name for Camomile tea) which—although not technically a Sherry—is made in the same district on sandy seaside soil and is likewise dry, though apt to be somewhat bitter; Amontillado (mountain Sherry), which reaches an even more desirable degree of dryness, with a top alcoholic content of 24 per cent; and Oloroso (perfume), which has the greatest body and the deepest color, and is always relatively sweet. Nearly all other names on Sherry labels are individual brand names or manufacturers' terms, except for Montilla, a wine from the inland city of Cordoba, often confused with Sherry. Montilla is a totally unfortified wine, slightly lighter than Sherry. Sold in tall bottles the shape of German Rhine wine bottles, at its best it is dry and elegant, and not too alcoholic. Among the more frequently seen brand names of Sherry are Cream Sherry and Brown Sherry. Both are basically Oloroso Sherry—sweetened and colored accordingly. Table Q lists the brands and manufacturers which are particularly recommended.

FINO	
Brand	*Manufacturer*
La Ina	Domecq
San Patricio	Garvey
Tio Pepe ("Uncle Joe")	Gonzalez Byass

MANZANILLA	
Prodigio	Domecq
Villamarta	Rivero

AMONTILLADO	
Amontillado	Duff Gordon
Amontillado Botaniz	Domecq
Amontillado Vina AB	Gonzalez Byass

OLOROSO	
Anniversary	Duff Gordon
La Raza	Domecq
(and any others by Domecq or Gonzalez Byass)	

MONTILLA	
Flor de Montilla	Carbonell

MADEIRA, MALAGA AND MARSALA

Whereas Port is a simple fortified wine, aged and blended in an almost elementary way, and Sherry is to be distinguished from it by the use of the *flor* yeast and the *solera* system of blending the oldest wines with the newest, Madeira is characterized by what is called the *estufado* method, a treatment which amounts, literally, to cooking the wine during the aging process.

The volcanic island of Maderia, which lies six hundred miles southwest of Lisbon off the African coast and is administered as part of continental Portugal, was first discovered by Portuguese fisherman early in the fifteenth century. Breathtakingly beautiful, extremely mountainous, ribbed with deep ravines and valleys, at the time of its discovery it was entirely covered by dense forests. Almost the first act of its colonizers was to burn them off—the fires lasted seven years!—and plant great sections of the island to vines. The soil of Madeira was well suited to the wine grape; the island has a hot growing season and plentiful rainfall twice a year, in October and March; it was not long before Madeira became known as one of the principal vineyard areas of Europe. Its trade in that day—once again—was in table wine. Madeira wines were not fortified until nearly three hundred years later.

The individualistically bitter and peculiar burnt taste that Madeira has today—contrasted with the sharp, "nutty" flavor of Sherry and the candid fullness or "winyness" of Port—is attributable to the special treatment it receives while aging in the cask. There is no reason to believe that Madeira, as originally fortified, tasted like this at all. After it became the practice to fortify the wine, it was found that Madeira (supposed to be the only wine that will live indefinitely in the bottle) was tremendously improved by long voyages. To the amazement of nearly everyone, when subjected to severe climatic changes, to the hot, putrid holds and constant rolling motion of ships, it became an entirely different (and far better) wine. A voyage between continents vastly improved it; a voyage around the world doubled—or sometimes trebled—its monetary value. Traveled Madeira, or *vinho do roda* (wine of the road), as it came to be called, gained such favoritism among connoisseurs that its producers set out purposely to devise a process to duplicate the effects of a long sea voyage. This is the origin of the *estufado* method used today, in which the casks of aging fortified wine are either left in the hot sun to bake or else stored, sometimes for as long as six months, in heated rooms with temperatures as high as 140 degrees Fahrenheit.

Madeira was once enormously popular in England, as well as in the United States in the early days of our history. But this vogue has greatly fallen off in recent years, and Madeira today, despite the promotional efforts of the Portuguese, only retains a really profitable market in Scandinavian countries. This decline may be attributed to several factors, one of which dates back to the middle of the last century, when these island vineyards were first heavily

204 The World of Wines

attacked by the mildew disease known as *oidium*, and then hit harder yet, some twenty years later, by the *phylloxera*. Thus, for many years good Madeira was almost unavailable—and the vacuum (or habit) was filled by other fortified wines. Another factor, of course, is the world-wide flagging taste for fortified dessert wines and *apéritifs*.

As with Ports, most of the best shippers of Madeira are of British origin, and such names as Blandy, Leacock, Cossart and Gordon are entirely typical on labels. With a few exceptions, such as "Rainwater Madeira," the wines take their nomenclature from grapes, of which there are four chief varieties, three red and one white: Sercial Madeira is dry and tangy; Bual (sometimes seen as Boal) is rich and fruity, perhaps the closest of all to a Red Port; Verdelho, from a white grape, is medium dry, with a pronounced tang; Malvasia (Malmsey) is rich and luscious, and considered the finest. "Rainwater Madeira" is something else again. Lighter both in color and texture than the average Madeira, it purportedly gained its name in the days when the wine was so universally popular in Colonial America. It is said that a certain Savannah importer, knowing that Madeira is always improved by extremes of heat and cold, stored his casks or "pipes" under the eaves. The tapped casks were drawn off by a pipe leading down to his shop—the wine always slyly referred to as "rainwater." The term was later adopted by the Madeira producers themselves for one of their lighter and drier products.

It is unfortunate that Madeiras, especially the dry ones (which show themselves to best advantage when slightly chilled), are now largely thought of in most civilized countries simply as "the best cooking wines." More true than false—they are excellent for this purpose. But their uses as *apéritifs* to wine drinkers should not be overlooked.

Two other European fortified wines, less well known, are Spanish Málaga and Sicilian Marsala. The former is made principally from Muscatel and Pedro Ximénez (Sherry) grapes, and comes from around the port of Málaga on Spain's southern coast. A dark-colored wine made from raisined grapes, with a taste faintly reminiscent of molasses, it has an unusually strong bouquet, and is the favorite sweet *vino generoso* of the Spanish nation. Likewise Marsala is the Italian's most desirable *vino di lusso*. Dark and usually very sweet (it is sweetened with cooked-down essence of grape juice mixed with alcohol), it is mainly used away from home as the perfect ingredient for veal scaloppini. One of the best producers exporting Marsala is the firm of Florio.

None of these European fortified wines, with the possible exception of Sherry, are ever really duplicated or equaled by their imitators in other lands. It is true that certain brands of South African and Australian Sherry have gained favor among adherents of the wines from Jerez—but this is perhaps the sole exception. California and New York State Sherry, when fabricated by a few vintners using the *flor* yeast and an abbreviated version of the *solera* system, is sometimes a good approximation—and a good drink. But most American Sherry is *cooked* like Madeira and *called* Sherry. Nor could anything be more of a double-barrelled misnomer than "California Solera Port." Most domestic Port is simply sweetened and fortified wine that is released to the consumer in its most youthful state—a concoction which has usually been fermented from grapes never heard of on the precipitous slopes or sizzling terraces of the Douro, much less benefited by even an approximation of the loving and prolonged care afforded genuine Port in the great winehouses of Vila Nova de Gaia. We repeat: as with all imitations—good, innocuous or simply bad—they would all stand up better under other labels. We are not agitating against them. Just let us not have anyone ask us, with a straight face, "Will you have a Sherry?"

SUMMARY

Fortified wines—table wines that have had brandy or alcohol added to bring their content to between 18 and 24 per cent—are useful both as dessert wines and as *apéritifs* before a meal with wine. Of the latter, the best are dry White Port (excellent on the rocks), Sherry and dry Madeira. To date, the finest White Port made for *apéritif* purposes is Cockburn's Dry Tang Apéritif.

Dessert Ports (reds) are generally called Ruby (quite sweet), and Tawny (less sweet). The most expensive Ports are Vintage Ports, which require many years in the bottle.

Traditionally, the best Sherries are the driest. One labeled Oloroso will probably be the sweetest available. Dry ones are Fino, Manzanilla, Montilla (actually an unfortified wine made by the Sherry process) and Amontillado. Some of the best manufacturers are: Domecq, Duff Gordon, Garvey and Gonzalez Byass. Sherries are always blends. A date on a label will simply indicate the age of the oldest Sherry in the blend—it may be only a few drops.

Madeiras are both dry and sweet, but never as sweet as Red Port. Of the four principal types, named after grapes, Sercial and Verdelho are dry, Bual (Boal) and Malvasia (Malmsey) are sweet. "Rainwater Madeira," a brand name, is light and medium dry.

Most American Sherries are only approximations of imported ones; domestic Ports are usually simply sweetened and fortified raw wines, lamentably lacking in age.

All fortified wines are better when slightly chilled and served in generous-sized glasses, to allow their bouquets to assert themselves.

TEN

Brandies

FINE CHAMPAGNE, *COGNAC AND ARMAGNAC*

Brandies, properly speaking, are spirits distilled from wine—and the two best are French. The first and finest are known generically as Cognacs; and the superlatives of these are called, somewhat confusingly, *Champagnes*. The Cognac district, which surrounds the little town of the same name, is to be found northeast of Bordeaux, close by the ancient fortress port of La Rochelle. At its very epicenter are two little areas known as Grande Champagne and Petite Champagne. When Cognacs from these two areas are blended—the ideal blend—they are entitled to the name *Grande Fine Champagne,*[1] the highest appellation of all. Progressing farther afield, as it is produced on poorer and poorer soil, the liquor is known as Cognac, Borderies, Fins Bois and Bons Bois, in that order. All these latter are usually simply called Cognac.

The white wines of the Cognac district are actually so mediocre that they are all but undrinkable. Curiously enough, this appears to have been anything but the case four hundred years ago, when white wines from the Charentais (as that part of France is called)

---

[1] Usually abbreviated and referred to as *Fine Champagne*. In a French café one simply asks for a *"Fine."*

were in great demand both in England and Holland. No one seems to know exactly what happened to this prosperous trade. One often accepted version, incongruous as it sounds, is that certain canny French vintners, seeking to save on transportation costs, concluded that "condensed" wines—that is, distilled—could be shipped abroad more economically, watered upon arrival, and neither the Dutch nor the English would know the difference. Another more plausible explanation is that each farmhouse of the Charentais of that day had its own little illicit still, the products of which eventually reached various ports on the coast and became understandably popular with sailors from visiting ships. The production of brandy thus turned out to be more profitable than wine. Whatever the explanation, brandy—known originally in France as *vin brûlé* (burnt wine)—in its unwatered state was avidly taken up first in Holland and then in England, and replaced Charentais table wines. The Dutch called it *brandewijn* (again meaning burnt wine); the British translated this to brandywine, and later simply to brandy.

The best evidence that Cognac originated as a product of small farms of the Charentais is the crude machinery by which brandy is distilled throughout this part of France. To this day even the best firms use primitive, copper "pot stills," of a design appreciably unchanged from five or six centuries ago. The wine is first fermented in the usual way, the two principal grapes being the St.-Emilion (no connection with the Bordeaux wine region) or Ugni blanc, and the Folle blanche (a grape we have already met in California). After several months in casks it is then subjected to two progressive distillations, the final result being a totally colorless and almost tasteless liquor with an alcoholic content of approximately 75 per cent. This liquor is then stored in casks wrought from charred oak of the nearby forests of Limousin and, depending upon the desired quality, aged from three to twenty-five years. The best unblended and undoctored Cognacs derive their color and flavor from the cask; and it is well to know that, after bottling, Cognac ceases to improve. This is a fact that pulls the props out from beneath the "Brandy of Napoleon," which—were it even to exist nowadays—would not be any better than the day it was bottled. "Napoleon Brandy" ranks high among some of the more transparent promotional myths of the industry.

True richness, mellowness and color come to all brandies only with many years in the cask, but because of a demand far exceeding the supply of good Cognacs and *Champagnes*, even the best firms blend and dilute with water, and color and sweeten the mixture with caramel—to cut the rawness and instill the proper "aged" hue and flavor. Thus the stars or symbols on a bottle of brandy, supposedly indicating age, may mean far less than one would think. One star is supposed to indicate that the Cognac has spent three years in the cask; each additional star theoretically means an added year—but a clever blending of spirits from several years, plus the requisite amount of caramel, can do wonders for a relatively newborn product. For the *Champagnes* (one should always remember that *Grande Fine Champagne* is the best) the producers have yet another series of symbolisms: *V.O.* (Very Old) stands for ten years or more in the cask; *V.S.O.* (Very Superior Old) for fifteen; *E.* (for Extra) is usually entirely superfluous. The highest appellation, *V.S.O.P.* (*P.* for Pale) is something else again. It *may* mean a liquor which is a better blend—and it may not.

It is not without significance that all these letter symbols—especially *P.* for Pale—stand for English words instead of French ones. Obviously, at some time in the annals of Cognacs, the producers of the Charentais, in too much of a hurry to age their products long enough in the cask to give them the traditional color and softness, must have sold someone on the idea that raw, pale brandy was the best! Genuine, well-aged *Grande Fine Champagne*, dark in color, strong-flavored and aromatic, is only suited to sipping and sniffing in small quantities. In fact, it is all but repulsive when diluted with water or soda—which is not the case with a brandy that is light and young, however raw. No wonder, then, that the Englishman came to drink his Very Superior Old Pale—which if taken straight would have removed the lining of his stomach with its rawness—with soda.

The other celebrated brandy of France, made in the *département* of the Gers in the Pyrénées, is Armagnac. This also is a twice-distilled liquid, from native Picpoul and Jurançon grapes, made in exactly the same way as Cognac—except that most Armagnac is still the direct product of small farms, bought and blended by the firms that bottle it after aging. By virtue of the loving care which

Armagnac receives from its individual rural producers, together with the fact that the demand has never exceeded the supply—the name is not as widely known throughout the world as that of Cognac, and few are imported to the United States—one will usually find it of excellent quality, and relatively inexpensive. After a long life in the cask, a fine Armagnac will have a deliciously individualistic, fruity bouquet—reminiscent of prunes. Armagnac, incidentally, is never selected by taste—but by smell. In the cafés of its home ground, the Béarn, it is not unusual to see the farmer sitting with his little flask over a coffee with the buyer, shaking out a few drops on the latter's palm, to be rubbed around, sniffed, assessed and bargained for.

Although a year on the label of a bottle of *Fine Champagne* Cognac or Armagnac may frequently be seen—as with *Solera* Sherry—it usually indicates the year of the oldest few drops in the blend. Certain small producers in the Cognac district do continue to turn out unblended and undoctored *Grande* or *Petite* (or *Fine*) *Champagnes* of certain years, known as *Naturs*. Brandy produced in this fashion is almost prohibitively expensive—and to the average brandy drinker, accustomed to the tastes and flavors of the standard, doctored blends, the *Naturs* may well be disappointing. Aging without any interference or treatment, except for the final addition of a certain amount of water to reduce its strength, results in a liquor that is unusually dry and sharp, and though appreciated by connoisseurs, is definitely an acquired taste.

OTHER BRANDIES

The reader should beware of anything simply marked *French Brandy*,[2] and try an import from some other country instead. Brandies from wine are made in almost every other wine-producing country in the world—and though they vary enormously, many of them are good. Both Portugal and Spain manufacture con-

[2] The terms Cognac, (*Grande*) *Fine Champagne* or Armagnac should at least appear on the label; without them, the liquor will be of no intrinsic value.

siderable amounts of brandy, much of which is used to fortify
Port, Sherry and Madiera. Spanish brandy in particular has many
enthusiasts, acquired during the last war, when French brandy
was unavailable. Unfortunately, the Spanish conception of the
term "brandy" is a rather loose one: it may simply mean a highly
fortified wine! Thus the reader is advised to stick religiously to
the best. These latter are almost invariably produced by the most
reputable Sherry houses: Carlos III (by Domecq), Carabella Santa
Maria (by Osborne) and Insuperable (by Gonzalez Byass) are
three of the best. Perhaps the most popular Spanish brandy is
Fundador, though its quality leaves much to be desired. Fundador's
Portuguese equivalent is known as Constantino. Italian brandy, the
two most popular of which are called Stock and Sarti, is by comparison mediocre. California makes far more "brandy" than France
—liquor which, were it ever properly aged, might well be redeemed.
Unfortunately, this never seems to happen, and most California
products are young, strong and harsh in taste, and give the im-
pression of being overpoweringly alcoholic. California producers
seem to pride themselves on this "purity."

In many countries of Europe a bastard type of brandy is distilled
from the *marc* or leftover "must" of the grapes, watered and re-
fermented after the juice for the wine has been pressed out. Known
specifically in France as *eaux-de-vie* (waters of life!),[3] it is coarse
and medicinal tasting at best, though a common drink with peasants
and low-income groups for the simple purpose of inducing a quick
state of intoxication—as a nocturnal stroll around any French port
will speedily bear out! Calvados, a French "brandy" made from
cider, can be delicious with sufficient age, carrying a delightful,
haunting aroma of apples. Other excellent European fruit brandies
include those made from cherries (Kirsch), from wild raspberries
(Framboise), from strawberries (Fraise)—not to mention France's
Prunelle and Poland's Slivovitz, distilled from fermented plums to
produce firewater with the power of an atomic submarine.

---

[3] Also often called *marc* in France, in Germany it is *Trestebranntwein* or
Trinkbranntwein, in Italy *grappa*. The Spanish equivalent is called *aguardiente*
(burning water), the Portuguese equivalent *agurdente*.

SUMMARY

The best brandies—distilled wines—are French Cognacs, the superlative of which is called *Grande Fine Champagne*. Almost all brandies are blends, and one should not be shocked to learn that even the best are generally doctored with caramel to give the color, richness and flavor that the public demands. A year on a French brandy label usually means nothing—unless it be a pure unblended product also labeled *Natur* (or "single cask")—a liquor which will be expensive and probably disappointing to those who are used to sweetened and otherwise doctored blends.

Brandy improves only in an oaken cask, never in the bottle; anything named "Napoleon Brandy," implying great age, is a hoax.

The second finest brandy of France, less well known, is called Armagnac, from the Pyrénées.

One should be wary of something simply labeled *French Brandy*. Imports from other countries—notably Spain, Portugal, Italy—are better. California "brandy" rarely receives proper aging. It has a taste and strength of flavor all of its own.

ELEVEN

The Service of Wines

SERVING WINES

Serving wine presents so many perplexing problems to so many people that it unfortunately often precludes the use of wine at all. Many of these perplexities may be solved by following a simple rule: given the facilities at hand, do the best you can. Wine is, after all, primarily for enjoyment—only secondarily is it for show.

The matter of glasses for wine is as good a case in point as any. One of the pleasantest things about wine is its bouquet—the sensation one receives as the glass is being brought to the lips. The sense of smell, with all of us, is very closely allied to taste. Thus the larger the glass (within obvious limits), the more ample the exposed surface of wine for evaporation and the more bouquet. One often hears that wine should be "allowed to breathe." Of equal importance is the reverse: the wine drinker should be allowed to breathe the wine! Hence wine is logically at better advantage when served in a tumbler than in a thimble. In Burgundy, for example, where great stress is laid on the bouquet of a wine, the traditional glass is the size of a small finger bowl.

If one does not own the exactly appropriate wineglasses, one will certainly have tumblers or water goblets. Their size will at least provide the surface for adequate evaporation. Save the decorous little long-stemmed glass thimbles someone gave you for a wedding present; they may make the dinner table pretty, but their true function is for *apéritifs* or after-dinner liqueurs. No wine will ever really be enjoyable in them; many a wine will not even taste like itself.

Eventually everyone who becomes fond of wine wishes to serve it at its best advantage. This does not involve expensive glasses. There are excellent, moderately priced glasses to be had which will cover all contingencies. The ideal all-purpose wineglass—suitable for any still or sparkling wine, or even brandy—is tulip-shaped, made of clear glass, and between five and six inches high. The length of the stem is immaterial (though this has its practical breakage problems in the washing of it), and can be left to one's own personal esthetic taste. But the glass itself should be wide-brimmed (two inches or more across) and large enough so that, if filled to the brim, it would hold at least six or seven ounces, preferably more. In Alsace and Germany, where the wines often approach the paleness of water, the traditional glasses are elaborately decorated. But the all-purpose wineglass should be of clear glass, so that along with the bouquet and the taste, one may have the added enjoyment of the wine's color. The tints and hues of wines are pretty.

The corollary to the rule of making the best of what's available is that no wineglass—whether it be the perfect one, the water globlet, or the thimble—should ever be filled much more than half full. Many people who do not understand the reason for this take it to be an affectation—or lay it to miserliness on the part of the host. But the custom has a very practical basis. The basic principle is that the unfilled top half of the glass channels and concentrates the wine's bouquet to the nose—whereas with a glass filled to the brim the bouquet obviously floats off in all directions and most of it is lost. This is why the tulip-shaped glass has become the traditional best: very much as with the flue rising from a fireplace, its inward-sloping brim concentrates the evaporating ethers, and the bouquet rises from it in a single invisible column.

There may be occasions when one will wish to serve two or more wines at the same meal—and here there are certain pertinent conventions which, if known, may save embarrassment or needless expense. If one perchance owns glasses of different sizes and is

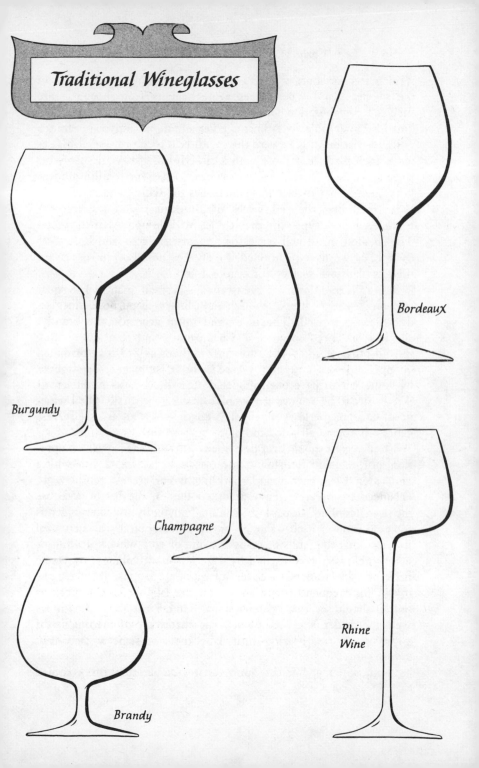

Traditional Wineglasses

Bordeaux

Burgundy

Champagne

Rhine
Wine

Brandy

serving two or more wines, a white wine is more appropriate in the smaller glass—whereas red wine benefits from having more surface for evaporation. Different glasses are certainly not necessary, but the dinner table always has a gayer and more festive appearance with a variation of glassware than with two or more similar glasses set at each place. For those with a closetful of glassware, use your largest, widest-brimmed, balloon-shaped glasses for red Burgundies, your slightly narrower and smaller ones for white wines and other reds (including the red wines of Bordeaux) and the longest-stemmed goblet types for the Rhine, Moselle and Alsatian wines. The smallest of all will serve for liqueurs, Sherries and Ports—although, as we have mentioned, fortified wines also are best when there is plenty of surface for evaporation.

Brandy is traditionally served (always in small quantity) in squat balloon-shaped "snifters," though an ordinary all-purpose wineglass does nearly as well. The older and more aromatic the brandy, the less one need serve. For Champagnes and sparkling wines, the all-purpose glass also does as well as any. Broad-brimmed "coupe" glasses customarily used for Champagnes—attributed by some wit to have been modeled after the breasts of Helen of Troy—are to be avoided if possible. As with the totally filled wineglass, Champagne loses much of is charm—as well as its effervescence—by being afforded too much surface for evaporation.

No *wineglass* should ever be chilled—this inhibits proper evaporation; nor, incidentally, should any glass ever be heated. But whites and *rosés*, Champagnes and sparkling wines are all considerably enhanced by a certain amount of cooling in the bottle. We use the term "cooling" instead of "chilling" advisedly. A wine which is too cold is never itself—though in this connection it may be useful to know that the faults of many a white or *rosé* wine, sparkling or otherwise, may be concealed by a good sound chilling (a favorite trick of wine waiters to cover up a poor vintage). By the same token, the frequently seen advice on the labels of a producer or bottler should serve as a danger signal. Unless it is a wine he knows well, the reader is advised to be somewhat wary of the quality of any white or *rosé* bearing on its label the words: *Serve very well chilled.*

Opinions vary, but the approximate temperature for a cooled

wine is in general between 40 and 45 degrees. This may be achieved in several ways: by putting the wine in a bucket of ice and water—or even better yet, snow and water—for half an hour or so; or in the refrigerator for about two hours; or in the freezing compartment for approximately half an hour. One should remember that any wine, once it has been overcooled or chilled, never really regains its original power and charm. Such is especially the case with wine that has been frozen—one of the main worries of importers who are oftentimes forced to bring wines across the Atlantic in winter.

With a few minor exceptions (Beaujolais is the principal one), red wine should be warm—but not *warmed* or heated. If it is practical to do so, the red wine one intends to drink should be allowed to remain for at least two hours in the room in which it will be consumed. But it should neither be left next to the stove, warmed with hot water nor put before an open fire! Wine brought suddenly to room temperature loses much of its vigor—as does wine served at a temperature appreciably higher than room temperature. Under ideal conditions, the wine should actually be a little cooler than the room itself. This may perhaps be accomplished by leaving it in the coolest part of the room—on the floor, say, away from heating units.

Should wine be opened ahead of time? All red wines are improved by having been opened an hour or so before the meal and allowed to breathe. This, of course, is never done in restaurants—unless one orders it so beforehand—and is often overlooked in the home. In our opinion, the practice is by no means as important as it is made out to be. Many lovers of wine, especially those who enjoy lingering over their glasses, experience much pleasure in all the different and intriguing stages of warming and aeration which wine poured directly from the newly opened bottle undergoes in the glass. The cardinal exception is a very old wine—for which more aeration is usually necessary than for a younger one. White wines should never be opened until just before serving.

Well-made red wines—especially aged ones—often throw a sediment, which is unpleasant if mixed with the contents of the bottle. Obviously, if one has bought a bottle at the corner liquor store and brought it home to drink that evening, there is nothing much to be done about it. But ideally, one should have bought it a few days, or preferably a week or so, ahead of drinking, to let the wine rest, with the bottle standing upright to allow the sediment to collect at the bottom. Just before drinking, one may—if one wishes—ease the bottle gently onto its side and lay it in a wine basket. The important point is not to joggle the wine any more than possible in pouring—whether it be in an upright position or in a basket. Or else one may decant it, a recommended practice for very old wine containing a great deal of sediment. The conventional way to decant is to pour the wine slowly, several hours before serving, into another receptacle—preferably a glass decanter—with a bright light or a candle behind the neck of the bottle. The decanting is stopped when the first sign of dregs appears. A simple glass decanter is always a useful accessory to any wine-drinking household.

This leads us to the by-no-means unimportant matter of corkscrews and uncorking. If one has gone to all the trouble to allow the dregs of the red wine to settle, obviously a battle between the bottle and the wine drinker using an inefficient corkscrew will negate all one's previous good intentions. Happily, the best corkscrews are both the simplest and the cheapest: those which resemble a fat pocketknife, with a small curved blade that folds into one end and a corkscrew into the other. Most liquor dealers or wine merchants will present you with one of these with their compliments. With the knife take away the foil around the neck of the bottle, and thoroughly wipe (or even wash) the exposed surface of the cork and the neck of the bottle. The corkscrew is then inserted directly down the middle of the cork—as far as possible without losing leverage. Most corks break not as a result of being faulty, but because the corkscrew has not penetrated deeply enough. Pull gently and evenly—and firmly.

One should remember that just because a cork breaks, or part of it appears to be rotten, it does not follow that the wine is spoiled. An almost invariable rule of thumb for knowing if a wine has been "corked," or spoiled, is to smell the wet end of the cork: if it smells of clean wine, the bottle probably is good. On the other hand, if it smells of musty cork, there are grounds for investigation of the wine itself.

Champagne and sparkling wines should never be opened with a corkscrew. After removing the wire and the foil, hold the bottle a little on its side (in your right hand), grasp the cork in your left hand and twist the bottle itself—*not* the cork. Use a towel or a cloth for a better grip, and for your own protection in case the bottle contains a flaw and should explode. As the bottle is thus twisted, ease the cork out gently. Well-cooled Champagne will open with a discreet pop and a faint whiff of blue smoke; but, if one *must* open a bottle of insufficiently cooled or warm Champagne, it is a part of wisdom not to aim the cork at a guest's eye—and one should count on a considerable wastage. Champagnes, and even wines, are sometimes served encased in a towel. This is, at best, an affectation; as well as an insult to one's guests, who deserve the courtesy of inspecting the label.

Although it is traditional for the host to pour—or to have poured —a small amount of wine into his own glass, this can often turn out to be an awkward and embarrassing practice. In which case it should be skipped—with the wine simply passing around the table from place to place. The reason for this custom, of course, is to ensure that the host's glass will receive any little fragments of cork floating in the bottle; also so that he may taste the wine and reject it, if necessary, before it is served to his guests. A far more gracious procedure, we think, is one by which the host tastes the wine when it is opened, away from his guests.

Purists shudder at the thought—but an opened bottle of any wine *may* be kept over for another meal or until the next day. White and *rosé* wine should be stored in the refrigerator, red wine in a cool place—both tightly corked. It should not be forgotten, however, that wine is a living thing, containing a minuscule number of residual live yeasts, and always prey to the vinegar-making bacteria. It will never keep longer than unpasteurized milk. Many white wines—especially the older and sweeter ones—also stand a chance of becoming *maderizé* (turning the color of Sherry and developing a bitter taste) when kept over; occasionally one even runs across a bottle of white wine that becomes *maderizé* within a few minutes after being opened. Should it be a wine you particularly like, remember to open the next bottle at the very last minute, and to consume it without delay. One's wine merchant should be informed of any such development, so that he may warn his other customers.

Finally, although the average person today will only want to serve one wine with a meal, there do exist certain customs having to do with sequences in serving wines—something that often has bearing on the menu one plans for a meal. In the ensuing pages the reader will find certain suggestions as to what wines go best with certain foods; but leaving aside, for the moment, the matter of appropriate fare, the following are the two traditional rules covering the serving of more than one wine at a meal. The first, best summarized as "youth before beauty," is that a less distinguished wine—meaning a lighter or a younger one, or one with a less pronounced taste, bouquet or body—precedes an older or heavier or stronger one. In this way one avoids what may turn out to be a disappointing anticlimax. The second rule is that a white wine almost always asserts its character and charm better when served before a red. The principal exception would be a sweet white wine, such as a Sauternes or a *Beerenauslese*—which are nearly always better suited to desserts, fruits and coffee.

WINES WITH FOODS

There are no inalterable rules about foods with wines, but there are many highways and byways to guide the reader toward a more complete enjoyment of wine with meals. Of one thing the wine drinker may be entirely certain: "hard liquors" never really mix with wine. Cocktails and strong alcoholic liquors served before a meal with wine tend to destroy one's taste for (and appreciation of) the wine—and this applies particularly to cocktails or drinks laden with sugar or fruit juices, such as an Old-Fashioned or a rum cocktail. A Dry Martini, on the other hand (in essence, a highly fortified Vermouth), is for some people less burdening to the palate. Others can get away with a whiskey, usually a Bourbon. But the ideal is dry Sherry or dry White Port, or a Vermouth or, if one can afford it, a glass of Champagne. This is not to say that there is anything criminal in having a strong drink before a meal with wine: only a warning that good wine will not bloom after hard liquor, and that it is therefore foolhardy to serve an expensive or choice wine at a meal which has been preceded by cocktails. Better to serve a modest Beaujolais or a humble *rosé*, and leave the Chambertin for another time.

Certain foods, too, definitely cloud the vision of a wine's beauty. These are principally overseasoned or spicy dishes, using curry, horseradish, mint, chutney, cloves—and even garlic. A Chablis or a Pouilly-Fuissé, or a dry German Riesling are notably excellent companions for oysters, clams and many other seafoods—but if one insists on Worcestershire, Tobasco or a strong cocktail sauce with seafood, it will be expedient to skip the wine with that course. Another incompatible with wine is vinegar and all foods which contain it, such as pickles. One may successfully substitute lemon juice for the vinegar in salad dressing—but pickled foods are an insurmountable problem. Not only do they contain vinegar, but also sugar, again an enemy of wine—and, as one will soon discover, only sweet dessert wines ever seem to go well with sweet or sugared dishes. A Sauternes or a *Beerenauslese* enhance ice cream and sherbet, puddings and sweet *soufflés;* but a red Bordeaux, a Chianti *Classico* or a Californian Pinot Noir have the opposite effect. Perhaps the chief exception is that sweet wines are oftentimes the most suitable for Chinese and Polynesian cookery.

The best friend at the table of all wines is cheese—delicious with red, white, *rosé*, dry or sweet—though we think the wine drinker will eventually discover that the stronger the cheese, the redder and heavier he will want the wine. For very strong cheeses, one of the fortified wines (Port, Maderia or Marsala) is probably the best accompaniment. Many people overlook the natural affinity that wines of one nation have with that nation's habitual foods. Italian dishes, for example, so often enhanced by strong tomato and meat sauces, cheeses and herbs, are gastronomic bedfellows of those relatively coarse and rough wines, particularly the reds, of that country—whereas a delicate French *Médoc* is hopelessly lost in their company. By the same token, an Italian Soave or a Riesling from California taste bland and inadequate with a rich, complicated French sauce; a Swiss cheese fondue attains true glory only when washed down by a Neuchâtel, a Fendant or a Dézaley. When serving dishes of a distinctly nationalistic character, the wine drinker will do well to keep this principle in mind.

There is, of course, the age-old saying that white wine is for white meat, red wine for red meat—"St.-Émilion with fur, Médoc with feathers!" is yet another classic gastronomic adage. These are all very well as general guides—yet there are many notable exceptions, including several classic French fish dishes with red-wine sauces, and some celebrated Germanic creations of venison or beef embellished with Riesling. White, red (St.-Émilion *or* Médoc) or *rosé* wine go well with any white-meat dish—whether it be chicken (feathers) or veal or rabbit (fur). Red wine is, of course, better with beef. Yet pork (a borderline white meat) and ham never seem to lend themselves to any still wine of any color. As an accompaniment to baked or broiled ham, most people settle for a sparkling white or a Champagne, or skip the wine entirely. Champagne and *rosé* wines, in the last analysis, are always common denominators: even though they do not blend ideally with all foods, they are rarely offensive or out of place, and one may be sure that they will at least taste like wine.

SUMMARY

Wine is primarily for enjoyment—only secondarily for show: just because one does not have the perfect glassware and the know-how of a connoisseur is no reason for not serving it. There are certain simple rules to heed: wine profits by evaporation in the glass, thus it is better served in a tumbler or a water goblet than in a thimble. It is not necessary to purchase a different type of wine-glass for every different type of wine. All-purpose wineglasses—suitable for red, white, *rosé* and sparkling wines—are not expensive. They should be tulip-shaped, at least two inches wide and hold six or seven ounces or more.

In serving wine, the glass should never be much more than half filled. This concentrates the bouquet.

If one serves two or more wines, a white is more effective if served before a red; similarly, a young or "lesser" wine before an older and "greater" one. White and *rosé* wines should be cooled (but not heavily "chilled"); red wine, except for Beaujolais, is best at slightly below room temperature.

The maxim that red wine goes with red meat, white wine with white meat is a sound rule—but not infallible. Chicken tastes well with both; pork and ham are best with a sparkling white. *Rosé* wines or Champagnes are often the most practical, harmonizing with almost any dish.

Beware of eating highly seasoned food with wines; overdoses of pepper, curry, pickles and vinegar do not mix with any wine.

The best drinks before wine are dry Sherries, dry White Ports, light Vermouth, Champagne. Cocktails containing sugar or fruit juices kill the wine's taste: to serve an expensive wine after any of them is foolhardy. If one must serve spirits, the universally acknowledged cocktail is a Martini.

TWELVE

The Selection and Storage of Wines

SELECTING WINES

In a recent catalogue of a well-known New York wine merchant, late (and by no means ready-to-drink) vintages of château-bottled wines such as Châteaux Latour and Margaux, along with Burgundy's venerable Musigny *Vieilles Vignes*[1] and many another, were all priced at more than $100.00 a case—some $20.00 in excess of the cost of this same merchant's good-quality Scotch. Not only are the prices of these wines about double what they would have been five years ago, the interesting thing is that they do not reflect any comparable shift in the respective economies of France or Germany, or any change in import duties, or any appreciable rise in the costs of transportation. Instead, they are largely the by-product of the bountiful (and considerably overrated) European wine crop of 1959, which received a booster of world-wide publicity worthy of Madison Avenue itself. In view of the American

[1] The above-mentioned section of the famous Côte d'Or vineyard, presently owned by the distinguished producer, Comte George de Vogüé, makes its wine from specially cultured old rootstock. The term is not to be confused with *Vieille Vigne Originelle Française non Reconstituée*—implying rootstocks of the pre-*phylloxera* era.

public's ever-growing demand for and appreciation of good wine, it would seem that these prices are here to stay—in fact they will probably go even higher. French and German producers, having discovered that their wines can bring such prices, would be fools to part with them for less. Another factor is the advent of the Common Market. As we have seen, Belgium, Germany and England have for many generations been among France's best customers for her finest wines. When and as the old tariff barriers are lifted, these countries will no doubt become better customers yet—and the United States will have to pay more.

Not only of major concern to those who drink wines are the staggering sums that the merchants demand for their brightest luminaries—nowadays tailored only to a Texas millionaire's expense account—but there is the additional frightening fact that these unrealistic values are being passed all down the line. Insignificant little St.-Émilions, hitherto unheard-of whites from the Loire, upstart Niersteiners, are being dusted off for display and totally undeserved promotion, offered to the public at ages far too young to be drinkable, and at prices way in excess of any conceivable intrinsic value. To date, this has not been as much the case with the vintages of Italy—or those of Spain, Portugal, Chile and certain other countries. Relatively few wines from South America and Iberia are presently imported into the United States—but their day is rapidly approaching, and the wine drinker will do well to follow an experimental path in his search for good values.

Unfortunately, the less expensive wines of France and Germany are not always—nor will they be—the answer. The promotion, propaganda and salesmanship staffs of many importers will do their best—but the truth is that much wine imported to the United States from these two countries is of extremely poor quality. It would not be so bad, perhaps, if these inferior products were offered to the public at something approaching their real value, say at $.50 a bottle instead of at $2.50. Though many a cloud has its silver lining. For even if they were inexpensive, they would constitute a further evil: so many of them are so poorly made or unskillfully blended, so bitter or acid or generally inferior, that they immediately kill off the taste of the beginner. The first sniff or sip—and one never wants to drink wine again!

These are in general wines which are blended and bottled by big firms, known to the trade as "monopoly wines." They come in bottles with ornate labels and superfluous promotional literature informing the consumer how delicious the wine is, with what foods it goes best, and—in the case of whites and *rosés* of exceptionally poor quality—instructing that the wine should be "very well chilled." They constitute the "lines" of wines, a term we have already employed in a comparable sense to the wine industry of California. What the reader should realize about these "lines" is that, unlike the wines which are selected by reliable importers, firms dedicated to maintaining a solid reputation with the public, the lines are tailored to the demand of continuous market, year on year. Like the Californian ones, they represent an attempt to include nearly everything. A line from a typical German shipper may embrace several grades of Liebfraumilch and Moselblümchen (usually overpriced), two Niersteiners and a Steinwein, generally labeled with a registered brand name—and be augmented by a few wines from recognized vineyards (*Lagen*), but rarely outstanding ones, and usually of a mediocre year. A typical French line must perforce include a regional Médoc, a Sauternes, a St.-Émilion, a Chablis, a Pouilly-Fuissé, a Rhône (usually some musty Châteauneuf-du-Pape) and an inferior *rosé* from Tavel, Provence or Anjou —not forgetting the perennial Beaujolais! They are of course all sold under the shipper's brand name—which by implication serves to assure the consumer that every wine in the line is as good as the other. The wine drinker should be ever alert to the fact that only rare bottles among these lines—even though they bear the endorsement of some well-known expert—represent good value. In fact, to those who would learn to appreciate wine, most of them can be so much high-priced poison.

There are several logical reasons why standardization in the world of wines does not work. To begin with, there is not—nor rarely has there ever been in history—enough good wine to go around. Secondly, the buying of good European wines has for generations been a traditional affair, the business of a proud hierarchy founded on generations-old friendships or family ties. The best European producers rarely have a surplus, and they nearly always receive a fair price for their good vintages—and are always able to sell their poor wines to the blenders. They would far rather let their prized products go to a friend or an old acquaintance—arriving at terms over a leisurely meal and a pleasant bottle —than haggle over prices with a stranger or the commercially minded representative of a large shipper whose purpose is to maintain an all-inclusive line. Thus the bottler of the line is in luck if he strikes gold with his Pouilly-Fuissé one year—and his Chablis and Médoc and Niersteiner of that same year may be something else again. Furthermore the line, like a theatrical show, must go on; its items must remain in the same general price range lest it lose prestige against its competitors, even though quality suffers.

The best importers rarely buy wines in poor years, even from their friends, and instead of accepting blindly what some shipper in Bordeaux, Beaune or Worms chooses to flood the market with each year, they make annual trips to Europe, picking and choosing here and there. Thus, for the consumer who wants a bottle of honest wine at an honest price, it is as important to gain a knowledge of the names of reliable importers as it is to be alert to the qualitative variations in the lines. A good way to accomplish this, of course, is to cultivate one's local wine dealer—or, better yet, to cultivate two or three. By spreading one's purchases among several, and by receiving advice from all, one soon learns to choose between the sheep and goats of the importers and foreign shippers. One final warning about the local liquor store: beware of dealers trafficking in "specials" and marked-down wines. A wine on sale at a reduced price almost always has something wrong with it—or will very shortly! And even on the rare occasions when one stumbles on a satisfactory "special," by the time one next visits the shop, the stock will in all probability be exhausted.

STORING WINES

A wine dealer may be of much value in storing a quantity of wine until one needs it. Nowadays only a few of us live where we may have a wine cellar or comparable storage facilities. A dark closet accomplishes the purpose in the case of a dozen or so bottles, especially a red wine that should settle for a while after joggling on its journey from the store—provided one intends to consume the wines within a month or two. But over a period of time wine ages prematurely and deteriorates rapidly when not stored at a reasonably constant temperature—ideally ranging between 55 and 60 degrees. Furthermore, it should be stored on its side, otherwise the cork dries and air, carrying vinegar-making and other harmful bacteria with it, enters to spoil the wine.

One's storage space should be neither too damp nor too dry, free of bright light, especially daylight—and vibration. Consequently, if one is without these facilities, or—even with them— if one lives near a subway or an express parkway or on a busy street, the solution is to have wines stored by one's local dealer at a nominal fee, bringing them home a few at a time.

Those of us who live where we may store our own wines properly are in luck. Wine is almost always cheaper when bought by the case, and waiting to purchase properly aged red wines from merchants is an expensive affair. Given all the above ideal conditions (correct temperature, no light or vibration, etc.) the following additional advice may be of value to the wine drinker contemplating a wine cellar of his own. One's bins should be square, but tipped to a diamond shape so that a corner is at the bottom—thus a single bottle constitutes the first tier. Additionally, bins should be large enough (at least fourteen inches square) to hold a full case of Burgundy or Champagne, the thickest bottles extant. Since white wines mature faster, lay them (on their sides) in the bins closest to the cool floor, with the reds on the top tiers. Fortified wines (Sherries, Ports, etc.) are traditionally stored upright, as are brandies and other spirits. A slight seasonal variation of temperature in your wine closet or cellar—one of 5 degrees, say—will do no appreciable harm, even though it is not ideal. The rule of thumb regarding temperature is that the warmer the storage area, the sooner the wine matures. But no wine profits by being forced to maturity. Thus a temperature of more than 70 degrees over a protracted length of time is apt to be ruinous.

Many wise wine drinkers, with or without their own cellars, supplement their memories (and greatly add to their pleasure in wine) by maintaining a cellar book or scrapbook of labels, in which they record the wine's cost, where it was purchased, notations on importers and the bottlers—as well as notes on the progress of successive bottles of wines that have been bought in quantity and laid down. For those who wish to acquire a knowledge of the subtleties of wines, such a practice can not be recommended too highly. It will soon be noted, too, that all wines, most especially the reds of Bordeaux, pass through inexplicable and alarming stages in the process of reaching their maturity—periodic set-backs of taste and character that are literally known in the trade as a "wine sickness." At its most serious stage, this becomes a condition when nothing but the bouquet (from an opened—and thus often wasted bottle) can inform the wine drinker that the wine is still sound. Usually the malady soon passes—but statistics or notes on this and many another development in the cellar are invaluable.

It should not be overlooked, either, that although half bottles are a great convenience, especially for a small family or for purposes of tasting and experimentation, the smaller the bottle the faster the wine matures. This is why one often finds stores having sales or "specials" on half bottles several years or so ahead of the logical time for a wine's maturity. As we have mentioned, the ideal size of bottle for almost any wine is the Magnum—constituting two full bottles. Unfortunately, it is impractical except for large functions or parties, though the farsighted master of his cellar will do well to have a few around.

In conclusion, one comes to the touchy matter of summarizing the rules of age and maturity. A reliable wine merchant will usually inform you when a wine is ready to drink—but for those with their own cellars who may not have access to such information, here are a few words of general advice. (See also pages 232-236.) As a rule, white wines may be consumed between two and six years of age; red wines—at least those made within the last decade—between four and ten. A fine red Bordeaux, especially a Médoc or a Graves, will have twice the life of a comparable Burgundy, the best of which latter are usually starting their prime at the age of ten. Well-made red Rhône wines, especially from the recognized vineyards of northern regions—the Côte Rôtie and Hermitage—improve in the bottle over many years, as do the superior (*Reserva*) reds of Spain,

Portugal and Italy. But these latter must be of superlative quality—
of a type rarely found, as yet, on export markets.

Few dry white wines—Californian, French, German, Italian,
Spanish or Portuguese—improve in the bottle, thus there is no valid
reason not to drink them young. But the sweetest ones from French
and German vineyards do indeed mellow and grow with time. For
immediate drinking, a Beaujolais or a *rosé* from any country may
always be relied on.

Vintages should be heeded, of course. That is why the charts are
prepared by experts and winehouses. But it must be borne in mind
that vintage years for California and for any European vineyard
south of Bordeaux are of no great or intrinsic importance. As one
works northward, however, they become of increasing significance
—their greatest value being, of course, as a guide to the proper
selection of an old wine, or a younger wine one wishes to buy and
lay down. Yet even so, at the risk of repetition, it cannot be emphasized too strongly that vintage charts and statistics must be
regarded with a well-cocked eye: like all statistics, they have their
outstanding exceptions. Through some freak of nature or some
particular skill on the part of a grower, fine wines—even in the
northernmost climes—are made in poor years. Only personal experimentation or a tip from a friend or one's wine merchant will find
them—but an abject slavery to any vintage chart is simple idiocy,
enabling the other fellow to get the real bargains and sometimes even
the best wines.

SUMMARY

In selecting wines, patronize *several* local dealers—the best and quickest way to learn the names of the reliable importers or firms which refuse to endorse poor-quality wines. One should be wary of the all-embracing "lines"—standardized brands or shippers carrying many or all types. These wines will be overpriced and usually of poor quality. The good importers rarely buy wines of poor years; and their purchases are usually based on personal relationships of many years' standing. It is their business not to let the consumer down.

Unless one has perfect facilities—a relatively dry storage area with an ideal constant temperature of between 55 and 60 degrees, without bright light and free from vibration—one should try to get a local dealer to store any wine one wants to buy by the case and lay down. Wine is usually cheaper bought by the case; a good red wine of a fine year can be expensive if one waits for the importer or dealer to age it for sale by the bottle. In storing one's own wines, lay the bottles on their sides. White wines mature faster than reds and should be closer to the floor.

Wine in half bottles matures faster than in full bottles; Magnums (two-bottle size) are the best but not always practical. One or two Magnums, however, should be available for "occasions."

Vintage charts have their uses, especially for the wines of France and Germany: but people who keep their noses glued to them often lose out. Some wines from poor years may be excellent bargains. One should consult one's local dealers; and keep one's ears open.

In general, white wines may be consumed between the ages of two and six; red wines between four and ten (the finest of Bordeaux and those of Spain, Portugal and Italy need more age). *Rosés* are ready to drink when bottled. None of them—and only a few whites—ever improve appreciably in the bottle. The notable exceptions are French white Hermitages, Sauternes and Barsacs, and German *Beerenauslesen* and *Trockenbeerenauslesen*.

General Characteristics of Recent Vintage Years

(L=long-lived. * indicates best year. + indicates good or fair years.)

FRANCE

BORDEAUX REDS

* 1953 A great year, nowadays difficult to find.

1954 Mediocre; not to be recommended.

* 1955 Fine, full wines, among the best on the market today.

1956 All but the best (and there were few good ones) are past their prime.

L + 1957 "Hard" wines, not yet ready to drink. They may or may not "come around"—except those from the best châteaux.

+ 1958 Well-balanced wines ready to drink now.

+ 1959 Most of them are lacking in "finesse" and are short-lived.

1960 Mediocre.

L * 1961 Generally excellent; best in St.-Émilion and Pomerol. Long-lived.

* 1962 Comparable to the 1955's. They will mature much earlier than the 1961's—some in two or three years.

1963 Variable and generally mediocre; the St.-Émilions and Pomerols will not equal the Graves or the Médocs.

+ 1964 Good, plentiful—but not great.

1965 A notably bad year.

1966 Good.

1967 Good, but not notable.

1968 Very bad indeed.

1969 Good. Probably will be better than 1967.

* 1970 Promises to be excellent. Should live long.

Note: For previous years watch for wines of 1945, 1947 and 1949.

BORDEAUX WHITES

* 1959 Except for the best-known Sauternes, the other white wines of Bordeaux were neither "typical" nor long-lived.

  1960 Mediocre throughout. Avoid even the celebrated names.

* 1961 Best white Bordeaux currently available.

  1962 Also good wines, though not of the outstanding quality of 1962 white Burgundies.

  1963 Growing conditions were most unfavorable, the wines poor.

+ 1964 See Bordeaux reds.

  1965 Ditto.

  1966 Good, not great.

  1967 Fair only.

  1968 Very poor indeed.

  1969 Vary from poor to mediocre.

* 1970 Graves should be very good; Sauternes superior.

BURGUNDY REDS

L * 1952 Long-lived, sturdy wines—hard to come by nowadays.

 * 1953 Wonderful if one can find them. But drink them now.

  1954 No.

 * 1955 Excellent wines, the survivors reaching their peak.

  1956 Few were estate-bottled. A very poor year.

L * 1957 Wines just coming into their own.

  1958 Generally poor.

 * 1959 Good, but not "the finest Burgundies of the century."

  1960 Much quantity, but no quality. Avoid them.

L * 1961 An outstanding year.

 * 1962 These are as fine as the 1961's. Produced in small quantity.

  1963 In general a poor year.

+ 1964 Plenty of them, and of fair quality.

  1965 Catastrophic.

+ 1966 Better quality than 1964.

  1967 Fair.

  1968 All but undrinkable.

L * 1969 Very excellent. Comparable to 1962.

  1970 A very fair year. Promises well.

BURGUNDY WHITES

+ 1959 Over-publicized even before the grapes were picked.

  1960 With a few notable exceptions, undistinguished.

L * 1961 Excellent and well-balanced; unusually long-lived.
   * 1962 Also excellent, especially those of Chablis.
  + 1963 Unexpectedly excellent as compared to the reds.
  + 1964 Unexpectedly good—short-lived.
     1965 No, except in Chablis.
  + 1966 Good quality, fruity.
     1967 Good. Some too high in acid.
     1968 Bad.
   * 1969 Quite superior, especially Pouilly-Fuissé.
   * 1970 Only a notch below 1969.

BEAUJOLAIS

L * 1961 Outstanding and long-lived.
  + 1962 Typical; pleasant. Ready for drinking now.
     1963 A poor year.
  + 1964 Good.
     1965 Very poor.
     1966 Fair.
     1967 Fair.
     1968 Poor.
   * 1969 Superior.
     1970 A satisfactory crop, but spotty in quality.

RHÔNE

   * 1955 Wonderful wines now at their best.
     1956 No good.
L + 1957 Slow to mature, now starting their prime.
   * 1958 Better than the 1959's, and still improving.
     1959 Good in Hermitage; only fair elsewhere. Short-lived.
  + 1960 A good year which will reach its peak soon.
L * 1961 Reds will be wonderful, but slow to mature.
  + 1962 Good *rosés* and whites. Somewhat less good reds.
     1963 Very few of them good enough for export.
  + 1964 Very good.
     1965 Poor—except for Châteauneuf-du-Pape.
L + 1966 Very good.
     1967 Good, but not outstanding.
     1968 Very poor.
     1969 Fairly good. Reds better than whites.
     1970 Same as above.

LOIRE

1959 They lacked character, and are not "typical."

1960 No.

* 1961 Consistently very good indeed—especially among the rarely found reds. The whites are now ready for drinking.

* 1962 Very good, especially in Pouilly, Sancerre and Quincy.

1963 Few good ones available.

+ 1964 A good year.

1965 Some are fair.

1966 Very fair.

1967 Fair only.

1968 Poor.

1969 Far better than the two preceding.

1970 Pouilly-Fumé and Sancerre good; others better.

ALSACE

1960 Poor throughout.

* 1961 A very good year.

* 1962 Outstanding wines: light and delicate.

1963 Generally mediocre except for a few *Grands Crus*.

1964 Passable year.

1965 Poor.

1966 Good.

1967 Not notable.

1968 A few rare ones were good.

1969 Very good.

1970 Promises very well.

CHAMPAGNE *(vintage wines only)*

* 1959 A very good year—but not a long-lived one.

1960 Lighter than the 1959's but of more than fair quality.

* 1961 A very good vintage.

* 1962 Also a very good year.

1963 Champagnes fared better than in other parts of France.

1964 Good.

1966 Excellent.

GERMANY
RHINE AND MOSELLE

+ 1958 A good year.

L * 1959 For the best and most expensive, a truly great year.

+ 1962 Rhine wines good; Moselles less so.
1963 Rhine wines fair; Moselles poor.
1964 Excellent in general.
1965 Many, unexpectedly, very good indeed.
L + 1966 Very good.

PORTUGAL AND SPAIN

Vintage years in both Portugal and Spain are of no consequence as such, except for that particular class of wines known in both countries as *Reservas*. The year of a *Reserva* may vary from vineyard to vineyard, even in the same region, and is always determined by the vineyard owner's (or producer's) personal assessment of the wine's merits.

ITALY

Only a very few Italian wines—the most carefully made reds, such as Chianti *Classico*, Barbaresco, Barolo, etc.—really merit a vintage year on the bottle, or the pains to lay them down. For these, the best years are: 1955, 1956, 1957, 1958, 1961, 1964 and 1965.

SWITZERLAND

Almost all years are good. 1965, a year of disaster in northern Europe (certain German wines excepted), was unusually good.

Bibliography

BOOKS ON WINES IN GENERAL

James, Walter. *Wine—A Brief Encyclopedia*. (New York: A. A. Knopf, 1960)
A comprehensive, and often amusingly anecdotal, collection.

Leedom, William S. *The Vintage Wine Book* (paperback). (New York: Vintage Books, 1963)
Concentrates on France, Germany and California, with cogent advice on buying and selecting wines.

Marrison, L. W. *Wines and Spirits* (paperback). (Baltimore, Md.: Penguin Books, 1962)
Excellent and readable reference work on wines of all countries.

Schoonmaker, Frank, and Tom Marvel. *Complete Wine Book*. (New York: Simon and Schuster, 1934)
Contains much material still valid today.

Schoonmaker, Frank. *Encyclopedia of Wine*. (New York: Hastings House, 1964)
Excellent, comprehensive reference book.

Simon, André L. *Dictionary of Wines, Spirits and Liqueurs*. (New York: Citadel Press, rev. ed., 1963)
Wines, wine terms and wine lore by the leading British authority on wines of the world.

Street, Julian. *Wines* (New York: A. A. Knopf, 1961)
Emphasis on French and German wines, Ports and Sherries, by the late dean of American writers on wines.

Wine and Food Association of Great Britain. *A Guide to Good Wine*. (London: Chambers, 1959)
Refreshingly written, informative chapters on most of the wines of Europe by various British experts.

BOOKS ON WINES OF INDIVIDUAL COUNTRIES

FRANCE

Churchill, Creighton. *A Notebook for the Wines of France.* (New York: A. A. Knopf, 1961)
Covers all the principal wine districts of France, with tables explaining classifications in each of the respective districts, and pages for the reader's use as a cellar book.

Cocks, Charles, and Edward Féret. *Bordeaux et Ses Vins* (in French). (Bordeaux: Féret et Fils, 11th edition, 1949).
For many years a standard and invaluable reference work on the châteaux of Bordeaux.

Dion, Roger. *Histoire de la Vigne et de Vin de France* (in French). (Paris: Dion, 1959)
A lengthy, comprehensive treatise on French vines and wines. Probably the most authoritative reference volume on the subject now extant.

Hallgarten, S. F. *Alsace and Its Wine Gardens.* (London: Deutsch, 1957)
Complete coverage of the fragrant wines of France's northernmost wine-growing district.

Jacquelin, Louis, and René Poulain. *The Wines and Vineyards of France.* (New York: G. P. Putnam Sons, 1962)
An ambitious collection of the names of all the vineyards of France (as well as the allowable wine grapes)—with its due share of omissions and inaccuracies.

Larmat, L. *Atlas de la France Vinicole* (in French). (Paris: L. Larmat, 1949 *et seq.*)
Les Vins de Bordeaux
Les Vins de Bourgogne
Les Vins de Champagne
Les Vins des Côtes du Rhône
Les Vins des Coteaux de la Loire
Les Eaux-de-Vie de France: Le Cognac
Invaluable and fascinating detailed maps of the important vineyard districts concerned, prepared under the auspices of L'Institut National des Appellations d'Origine.

Lichine, Alexis, and William E. Massee. *The Wines of France.* (New York: A. A. Knopf, rev. ed., 1960)
A full coverage of all the principal wines of France. Mr. Lichine

is the owner of vineyards in Bordeaux and the Côte d'Or, as well as being in the import trade.

Poupon, Pierre, and Pierre Forgeot. *Les Vins de Bourgogne* (in French). (Paris: Presses Universitaires de France, 1959)
An authoritative volume on the wines, their *appellations* and comparative ranking from Chablis to the Beaujolais.

Rodier, Camille. *Le Vin de Bourgogne* (in French). (Dijon: L. Damidot, 1948)
Historically (and otherwise) a standard reference work for the wines of the Côte d'Or.

———*Le Clos de Vougeot* (in French). (Dijon, 1959)
History and lore (with prints, maps and drawings) of one of the Côte d'Or's oldest and most celebrated vineyards.

Roger, J. R. *The Wines of Bordeaux.* (New York: E. P. Dutton, 1960)
A comprehensive volume on Bordeaux wines, especially recommended for those without sufficient mastery of the French language to profit from the classic by Cocks and Féret.

Shand, P. Morton. *A Book of French Wines.* (New York: A. A. Knopf, 1960)
Wines of France by a British expert, including a summary of the *Appellations Contrôlées* laws.

Simon, André L. *Champagne.* (New York: McGraw-Hill, 1963)
A history of Champagne and the various theories of how it came to be. Illustrated with color photographs and interlarded with many statistics, including vintage years from 1800 to 1961.

GERMANY

Andres, Stefan. *Die Grossen Weine Deutschlands* (in German). (Berlin: Verlag Ullstein, 1960)
By a well-known German authority—also beautifully illustrated. Many recommended (and excellent) vineyards do not appear in the majority of English-language volumes. A collector's item for anyone whose chief interest lies in German wines.

Langenbach, Alfred. *German Wines and Vines.* (London: Vista Books, 1962)
A fine companion piece to Schoonmaker's volume on German wines, by a British expert. Recommendations as to the best vineyards do not necessarily coincide.

Schoonmaker, Frank. *The Wines of Germany.* (New York: Hastings House, 1956)

Schoonmaker probably knows more about German wines than any English-speaking individual alive today. A brief, thorough and readable reference.

Simon, André L., and S. F. Hallgarten. *The Great Wines of Germany.* (New York: McGraw-Hill, 1963)
Coverage from yet another viewpoint. Superbly illustrated with color photographs—but more than one-third of the volume contains production and other statistics of no real interest to the layman.

ITALY

Layton, T. A. *Wines of Italy.* (London: Harper, 1961)
A complete—if sometimes excessively anecdotal—work on Italian wines.

HUNGARY

Halász, Zoltán. *Hungarian Wine Through the Ages.* (Budapest: Covina Press, 1962)
A highly interesting account of wines from a country which, before the *phylloxera* period, ranked fourth in European production.

UNITED STATES

Melville, John. *Guide to California Wines* (paperback). (San Carlos, California: Nourse Publishing Co., 1960)
The most complete coverage of California's vineyards and wine industry in print at this time.

Wagner, Philip M. *American Wines and Wine-Making.* (New York: A. A. Knopf, 1961)
In addition to specific recommendations for operating one's own vineyard, contains an excellent account and estimation of all United States wines, from California to New York State.

PORTUGAL

Valente-Perfito, J. C. *Let's Talk About Port.* (Oporto: Instituto do Vinho do Porto, 1948)
History of Port, description of the Douro Valley where it is made and the great winehouses in Oporto where it is aged and blended.

SPAIN

Croft-Crooke, Rupert. *Sherry*. (New York: A. A. Knopf, 1956)
The making of Sherry as done in the Jerez region of Spain. Contains an excellent account of the *solera* system of blending.

BOOKS FOR GENERAL READING

Allen, H. Warner. *Romance of Wines*. (London: Constable, 1931)
Anecdotes, appraisals and tales of wine drinking by a British expert of the old school.
———. *Natural Red Wines*. (London: Constable, 1951)
Based on a lifetime experience of drinking red wines of most European countries.
———. *The History of Wine*. (New York: Horizon Press, 1961)
An authoritative volume of the history of wines from the beginning of recorded history to modern times.
Chamberlain, Samuel. *Bouquet de France*. (New York: Gourmet, 1952)
The foods, the wines and ways of France.
———. *Italian Bouquet*. (New York: Gourmet, 1958)
Italian companion piece to the same author's volume on France.
Root, Waverley.*The Food of France*. (New York: A. A. Knopf, 1958)
Represents years of research into provincial dishes and wines of the less traveled corners of France.
Saintsbury, George. *Notes on a Cellar-Book*. (London: Macmillan, 1964)
Classic work on the enjoyment and appreciation of wines and liquors by a celebrated British connoisseur who lived primarily during the latter half of the Nineteenth century.
Scott, J. M. *The Man Who Made Wine*. (New York: E. P. Dutton, 1954)
A delightful, charmingly fictionalized account of wine making and life in the vineyards of Bordeaux. Good reading for *any* wine lover.
Seltman, Charles. *Wine in the Ancient World*. (London: Routledge and Kegan Paul, 1957)
Wine-drinking habits of the ancients, with emphasis on Greece and Rome.
Winkler, A. J. *General Viticulture*. (University of California Press, 1962)
Comprehensive compilation of contemporary practices in wine making; description of various wine grapes and table grapes; a manual for vineyardists.

Pronouncing Glossary of Wine Terms and Names

ABBREVATIONS

Fr.–French   *Ger.*–German   *Port.*–Portuguese
It.–Italian   *Hun.*–Hungarian   *Sp.*–Spanish

abboccato (ah-bo-*kaht*-oh) (*It.*)— Sweet; sweetish.

adamado (ah-dam-*ad*-oh) (*Port.*)— sweet; literally: "for ladies."

adegas (eh-*day*-gash)—Portuguese winehouse; producer's cellars.

Alella (Al-*aye*-ya)—Spanish wine, made near Barcelona.

Alevesa (Al-ay-*vay*-sah)—section of Spanish Rioja region, east of Ebro River.

Aligoté (Al-ee-*got*-ay)—white (and inferior) Burgundy grape.

Aloxe-Corton (Al-*laws* Kor-taw)— Burgundy commune (Côte de Beaune).

alta (*al*-tah) (*Sp.*)—high; upper: as in Rioja Alta.

Amontillado (Ah-mont-ee-*ah*-doe) —popular type of dry Sherry.

Anjou (Anh-*zhoo*)—wine (and region) of lower Loire (France).

apéritif (a-pair-ee-*teef*) (*Fr.*)—before-meal drink, usually fortified wine.

Appellations Contrôlées (Ap-pell-*ass*-see-yaw Kawn-troll-*ay*)—regulations pertaining to principal vineyards and wines (France).

Arbois (Arr-*bwa*)—wine (and commune) of Jura (France).

Arinto (Ar-*reen*-too)—Portuguese white-wine grape, kin of Riesling.

Armagnac (Ar-man-*nyack*)—brandy (and region) of Pyrénées (France).

Asti Spumante (*Ahs*-tee Spoo-*man*-tay)—popular Italian sparkling wine, Piedmont region.

Auslese (*Ows*-lay-seh) (German)—

wine from specially picked, ripe grapes.

Ausone (Oh-*sohne*)—(Château) "1st Growth" St.-Émilion (Bordeaux).

Badacsonyi Kéknyelü (*Bahd*-ac-*cho*-ny Kek-en-ay-loo)—Hungarian white wine, traditionally sweet.

baja (*ba*-hah) (*Sp.*)—lower: as in Rioja Baja.

Barbaresco (Bar-bar-*ess*-co)—Italian red wine, Piedmont region.

Barbera (Bar-*bair*-ah)—Italian grape and generic red wine; also Californian.

Bardolino (Bar-doe-*leen*-oh)—Italian red wine, made near Verona.

Barolo (Bar-*oh*-lo)—Italian red wine, Piedmont region.

Barsac (*Bar*-sack)—subdivision of Sauternes region (Bordeaux).

Bâtard-Montrachet (Bah-*tar* Mawrahsh-*ay*)—Burgundy vineyard, part of Montrachet "group" (Côte de Beaune).

Beaujolais (Bo-zho-*lay*)—southern Burgundy red wine (and region).

Beaune (Bone)—principal town of Côte d'Or (Burgundy); (Côte de) southern half of this region.

Beerenauslese (*Beer*-en-*ows*-lay-seh) (*Ger.*)—wine from individually picked, overripe grapes.

Berg (Bairg) (*Ger.*)—hill or mountain; steep hillside.

Bergerac (*Bair*-zhair-ack)—wine (and wine town), Dordogne (France).

Beugnon(s) (Bun-*nyaw*)—"2nd Growth" Chablis vineyard.

Beychevelle (*Bay*-sheh-vell)—(Château) "4th Growth" Médoc (Bordeaux). Unofficially considered a "2nd."

Bèze (Clos de) (Klo-deh-Baihz)—classic Burgundy vineyard of Chambertin "group."

Blanc de Blancs (Blahw deh Blahw) (*Fr.*)—predominantly a Champagne term, indicating wine made from white grapes only.

Blanchots (Blahw-*show*—"1st Growth" Chablis vineyard.

blanco (*blan*-koe) (*Sp.*)—white (wine).

Blaye (Côtes de) (Coat deh Bly)—wine region of Bordeaux.

Bocksbeutel (Box-boy-tell) (*Ger.*)—squat, flagon-shaped bottle, used for Frankenwein and Steinwein.

bodega (bo-*day*-ga) (*Sp.*)—winehouse; producer's cellars.

Bonnes-Mares (Bohn-*Mar*)—famous Burgundy vineyard (Côte de Nuits).

Bordeaux (Boar-*doh*)—French port; wine from Bordeaux district.

Bourg (Côtes de) (Coat deh Boorg)—wine region of Bordeaux.

Bourgogne (Bur-*goyn*) (*Fr.*)—Burgundy; (*vin de*) wine thereof.

Bourgros (*Boor*-grow) — "1st Growth" Chablis vineyard.

bouteille(s) (boo-*tay*) (*Fr.*)—bottle(s).

Boxbeutel—see *Bocksbeutel*.

Brouilly (also Côte de Brouilly) (Brue-*ee*)—two of the nine principal (superior) subdivisions of Beaujolais (France).

brut (*broo*-t)—Champagne or sparkling-wine term: very dry.

Bual (Boo-*al*)—Madeira type most comparable to Red Port.

Bucelas (Boo-*sell*-ush)—wine (and region) of central Portugal.

Cabernet (Kab-err-*nay*)—red-wine grape, basically of Bordeaux.

Calvados (*Kal*-va-dohs) (*Fr.*)—spirits distilled from cider.

Carcavelos (Kar-kar-*vell*-oush)—Portuguese sweet wine.

Cassis (Kah-*see*)—currant liqueur (Burgundy); Mediterranean wine town (and wine).

caves (kahv) (*Fr.*)—cellars; wine storehouses.

Cérons (*Sair*-ahw)—white-wine region of Bordeaux.

Certan (*Sair*-tanh)—(Château) "1st Growth" Pomerol (Bordeaux).

Chablis (Shab-*lee*)—northern Burgundy white-wine region.

Châlon (Shall-*onh*)—vineyard (Château) of Jura (France); Chalon: wine town, southern Burgundy.

Chalonnaise (Shall-awn-*ays*)—southern Burgundy wine region.

Chambertin (*Shawm*-bair-tanh)—classic Burgundy red-wine vineyard.

Chambolle-Musigny (Sham-*bowl* Mew-*seen*-yee)—Burgundy commune (Côte de Nuits).

Champagne (Shawm-*pahn*) (*Fr.*)—sparkling wine from French Champagne district (or foreign imitations); brandy from superior part of Cognac.

Chardonnay (Shar-dawn-*ay*)—Burgundy white grape, sometimes called Pinot Chardonnay; commune of southern Burgundy.

Charlemagne—*see* Corton-Charlemagne.

Chassagne-Montrachet (Shass-*ahn*-Maw-rash-*ay*)—Burgundy commune sharing (with Puligny) the great Montrachet vineyard.

Chasselas (*Shas*-sel-ah)—common white-wine grape, principally used in Germany, Switzerland, and France.

château(*x*) (shat-*oh*) (*Fr.*)—wine-producing estate(s) or vineyard(s).

Châteauneuf-du-Pape (Shato-*nuhf*-duh-*Papp*)—French Rhône wine.

Chenin Blanc (*Shen*-anh Blahw)—white-wine grape, basically of the Loire (France); also used in California.

Cheval-Blanc (Shev-*al-Blahw*)—(Château) "1st Growth" St. Émilion (Bordeaux).

Chevalier-Montrachet (Shev-*al*-yay Maw-rash-*ay*)—Burgundy vineyard, part of Montrachet "group."

Chianti (Key-*an*-ti)—Italian wine and region (central Italy).

Chinon (*Sheen*-anh)—wine town of central Loire (France).

classé (class-*say*) (*Fr.*)—officially classified: as in *Cru Classé*.

clairet (klair-*ay*) (*Fr.*)—original term for claret; light-colored red wine.

claret—red Bordeaux wine.

clos (klo) (*Fr.*)—vineyard; literally: "yard."

Cognac (*Ko*-nyack)—French brandy from district of same name.

Colares (Koe-*lar*'sh)—wine (and region) of central Portugal.

colheita (kool-*yea*-tah) (*Port.*)—vintage year; vintage.

consumos (kanh-soom-*oush*) (Port.)—common wines: *ordinaires*.

Cornas (Kor-*nar*)—wine commune of Rhône district (France).

Corton-Charlemagne (*Kaw*-taw-*Schar*-leh-man)—classic (red and white wines) Burgundy vineyard.

cosecha (ko-*say*-chah) (*Sp.*)—vintage; vintage year. cosechado (ko-say-*char*-doh): "of the vintage of ——"

côte(*s*) (coat) (*Fr.*)—hillside; wine-growing area.

Côte d'Or (Coat *dohr*)—traditional (central) Burgundy region.

Côte Rôtie (Coat Roat-*ee*)—Rhône red-wine region (France).

cru (krew) (*Fr.*)—growth, crop; wine from a specific vineyard.

crust—stringy sediment (dregs) in old bottles of Port.

cuvée (*Fr.*)—see *Têtes de Cuvée.*

Dão (Downh)—Portuguese wine (and region) of Central Portugal.

doce (dohs) (Port.)—sweet.

Dolcetto (Dol-*chett*-oh)—Italian red-wine grape; generic wine.

Dole (*Doe*-l)—Swiss red wine, Canton of Valais (Val-*ay*).

Dom Pérignon (Dom *Pair*-ee-nyaw) —Benedictine monk, often called the "inventor of Champagne"; Champagne brand name.

domaine (doe-*mane*) (*Fr.*)—vineyard; control or management of several vineyards.

Dordogne (Door-*doyn*)—river of Bordeaux district; wine region.

Douro (*Door*-roe)—river and wine region of central Portugal, principally producing Port.

doux (doo) (*Fr.*)—predominantly a Champagne or sparkling-wine term: usually denotes sweet or sweetish.

d'Yquem (dee-*kem*—(Château) "1st Growth" Sauternes (Bordeaux).

eaux-de-vie (oh-deh-*vee*) (*Fr.*)— spirits distilled from crushed grape leavings; distilled spirits in general.

Échézeaux (also Grands Échézeaux) *Esh*-ay-zo)—famous Burgundy vineyards (Côte de Nuits).

Echt (Ekt) (*Ger.*)—unsugared wine; genuine; "natural."

edelfaüle (*Aye*-dell-fohl) (*Ger.*)—

"noble rot"—equivalent to French *pourriture noble.*

Edelzwicker (*Aye*-del-zwick-er)— Alsatian blended wine from "noble" (superior) grapes.

éggrapoir (aye-grapp-*pwar*)—revolving cylindrical machine separating grapes from stems and stalks.

Egri Bikavér (*Egg*-ree *Bee*-kah-veer) —Hungarian red wine ("Bull's Blood").

Eiswein (*Ice*-vine) (*Ger.*)—sweet wine from frostbitten grapes.

Entre-Deux-Mers (*Awn*-trer-Deh-*Mair*)—wine region (Bordeaux).

Ermitage (*Air*-mee-tahge)—Swiss white wine.

escogida (ess-co-*hee*-dah) (*Sp.*)— specially selected.

especial (ess-spay-see-*al*) (*Sp.*)— special (Chilean). *espumantes* (ess-poo-*mant*-esh) (*Port.*)—sparkling wines.

estufado (esh-too-*fah*-dou) (*Port.*) —method of heating Madeira during aging process.

Étoile (Aye-*twall*)—wine (and commune) of Jura (France).

exceptionnelle (ess-*sep*-tyon-el) (*Fr.*) —special; exceptional: as in *Cru Exceptionnelle.*

Fass (Fahss) (*Ger.*)—cask or barrel.

feine (fine) (*Ger.*)—fine or excellent.

feinste (*fine*'st) (*Ger.*)—finest, most excellent.

Fendant de Sion (Fawn-*daw* der *See*-anh)—Swiss white wine.

fiaschi (fee-*as*-kee) (*It.*)—straw-wrapped, flagon-shaped bottles, usually used for Chianti.

finesse (fee-*ness*) (*Fr.*)—delicacy or elegance (of a wine).

Fino (*Fee*-no)—type of common Sherry: very dry.

Fixin (*Fee-sanh*)—commune of Côte de Nuits (Burgundy).

flasche (*flash*-eh)—typical tall, slim German wine bottle.

Fleurie (Flur-*ee*)—one of nine principal (superior) subdivisions of Beaujolais (France).

flor (flor) (*Sp.*)—yeast or bacteria producing a whitish crust on wine's surface; encouraged in production of Sherry.

Folle Blanche (Foll *Blawnch*)—white grape of Cognac (France); also Californian.

Frankenwein (*Fran*-ken-vine)—wine from Franconia (Germany).

Frascati (Frahs-*kaht*-ee)—Italian wine from vicinity of Rome.

Freisa (*Fray*-sa)—Italian red-wine grape; generic wine.

frizzante (free-*zhan*-tee) (*It.*)—slightly sparkling; *pétillant.*

Fronsac (Côtes de) (Coat deh *Fronsack*)—wine region (Bordeaux).

fuder (*foo*-der) (*Ger.*)—cask or barrel.

Furmint (*Foor*-mint)—Hungarian grape, principally used for Tokay.

Gamay (*Gam*-may)—red-wine grape of Beaujolais (France).

garrafeira (garr-ah-*fay*-ra) (*Port.*)—selected; specially chosen.

Gattinara (Got-ee-*nahr*-ah)—Italian red wine, Piedmont region.

generic—(*Eng.*) wine term meaning "type" (deriving from a well-known area); often "borrowed": as with "California Burgundy," "Chilean Chablis," etc.

Gevrey-Chambertin (*zhev*-ray-*Shawm*-bair-tanh)—Burgundy commune containing the famous Chambertin vineyard.

Gewürztraminer (Ger-*wurtz*-*trah*-min-er)—white-wine grape, version of Traminer (*q.v.*).

Gran Vino (Gran *Vee*-no) (*Sp.*)—fine or "great" (Chilean).

Grand (Grahw) (*Fr.*)—large; superior or "great," usually unofficial.

grappa (*gra*-pa) (*It.*)—distilled grape spirits. (See *marc*).

Graves (Grahv)—red- and white-wine region (Bordeaux).

Grenache (Gren-*ahsh*)—wine grape, principally a source of *rosés.*

Grenouilles (gren-*wee*)—"1st Growth" Chablis vineyard.

Grignolino (Grin-nyo-*leen*-no)—Italian red grape; generic wine.

Grillet (Château) (*Gree*-yay)—white-wine Rhône vineyard (France).

Gruaud-Larose (Grew-oud-La-*rose*)—(Château) "2nd Growth" Médoc (Bordeaux).

grünlach (groin-lahk) (*Ger.*)—"green seal." *See* Johannisberg (Schloss).

Haro (*Ah*-roe)—principal wine town of the Rioja region (Spain).

Haut-Brion (Oh-bree-*yohw*)—(Château) "1st Growth" Graves (Bordeaux).

Haut-Médoc (Oh-May-*dock*)—superior wine region (Bordeaux).

Hermitage (*Air*-mee-tarhge)—region of Rhône district (France).

hochfeinste (hock-fine'st) (*Ger.*)—finest; most superior.

Hochheim (*Hock*-hyme)—famous wine town of German Rheingau.

hospice (aw-*spees*) (*Fr.*)—hospital, almshouse; in France frequently supported by income from vineyards (Hospice de Beaune, etc.).

Hunawihr (*Hun*-a-veer)—wine town of Alsace (France).

Jerez de la Frontera (Hair-*eth* day lah Fron-*tair*-ah)—Sherry town; region of southwest Spain.

Johannisberg (Schloss) (Schlohs Yo-*hann*-is-bairg)—a universally famous vineyard, Rheingau region (Germany).

Josephhof (*Yo*-sef-hoef)—German vineyard, Moselle region.

Jurançon (*Jur*-anh-saw)—wine (and region) of Pyrénées (France).

Kabinett (or *Cabinet*) (Ka-bin-*et*) (*Ger.*)—specially reserved.

Keller-Abfülling (*Kell*-er-Ahb-*fuel*-ung) (*Ger.*)—estate-bottled.

könsumwein (kon-sum-vine) (*Ger.*)—common wine; *ordinaire*.

Lacryma Christi (*La*-cream-ah *Krees*-tee)—wine from slopes of Vesuvius; term for generic Italian sparkling wine.

Lafite-Rothschild (La-*feet*-Raw-*sheeld*)—(Château) "1st Growth" Médoc (Bordeaux).

Lage (*Lahg*-eh) (*Ger.*)—Vineyard (plural: *Lagen*).

Lagrein Rosato (La-*grain* Rosa-*ah*-toe)—*rosé* wine, Italian Tyrol.

Lascombes (Lass-*kawmb*)—(Château de) "2nd Growth" Médoc (Bordeaux).

Latour (La-*toor*)—(Château) "1st Growth" Médoc (Bordeaux).

Latricières (La-tree-see-*air*)—Burgundy vineyard of Chambertin "group" (Côte de Nuits).

Léoville-Lascases (*Lay*-oh-veel-Las-*cass*)—Château) "2nd Growth" Médoc (Bordeaux).

Liebfraumilch (*Leeb*-frow-milch)—popular generic Rhine wine.

liqueur (lee-*ker*)—sweet cordial or after-dinner drink.

liquoreux (lee-ker-*err*) (*Fr.*)—sweet; "luscious"; dessert wine.

Lirac (*Lee*-rack)—Rhône commune, principally noted for *rosés*.

Listrac (*Lees*-track)—subdivision of Médoc (Bordeaux).

Lussac (*Lew*-sack)—subdivision of St.-Émilion (Bordeaux).

Mâconnais (*Mack*-awn-ay)—southern Burgundy wine region.

Madeira (Mad-*air*-ah)—apéritif or dessert wine (Portuguese).

maderizé (mad-air-*ee*-zay) (*Fr.*)—oxidized white wine, dark and bitter. Literally: like Madeira.

Magnum—two-bottle size.

Manzanilla (*Man*-tha-*nee*-yah)—sherry-like wine (Spanish).

marc (maa) (*Fr.*)—spirits distilled from the "must" or leavings of pressed grapes.

Marcobrunn(er) (*Mark*-o-*bruhn*)—German vineyard, Rheingau region.

Margaux (Mar-*go*)—subdivision of (and "1st Growth" Château in) Médoc (Bordeaux).

marque déposée (mark *day*-poe-*say*) (*Fr.*)—registered brand name.

Marsala (Mar-*sah*-la)—Italian fortified sweetish wine from Sicily.

Mateus (Mat-*ay*-osh)—Portuguese *rosé* from Douro region.

Mazoyères (Mah-zoy-*air*)—famous Burgundy vineyard in Chambertin "group" (Côte de Nuits).

media (*may*-dee-ah) (*Sp.*)—middle; central: as in Rioja Media.

Médoc (*May*-dock)—Bordeaux wine region: technically includes both Médoc and Haut-Médoc.

méthode champenoise (*may*-tohd shaw-pan-*warhz*) (*Fr.*)—traditional French process for making Champagne.

Meursault (*Mair*-so)—Burgundy commune (Côte de Beaune).

mise (meeze) (*Fr.*)—literally: put or placed. *Mise en Bouteilles au Château:* bottled at the chateau; estate-bottled.

Mittelwihr (*Mit*-el-veer)—wine town of Alsace (France).

Monbazillac (More-*baz*-ee-ack)—wine (and region) of Dordogne (France).

monopole (mon-o-*pole*) (*Fr.*)—monopoly on a wine, vineyard or brand name.

Mont-de-Milieu (*Maw*-deh-Meel-*yehr*)—"2nd Growth" Chablis vineyard.

Montilla (Mawn-*tee*-yah)—unfortified Sherry-type wine (Spain).

Montrachet (Maw-rash-*ay*)—classic white-wine Burgundy vineyard.

Moscatel (Moosh-kah-*tel*)—Portuguese dessert wine; region (Setúbal) south of Lisbon.

Mosel (*Mos*'l)—Moselle: German wine region.

Moselblümchen (Mos'l-*bloom*-shen) —generic term for Moselle wine, usually a blend.

Moulin-à-Vent (*Moo*-lanh-a-*Vaw*) —one of nine principal (superior) subdivisions of Beaujolais; name of outstanding vineyard of same area.

Moulis (Moo-*lee*)—subdivision of Médoc (Bordeaux).

mousseux (moo-seh (*Fr.*)—sparkling wine.

Mouton-Rothschild (*Moo*-taw-Raw-*sheeld*)—(Château) "2nd Growth" Médoc (Bordeaux). Unofficially considered a "1st."

Moutonne (La) (Lah Moo-*tawn*)—"1st Growth" Chablis vineyard.

Muscadet (Moos-kah-*day*)—white wine (and region) of lower Loire.

Musigny (Mew-*seen*-yee)—Burgundy vineyard (Côte de Nuits).

Nahe (Nahh)—German wine region, west of the Rhine.

Natur (Nature) (Nat-*tour*) (*Fr.*)—brandy (*Champagne*) term, denoting unblended or from a single cask; sparkling wine (Champagne) term, usually meaning unsugared or "natural."

Naturwein (Na-*toor*-vine) (or *Naturrein*) (Na-*toor*-rine) (*Ger.*)—unsugared or unsweetened; "natural" wine.

Néac (Nay-*ack*)—minor wine region (Bordeaux).

Nebbiolo (Nebb-ee-*oh*-lo)—Italian grape; generic red wine; Nebbiolo *Spumante:* sparkling Nebbiolo.

Neckar (*Neck*-er)—small German wine region, east of the Rhine.

négociants (nay-*go*-see-aw) (*Fr.*)—producer, bottler, shipper; "middle-man."

Nemeskadar (*Nem*-esh-kah-dar)—Hungarian red wine.

Nierstein (*Neer*-styne)—wine town, Rheinhesse region (Germany).

Nozet (Château de) (No-*zay*)—vineyard (Pouilly-Fumé), upper Loire.

Nuits (Côte de) (Coat-deh-Nwee) —Northern section of Côte d'Or (Burgundy).

Nuits-St.-Georges (Nwee-San-*zhorge*)—Burgundy commune (Côte de Nuits).

oeil-de-perdrix (*oye*-der-pair-*dree*) (*Fr.*)—traditional term for *rosé*.

Oloroso (Oh-lo-*ro*-so)—sweet Sherry type.

Original-Abfüllung (Or-*ig*-in-al-Ahb-*fol*-ung) (*Ger.*)—estate-bottled.

Orvieto (Or-vee-*ate*-oh)—white wine (and region) of central Italy.

Palomino (*Pahl*-oh-*meen*-oh)— white wine grape, used for Sherry.

Parsac (*Par*-sack)—subdivision of St.-Émilion (Bordeaux).

pasado (pas-*sah*-doe) (*Sp.*)—"old" (wine); generally invalid term.

Passe-Tous-Grains (Pass-Too-Granh) (*Fr.*)—inferior type of Burgundy, usually a blend from two red grapes.

pastos (*pass*-tose) (*Sp.*)—common wines; *ordinaires*.

Pauillac (*Poy*-yack)—subdivision of Médoc (Bordeaux).

Pedro Ximenez (*Pay*-droe *Hee*-may-neth)—white grape, used for Sherry.

Periquita (Pair-ee-*kee*-tah)—Portuguese red grape; generic wine.

pétillant (*pet*-ee-anh) (*Fr.*)—slightly sparkling; fizzy.

petit (p'tee) (*Fr.*)—minor, secondary; *Petit Chablis:* "3rd Growth" Chablis.

Pétrus (*Pay*-troos)—(Château) "1st Growth" Pomerol (Bordeaux).

phylloxera (fill-*ox*-era)—vine louse of North American origin.

Pichon-Longueville (*Pee*-shaw-*Long*-eh-veel)—(Château) "2nd Growth" Médoc (Bordeaux).

Pinot blanc (*Pee*-no blahw)—French white grape; Californian varietal wine.

Pinot noir (*Pee*-no nwar)—principal Burgundy red grape; Californian wine.

Pomerol (Pom-air-*oll*)—wine district (Bordeaux).

Pommard (Po-*mar*)—Burgundy commune (Côte de Beaune).

Pouilly-Fuissé (*Poo*-ee-Foo-*ee*-say)

—white wine (and region) of southern Burgundy.

Pouilly-Fumé (*Poo*-ee-*Foo*-may)— white wine (and region), upper Loire (France).

pourriture noble (pur-it-*ur nob'l*) (*Fr.*)—"noble rot" or mold that settles on ripe grapes, responsible for sweet wines.

premier (*prem*-yay) (*Fr.*)—first, foremost: as in *Premier Cru.*

Puligny-Montrachet (Pooh-*leen*-ye-Maw-rash-*ay*)—Burgundy commune (Côte de Beaune).

puttonys (*put*-on-yus) (*Hun.*)— term used to indicate degree of sweetness of Tokay wine.

Quarts-de-Chaume (Kah-deh-*Shome*)—famous sweet-wine vineyards of Anjou (Loire).

Quincy (*Kan*-see)—white-wine region of upper Loire (France).

quinta (*keen*-tah) (*Port.*)—winehouse; producer's cellars.

reserva (ray-*ser*-vah) (*Sp.*)—"Reserve"; specially aged.

reservado (ray-sehr-*vah*-doe) (*Sp.*) reserve; selected (Chilean).

réserve (ray-zerv) (*Fr.*)—special; specially selected.

Rheingau (*Rine*-gow)—most celebrated German wine region.

Rheinhesse (*Rine*-hesser)—German wine region, west bank of Rhine.

Rheinpfalz (*Rine*-falz)—German wine region, adjoining Alsace.

Rhône (Rohn)—river of south central France; wine from its valley.

Ribeauville (*Ree*-bo-veel)—wine town of Alsace (France).

Ribero (Ree-*bair*-oh) or Ribeiro (Ree-*bay*-roh)—wine from Province of Galicia (northwest Spain).

Richebourg (*Reech*-boor)—Burgundy vineyard, part of Romanée "group" (Côte de Nuits).

Riesling (*Rees*-ling)—white wine grape, basically German; varietal wine.

Rioja (Ree-*oh*-ha)—superior wine region of northern Spain.

Riquewihr (*Reek*-veer)—wine town of Alsace (France).

riserva (ree-*sair*-vah) (*It.*)—"reserve"; specially selected.

Roche (Clos de la) (Clo-deh-la-*Rawsh*)—Burgundy vineyard (Côte de Nuits).

Romanée-Conti (*Ro*-man-ay-*Kawn*-tee)—celebrated Burgundy vineyard (Côte de Nuits).

Romanée-St.-Vivant (*Ro*-man-ay-San-*Vee*vaw)—Burgundy vineyard (Côte de Nuits).

rosé (rose-*aye*) (*Fr.*)—pink or rose-colored wine.

roslach (*rose*-lahk) (*Ger.*)—"rose" or "pink seal." *See* Johannisberg (Schloss).

rötlach (*roht*-lahk) (*Ger.*)—"red seal." *See* Johannisberg (Schloss).

Ruwer (*Rew*-er)—wine-producing tributary of the *Mosel* (Germany).

Saar (Tsar)—wine-producing tributary of the *Mosel* (Germany).

St.-Amour (*Sann*-tah-*moor*)—One of nine principal (superior) subdivisions of Beaujolais (France).

St.-Émilion (Sant-Ay-*meel*-yaw)—wine region (Bordeaux).

St.-Estèphe (San-Ay-*steff*)—subdivision of Médoc (Bordeaux).

St.-Georges (San-*zhorge*)—subdivision of St.-Émilion (Bordeaux); Burgundy vineyard (Côte de Nuits).

St.-Julien (San-Zhool-*yanh*)—subdivision of Médoc (Bordeaux).

Ste.-Croix-du-Mont (Sant-*Kwa*-deh-*Maw*)—wine region (Bordeaux).

Sancerre (Saw-*sayr*)—white wine (and region) of upper Loire.

Saumur (So-*muyr*)—wine (and region) of central Loire.

Sauvignon (*So*-veey-naw)—white grape, basically of Bordeaux.

Savennières (Sa-veh-*nyair*)—famous wine commune of lower Loire.

Schlossabzug (*Schlohs*-ab-*zug*) (*Ger.*)—estate-bottled.

sec (sek) (*Fr.*)—dry; Champagne or sparkling-wine term: usually denotes moderately dry, sweeter than *brut.*

secco (*sek*-ko) (*It.*)—dry.

Sekt (Sekt)—generic term for German sparkling wine.

Sémillon (*Sem*-ee-yaw)—white grape, basically of Bordeaux.

Sercial (*Sir*-seal)—dry type of Madeira.

Sipon (Chi-pon)—Yugoslavian grape (and white wine).

Soave (*Swa*-vay)—Italian white wine from vicinity of Verona.

solera (*sol*-air-ah) (*Sp.*)—system of casks arranged in tiers for blending and aging Sherry.

Spätlese (*Spate*-lay-seh) (*Ger.*)—wine from late-picked grapes.

spritzig (*sprit*-zig) (*Ger.*)—slightly sparkling; *pétillant.*

spumante (spoo-*man*-tay) (*It.*)—sparkling.

Steinberg (*Styne*-bairg)—celebrated German Rheingau vineyard.

Steinwein (*Styne*-vine)—German generic term for wine from the Würzburg section of Franconia.

Stück (Stueck) (*Ger.*)—cask or barrel.

Supérieur(e) (soo-pair-ee-*yur*) (*Fr.*)

—usually denotes wine of higher alcoholic content.

Sylvaner (Sil-*vahn-er*)—white wine grape, basically German.

Szamarodni (Sah-moor-*od*-nee)— Hungarian: dry Tokay.

Tâche (La) (La-*Tash*)—Burgundy vineyard, part of Romanée "group."

Tart (Clos de) (Clo-der-*Tar*)—Burgundy vineyard (Côte de Nuits).

Tavel (Tav-*ell*)—Rhône commune, traditional source of best French *rosés*.

terroir (tear-*wahr*) (*Fr.*)—special, individualistic quality of wine, attributable chiefly to soil-type.

Tête(s) de Cuvée (*Tayt*-der-Koo-*vay*)—traditional Burgundian term for finest vineyard(s).

Tokay (*Tow*-kai)—celebrated Hungarian white wine.

Tokay Aszú (*Tow*-kai Ah-*shu*)— sweet Tokay.

Traminer (*Trah*-min-er)—white-wine grape; excels in Alsace and Germany.

Trockenbeerenauslese (*Trock*-en-beer-en-*ows*-lay-ser) (*Ger.*)— wine from late-picked, raisin-sweet grapes.

Valdepeñas (*Val*-day-*pain*-yas)— wine (and region) of central Spain.

Valmur (Vawl-*meeur*)—"1st Growth" Chablis vineyard.

Valpantena (Val-pant-*ain*-ah)—Italian red wine from near Verona.

Valpolicella (Val-po-lee-*chell*-ah)— Italian red wine (Verona).

varietal—(*Eng.*) wine named after predominant grape: Alsatian "Traminer," Californian "Riesling," etc.

Vaudesir (Vo-day-*zeer*)—"1st Growth" Chablis vineyard.

velho (*ver*-lyou) (*Port.*)—old; aged.

vendange (vawn-*dawj*) (*Fr.*)—harvest, harvesttime.

Verdelho (Ver-*dell*-you)—Madeira grape (and wine: medium dry).

Verdicchio (di Jesi) (Ver-*dee*-kee-oh)—Italian white wine made near Venice.

Verdiso (Vair-*dees*-zo)—Italian white-wine grape; wine of the same name.

viejo (vee-*ay*-ho) (Sp.)—"old" wine.

vieux (vyeh) (*Fr.*)—old.

village(s) (veel-*ahzh*) (*Fr.*)—village(s); when hyphenated with another name, usually denotes a more extensive geographical source (area). (Ex. *Beaune* is classified higher than *Beaune-Villages*.

vin (*vanh*) (*Fr.*)—wine; *v. gris* (gree): a *rosé* of usually inferior quality; *v. jaune* (joan): yellow Sherry-type wine of Jura; *v. de paille* (*der pie*): sweet wine from raisined grapes; *v. du pays* (due pay-*ee*): local or country wine.

vino (*vee*-no) (Sp.)—wine; *v. de pasto* (*pas*-toe): common wine, *ordinaire; v. del pais* (dell-pie-*ess*) or *v. de la tierra* (day lah tee-*air*-ah): regional or country wine.

vinho (*veen*-you) (*Port.*)—wine; *v. branco* (*brank*-ou): white wine; *v. de consumo* (deh kanh-*soom*-ou): common wine, *ordinaire; v. generoso* (jeh-neh-*rah*-gou): fortified wine; *v. maduro* (mad-*oor*-ou): *rosé; v. de mesa* (deh *may*-zer): table wine; *v. tinto* (*teen*-tou): red wine.

Vinho Verde (*Veen*-you *Ver*-der) —"new wine"; wine region of northern Portugal.

Vitis labrusca (*Wee*-tiss la-*brus*-ka) table or "fox" grape.

Vitis vinifera (*Wee*-tiss weenie-*fair*-ah)—wine grape.

V.O.—brandy (*Champagne*) term: "Very Old"; *V.S.O.*: "Very Old Superior"; *V.S.O.P.*: "Very Old Superior Pale."

Vollrads (Schloss) (Schlohs *Vawl*-rads)—famous German Rheingau vineyard.

Volnay (Voll-*nay*)—Burgundy commune (Côte de Beaune).

Vosne-Romanée (*Vohn*-Ro-man-ay) —Burgundy commune, containing the celebrated Romanée vineyards.

Vougeot (Clos de) (*Klo*-der-Vou-*zhow*)—classic Burgundy vineyard.

Vouvray (*Voo*-vray)—white wine (and region), central Loire (France).

Weinstrasse (*Vine*-strass-eh)—principal group of wine-producing villages of Rheinpfalz (Germany).

Xampáns (*Sham*-pong) (*Sp.*)— "Champagne."

Zwicker (*Zwick*-er)—Alsatian common wine or *ordinaire*.

Index

ABBREVATIONS

App. Cont.–*Appellation Contrôlée*
class.–classification, classified
co.–county
com.–wine commune or village
dist.–district
ch.–château
fort.–fortified
prov.–province
reg.–region
sh.–shipper, producer, *négociant*
subreg.–subregion
vyd.–vineyard

Aus.–Austria
Calif.–California
Fr.–France
Fr.–French
Ger.–Germany
Ger.–German
Gr.–Greece
Gr.–Greek
Hun.–Hungary
Hun.–Hungarian
It.–Italy
It.–Italian
Port.–Portugal
Port.–Portuguese
Sp.–Spain
Sp.–Spanish
Switz.–Switzerland
Yugo.–Yugoslavia

abboccato (*Sp.*), 121
Abtsberg (vyd.) (Ger.), 116
Achkarren (com.) (Ger.), 109
adamado (Port.), 133
ADEB (Fr.) (*Association pour le Développement de l'Exportation du vin de Bordeaux*), 27n
adega (Port.), 139, 149
Adega Cunhas (sh.) (Port.), 140
aguardiente (*Sp.*), 211n
Ahr (reg.) (Ger.), 109
Aigle (wine) (Switz.), 155, 162
Aix-en-Provence (city) (Fr.), 73
Alameda (co.) (Calif.), 171; wines of, 177
Alella (wine) (Sp.), 145, 151
Alevesa (subreg.) (Sp.), 148

Alexander (grape), 178
Algarve (prov.) (Port.), 141, 142
Algeria, 6, 11, 67
Alicante (wine) (Sp.), 145, 151
Aligoté (grape), 52n
Almadén Vineyards (Calif.), 172, 177, 179, 192
Aloxe-Corton (com.) (Fr.), 49-50, 57
Alsace (dist.) (Fr.), 10, 14n, 24, 86; wines of, 85, 92
Altärchen (vyd.) (Ger.), 115
Alvarelhão (grape), 138
Alves, J. Camillo (sh.) (Port.), 141
Amontillado (Sherry), 201, 202
Amoureuses, Les (vyd.) (Fr.), 56
Amphora (*Gr.*), 159

253

Meier Wine Cellars (Ohio), 180
Melinots (vyd.) (Fr.), 44
Melon (grape), 80; *see* Muscadet
Mendocino (co.) (Calif.), 168
Mercurey (com.) (Fr.), 59, 64, 65
Merlot (grape), 28, 158, 162
de Mérode, Prince (sh.) (Fr.), 66
méthod champenoise (Fr.), 121, 186
Methuselah, 190
Meursault (com.) (Fr.), 53, 54, 59
Meursault-Charmes (vyd.) (Fr.), 53n
Meursault-Genevrières (vyd.) (Fr.),
 53n
Mexico, 7
Minho (reg.) (Port.), 134; *see* Vinhos
 Verdes
Mise en Bouteilles au Château (Fr.), 22;
 see château-bottled wines
Mise en Bouteille au Domaine (or à la
 Propriété), 41; *see also* estate-bottled
Mittehölle (vyd.) (Ger.), 114
Mittel-Mosel (subreg.) (Ger., 108
Mittelwihr (com.) (Fr.), 92
Moët et Chandon (sh.) (Fr.), 190
Moillard-Grivot (sh.) (Fr.), 66
Moillard, J., (sh.) (Fr.), 66
Monbazillac (reg.) (Fr.), 88, 89, 92, 93
Monnot, Julien (sh.) (Fr.), 66
monopole (Fr.), 14, 26; "monopoly
 wines," 226
Montagne (subreg.) (Fr.), 27
Montagny (com.) (Fr.), 60, 65
Montée de Tonnerre (vyd) (Fr.), 44
Montilla (wine) (Sp.), 201, 202
Montlouis (com.) (Fr.), 78, 79, 84
Mont-de-Milieu (vyd.) (Fr.), 44
Montrachet (vyd.) (Fr.), 15, 40, 46, 47,
 53, 55, 68
Mont-Luisants Blanc (wine) (Fr.), 57
Montmains (vyd.) (Fr.), 44
Mont-Redon (Domaine de) (vyd.)
 (Fr.), 76
Morey-St.-Denis (com.) (Fr.), 47, 53,
 56-57
Morgeot (vyd.) (Fr.), 59
Morgon (*App. Cont.*) (Fr.), 65
Morocco, 11
Moscatel de Setúbal (wine) (Port.),
 133, 137, 142
Moscatello (wine) (It.), 120
Moscato (fort. wine) (It.), 125
Mosel, (river & reg.) (Ger.), 94; *see
 also* Moselle
Moselblümchen (wine) (Ger.), 95, 96,
 108, 122

Moselle (river & reg.) (Ger.), 6, 94,
 95, 103, 107, 110; principal wines of,
 115; *see also* Mosel
Mosel-Saar-Ruwer (class.) (Ger.), 107;
 see also Moselle
de Moucheron, Comte (sh.) (Fr.),
 66
Mouilles, Les (vyd.) (Fr.), 64
Moulin, Le (vyd.) (Fr.), 64, 75
Moulin-à-Vent (*App. Cont.*) (Fr.), 61,
 64; (vyd.) (Fr.), 64
Moulis (subreg.) (Fr.), 27, 28
Mourvèdre (grape), 70
mousseux (Fr.), 8n, 179, 187, 191
Moutonne, La (vyd.) (Fr.), 44
Mugneret, F. (sh.) (Fr.), 66
Mugnier, F. (sh.) (Fr.), 66
Müllar-Thurgau (grape), 99, 103
Mumm (sh.) (Fr.), 190
Mûrets (vyd.) (Fr.), 75
Murgers, Les (Aux), (vyd.) (Fr.),
 57
Murrieta, Marqués de, (sh.) (Sp.),
 148n, 151-152
Muscadelle (grape), 29n
Muscadet (grape), 80; (reg.) (Fr.),
 80-81, 84
Muscat (grape & wine), 87, 92, 138,
 154
Muscat de Frontignan (wine) (Fr.),
 38
Muscat of Samos (wine) (Gr.), 163
Muscatel (grape), 204
Musigny (vyd.) (Fr.), 47, 55
Musigny Blanc (wine) (Fr.), 47, 68

Nachkenheim (com.) (Ger.), 113
Nahe (reg.) (Ger.), 102, 104, 109;
 wines of, 116
Napa (co.) (Calif.), 171; wines of,
 177
Naples (city) (It.), 118
Napoleon, 47, 66, 105n; "Brandy," 208
Natur (Ger.) (class.), 99; Champagne,
 210; *Nature* (Calif.), 192
Naturrein (Ger.), 99; *Naturwein*, 99
Néac (reg.) (Fr.), 27
Nebbiolo (grape & wine), 118, 121,
 128; N. *spumante*, 121
Nebuchadnezzar, 190
Neckar (reg.) (Ger.), 103; wines of,
 113
Nemeskadar (wine) (Hun.), 157, 162
Nerthe, de la, Marquis, 70